Perspectives on Educational Management and Leadership

Also available from Continuum

Analysing Underachievement in Schools - Emma Smith
Private Education - Geoffrey Walford
Pedagogy and the University - Monica McLean
Education and Community - Dianne Gereluk

Perspectives on Educational Management and Leadership

Syllables of Recorded Time

Les Bell

continuum

Continuum International Publishing Group
The Tower Building
11 York Road
London
SE1 7NX

80 Maiden Lane, Suite 704
New York, NY 10038

www.continuumbooks.com

British Library Cataloging-in-Publication Data
A catalogue record for this book is available from the British Library.

ISBN: 978-0-8264-8831-2 (hardcover)

Library of Congress Cataloging-in-Publication Data
A catalog record for this book is available from the Library of Congress

Typeset by Data Standards Ltd, Frome, Somerset, UK.
Printed and bound in Great Britain by Biddles Ltd, Kings Lynn, Norfolk

This book is dedicated to Professor Ray Bolam who died suddenly in August 2006. I was proud to call him colleague and privileged to call him friend. He will be much missed and long remembered.

Contents

List of Tables   ix
Acknowledgements   x

Introduction: A Syllable of Recorded Time   1

Part 1: Context and Concepts   9
1   All Our Yesterdays: the Development of Educational Policy
    in England, 1960–2006   11
2   I'll Do, I'll Do, and I'll Do: Organizational Culture,
    Schools and Teachers' Work   33
3   I Have Thee Not, and Yet I See Thee Still: the School as an
    Ambiguous Organization   48

Part 2: Leading and Managing Staff in Schools   61
4   The Cloudy Messenger: a New Role in Schools
    – the Case of the TVEI Co-ordinator   63
5   A Walking Shadow: the Emergence of Middle Leadership in
    Schools and Colleges   76
6   We Will Perform in Measure: Accountability,
    Performance and School-based Management   90
7   Which Grain will Grow and Which will Not:
    the Management of Staff – Some Issues of Efficiency
    and Cost-Effectiveness   103

Part 3: Management and Leadership in Primary Schools   115
8   Service in Every Point Twice Done: Primary Schools
    and the Nature of the Education Marketplace   117
9   Leave no Rubs nor Botches in the Work: Primary Heads,
    Governors and Institutional Autonomy   129
10 A Tale of Some Significance: Primary Headship and
    Strategic Planning in England   140
11 What's Done is Done: the Impact of Educational Policy
    on Headship in Primary Schools in England 1994–2001   159

End Piece: Bring Me No More Reports   173
12   Strategic Planning in Education: Full of Sound and Fury,
     Signifying Nothing?   175

Bibliography   189
Index   209

List of Tables

1.1	The Social Democratic Phase 1960–73	13
1.2	The Resource Constrained Phase 1973–87	15
1.3	The Market Phase 1988–96	20
1.4	The Targets Phase 1997 onwards	25
2.1	Characteristics of the three constituent schools and the newly formed school	39
3.1	A comparison of the characteristics of bureaucracy and an ambiguous organization	58
4.1	Characteristics of TVEI school co-ordinators in Addleton LEA	72
10.1	Models of planning	143
10.2	Dimensions of planning in six English primary schools	157

Acknowledgements

I am indebted to my friends Gunnar Graff (Chief Educator at the Rektorsuitbilbingen, Stockholm) and Anita Segerstad (Director of Education with responsibility for school management training, Uppsala University) for sharing their ideas about policy formulation and implementation with me. Their conceptual insights helped me to formulate the framework for analysis touched upon in the Introduction and developed more fully in Bell and Stevenson (2006).

Chapter 1 was first published as 'Back to the future: the development of educational policy in England', *Journal of Educational Administration*, 37 (3 & 4), 1999, pp. 200–28. I am grateful to Emerald Publishing Group Limited for permission to publish that material in this volume. I am also grateful to Mike Aiello for his help in formulating the details of the fourth policy phase (although I have now changed its title and restructured the argument) and to Professor Mike Bottery for his stimulating paper on the distinctions between the education policies of the New Right and New Labour. Dr Evonne Edwards, then my graduate student, made me reflect upon the ways in which educational policy in the 1960s helped to shape that of the late 1990s.

A shorter version of Chapter 2 was first published as 'When worlds collide: school culture, imposed change and teacher's work', in F. Crowther, B. Caldwell, J. Chapman, G. Lakomski and D. Ogilvie (eds), (1994) *The Workplace in Education: Australian Perspectives. First Yearbook of the Australian Council for Education Administration*, Sydney: Edward Arnold, pp. 52–9. I am grateful to the Australian Council for Educational Leadership for permission to publish that material in this volume and to the Nuffield Foundation for funding the research project on which the chapter is based.

Some of the material for Chapter 3 was first published as 'The school as an organisation: a re-appraisal' in A. Westoby (ed.), (1987) *Culture and Power in Educational Organisation: a Reader*, Milton Keynes: Open University Press, pp. 3–14, and other parts were published as 'The school as an organisation: a re-appraisal', *British Journal of Sociology of Education*, 1 (2), 1980, pp. 183–93. I am grateful both to Open University Press and Taylor and Francis for permission to publish that material in this volume.

A shorter version of Chapter 4 was first published as 'An investigation of a new role in schools: the case of the TVEI co-ordinator', in T. Simkins (ed.), (1985), *Research in the Management of Secondary Education, Sheffield Polytechnic Papers in Educational Management*, (59), pp. 55–68. I am grateful to Sheffield Hallam University for permission to publish that material in this volume. I am also grateful to my former colleague Martin Merson at the University of Warwick for access to his data on TVEI school co-ordinators from which I obtained information about co-ordinators' experience, qualifications and the time allocated to TVEI activities.

An earlier version of Chapter 5 was first published as 'Cross-curriculum co-ordination', in D. Middlewood and N. Burton (2001) *Managing the Curriculum*, London: Paul Chapman, pp. 135-54. I am grateful to Paul Chapman Publishing for permission to publish that material in this volume.

Chapter 7 was first published as 'The management of staff: some issues of efficiency and cost-effectiveness', in L. Anderson and M. Coleman (eds), (2000), *Managing Finance and Resources in Education*, London: Paul Chapman, pp. 186-99. I am grateful to Paul Chapman Publishing for permission to publish that material in this volume.

Chapter 8 was first published as 'Primary schools and the nature of the education market place', in T. Bush, L. Bell, R. Bolam, R. Glatter and P. Ribbins, (eds), (1999), *Educational Management: Redefining Theory, Policy and Practice*, London: Paul Chapman Publishing, pp. 59-73. I am grateful to Paul Chapman Publishing for permission to publish that material in this volume.

Chapter 9 was first published with David Halpin as 'Primary heads, governors and institutional autonomy', in K. Stott and V. Trafford (2000), *Partnerships: Shaping the Future of Education*, London: Middlesex University Press, pp. 55-68. I am grateful both to David and to Middlesex University Press for permission to publish this material in this volume.

Chapter 11 was first published with Avril Rowley as 'The impact of educational policy on headship in primary schools in England, 1994-2001', *Journal of Educational Administration*, 40 (3), 2002, pp. 195-210. I am grateful both to Avril and to Emerald Publishing Group Limited for permission to publish that material in this volume.

Chapter 12 was first published as 'Strategic planning in education: full of sound and fury, signifying nothing?' *Journal of Educational Administration*, 40 (5), 2002, pp. 407-24. I am grateful to Emerald Publishing Group Limited for permission to publish that material in this volume.

I am grateful to my colleague and co-researcher Professor David Halpin, now of the Institute of Education, University of London, for agreeing to the use of some of the data collected as part of our jointly held ESRC Project on primary school management on which Chapters 8 and 9 are based and which is used in part of Chapter 11, and also to the Economic and Social Research Council (R000 22 1271) for funding that research.

I acknowledge the debt I owe to all the heads and teachers who gave up their time to take part in the various research projects reported here and, in particular, the headteachers of the primary schools who feature in Chapters 8 to 11, many of whom have been the subject of my quest for data since 1987.

I am also grateful to Penny Brown of Good Impressions Editorial Services (www.good-impressions.net) for her copy-editing and proof reading of much of my work since 1995, for her comments on earlier drafts of many of the chapters in this book and for her proof reading and copy-editing of this manuscript - and for her technical assistance, especially in compiling the bibliography from a range of different sources.

Introduction: a Syllable of Recorded Time

In 2005 I took the decision to take early retirement in 2006. It had long been my ambition to produce as my last academic book a volume of articles, mainly already published elsewhere but brought up to date, that reflected my work over the four decades in which I have been involved in the field of educational management and leadership. I am grateful to Continuum Books for giving me the opportunity to achieve this ambition, at least in part. Although this is my 'syllable of recorded time' (*Macbeth*, Act V, Scene v), this is not a book about the past. It is written for the future. Indeed, many of the chapters develop an argument about alternative approaches to management and leadership that either are already being adopted or might usefully be adopted in order to cope with the ever-increasing demands being placed on those who work in education. One of the basic themes of this book is that by understanding how educational policy has developed over time, it is possible to be better placed to respond to both current and future policies. It focuses, therefore, on management and leadership practices as well as policy issues.

A second theme of this book is that educational policy is not shaped in a random manner and nor is it isolated from the mainstream of political ideas. All policy is derived from values that inform the dominant discourses in the socio-political environment and the values that are derived from that discourse. It is the trends that emerge, based on these discourses, that establish the strategic direction for policy and translate this into broad policy statements. These statements are then applied to different domains such as health, economy and education. The parameters for policy in any one of these spheres of activity are defined by the organizational principles and the operational practices and procedures, which are the detailed organizational arrangements that are necessary to implement the policy at the regional or even institutional level (see Bell and Stevenson 2006). What this means is that the strategic direction that shapes what schools and colleges set out to do, the principles on which schools and colleges are organized and the operational practices in those schools and colleges are derived from policy which, in turn, is shaped by the dominant discourses in the socio-economic environment. So in the 1960s the dominant theme was equality of opportunity, which gave rise to the development of comprehensive schools and the raising of the school leaving age. This was followed by a strict fiscal regime generated by the oil crisis and poor economic performance. In education this produced school closures and teacher redundancies. By the late 1980s, the operation of market forces brought league tables, inspection and competition between schools, followed by planning driven by target setting, a product of the emphasis placed by the New Labour government on the link between education and economic performance.

The book sets out to show how many of these policies impact directly on the working lives of those in educational institutions today. Performance management, strategic planning, target setting, bidding for special funds, the emphasis on pupil attainment, the control over curriculum content and pedagogy, accountability, autonomy and even the nature of the national curriculum are all derived from debates about education policy that can be traced back to the 1960s and beyond. To understand these debates is to have a better understanding of where we are now and of how we might respond to what is currently happening in our schools and colleges. A third theme of this book, therefore, is that while leadership and management in schools is derived from the policy contexts within which educational institutions are located at any particular time, if staff in those schools and colleges understand the nature and importance of the dominant discourses that have shaped those policies, they can be more than passive recipients of policy. Indeed, they can shape policy to suit the needs of their own situations.

In preparing this Introduction I was surprised to recognize that my own work in the field was almost contiguous with the development of the field itself. Educational management as an academic discipline and as a priority area for the professional development of teachers has expanded and developed considerably since the mid-1970s, when I first studied with Len Watson and his team at the then Sheffield City Polytechnic. My work has had two main strands, much like the field itself: that of the writer and researcher, and that of the tutor, trainer and teacher. Much of the work in educational management and leadership has fallen either into the category of academic study or that of training. At times, the boundary between the two categories has been extremely permeable. Since the 1960s education has been subject to vast and almost continuous change, largely because of the activities of educational policy makers. Many people working in the field of educational management and leadership have sought both to analyse and comment on such changes, while also seeking to develop concepts and theories that might help to enhance our understandings of both the processes of school leadership and of management and the policy context within which those processes are located. At the same time, many of us have been involved in providing training and in-service support to enable colleagues in schools and colleges to implement, adapt or even resist policies and procedures in their own institutions. Through my work I have sought to help colleagues in schools (and colleges and universities) at home and abroad to understand (and perhaps anticipate) educational policy and policy shifts and to try, through research and professional development, to help them cope with such changes. My aim has been to enable staff in schools to make the most of the opportunities that educational policy changes offered in order to achieve those objects that they deemed best for children rather than policy makers. I have also tried to understand what it is that school leaders actually do rather than what they are expected or supposed to do, what works for them, what lessons might be learned from such insights and to locate these understandings within conceptual frameworks derived from analysis of research data. Thus the two strands of my work are closely interconnected. However, it proved impossible to encompass both aspects in one volume, so the chapters in this book focus on educational management and leadership rather than on professional development. For reasons of lack of space I have chosen to concentrate here on the UK aspects of my work, leaving out almost all reference to its international dimensions. To the extent that this book reflects the work I have done over four decades and my contribution to the development of the field of educational management and leadership, it is a syllable of my recorded time.

This book also gives me an opportunity to express my gratitude to all my friends and colleagues in local education authorities, schools and in the field of educational management and leadership with whom I have worked over the years. It all started in the 1960s with Robert Pinker and the staff of the Sociology Department at Goldsmiths College, University of London, who introduced me to organization theory. It was while I was a part-time student at Goldsmiths that I first met Brian Davies, until recently Professor at the University of Cardiff, who became a friend and mentor throughout most of my career. In the early 1970s I was fortunate enough to study with Wilfred Harrison and Malcolm Anderson in the Politics Department at the University of Warwick who both endeavoured to teach me the skills of critical analysis, and with Leslie Perry who introduced me to the literature on educational administration and gave me my first research grant. My Ph.D. supervisor, George Bain, shared his talents as a supervisor with me and showed me the importance of locating any analysis of practice within a robust conceptual framework. It was Len Watson who really sparked off my interest in the relationship between the theory of educational management and its practice in schools and from whom I learned the importance of theoretical models. Len's recent death has deprived us of a stalwart supporter of the importance of linking our theory to our practice. I will miss him greatly. It was during my time as a student with Len Watson that I first met Ray Bolam, who was then an external examiner for the Sheffield City Polytechnic M.Sc. (Educational Management) programme. At about the same time I joined BEMAS (British Educational Management and Administration Society) and came to know Ron Glatter and Tony Bush and, through a mutual friend, Peter Ribbins. My work has benefited significantly from my friendship with this group from that point. By the late 1980s David Halpin had joined the Education Department at the University of Warwick and together we developed a research agenda that helped me to continue a study of primary school headteachers that started in 1987 and is still ongoing.

In 1994 I moved to Liverpool John Moores University to become Professor of Educational Management and Director of the School of Education and Community Studies. Here I had the opportunity to establish a new master's degree programme in educational management and to work with two outstanding colleagues who are not widely known, Mike Aiello and John Latham. John helped me further with my analysis of the role of primary heads while Mike made an insightful contribution to the conceptual framework that is developed in Chapter 1 of this book. Soon after I moved to Liverpool, Ray Bolam, Tony Bush, Ron Glatter, Peter Ribbins and I came together when, in 1997, after a discussion between Tony and Ray, we organized a seminar series funded by the Economic and Social Research Council (ESRC) to review the academic discipline of educational management and to take into account the many developments in policy, practice, theory and research since educational management first became established in the United Kingdom in the 1970s (see Bush, Bell, Bolam, Glatter and Ribbins 1999). This seminar series resulted in the five of us, now termed – by ourselves – 'The Five Old Farts of Educational Management', establishing the Standing Conference for Research in Educational Leadership and Management (SCRELM). SCRELM obtained a grant from the EPPI-Centre at the University of London to conduct a literature review of the field (see Bell, Bolam and Cubillo 2003). This work brought me into closer contact with colleagues such as Mike Bottery, Peter Earley, Helen Gunter and Geoff Southworth who have all influenced my thinking. However, it was with Ray Bolam that I worked most closely. His tragic death in August 2006 as I wrote this Introduction, has deprived us all of a wonderful friend and colleague whose insights, warmth and humour have enriched the lives of all of us who were fortunate enough to know him. This book is dedicated to him. He will be very greatly missed.

From the late 1970s the continued professional development aspect of my work flourished, partly through the B.Phil. and MA programmes at the University of Warwick and through the increasing opportunities for funded short courses in educational management for heads and senior staff in schools. Derek Wilmer, then Senior Inspector of Schools in Warwickshire and a most far-sighted man, invited me to help him run one of the first management courses for primary headteachers in 1978. We established a relationship which continued until his retirement from Warwickshire LEA. By the early 1980s I was tutoring management training courses for a number of LEAs. It was at this time that I encountered Kinsley Bungard, an unusual man who is, undoubtedly, the best management trainer I have ever met. We worked together throughout the 1980s and into the 1990s. In this period I came to know and work closely with a number of outstanding school colleagues including Angela Bird, David Higham, Martin Jackson, Ken Lambert, Joan Martin, Eric Needham and Chris Rhodes. From these people I gained a deeper understanding of the world of schools generally and the role of the headteacher in particular.

As my own understandings developed, the field of educational management and leadership itself changed. It had expanded significantly from the middle of the 1970s but its beginnings can be traced as far back as 1913. One of the first remotely academic references to schools and their management sought to apply the principles of management to the problems of city school systems. This paper, clearly then at the cutting edge of thinking, was written by Bobbit and published in *The Supervision of City Schools* by the University of Chicago in 1913 (Bobbit 1913). In Britain there are some oblique references to the management of schools, mainly in the context of school governors and managers in the Cross Commission (1888) and in the voluminous correspondence about the model *Regulations for Secondary Schools* published by Morant, the first Permanent Secretary of the Board of Education in 1904 (quoted in Baron and Howell 1974). Apart from that, the silence on this topic is deafening. It is even impossible to find anything except the most transitory reference to school management and organization in the 1944 Education Act.

The first specialist educational management courses were offered by the Institute of Education, University of London in the late 1960s, followed by similar developments in Birmingham and Sheffield. Much of the content of these early courses was derived from research on industrial and commercial organizations, although a view was rapidly emerging that education should not be treated as simply another field within which general principles of management could be applied. Rather it should be seen as a separate discipline with its own concepts, theories and related practice. As early as 1969 one of the founding fathers of the study of educational management and administration in Britain, George Baron, commenting on the current state of the discipline, could write:

> There are two major tasks that lie ahead ... The first is that of making known and demonstrating the relevance of concepts and approaches that already exist within the social sciences and that have a bearing on the study of educational policy and administration ... The second task is ... to construct a body of case studies from which systematic content can be developed. (Baron and Taylor 1969, pp. 13–14)

Already Eric Hoyle at Bristol was taking up the challenge with his work on organization theory and curriculum change (Hoyle 1965, 1969, 1973). Two years later the British Educational Administration Society, later to become the British Educational Leadership, Management and Administration Society (BELMAS) was formed. Its founding group consisted of a combination of academics, chief education officers and other LEA administrators and a few doughty practitioners. It produced a journal, now called *Educational Management Administration and Leadership* (EMAL). The first editor was Meredydd Hughes who played a leading role in the third International Intervisitation Programme on Educational Administration, held in the United Kingdom in 1974. Hughes became Professor of Educational Administration at the University of Birmingham and made a major contribution to the development of our understanding of school management. Several of the leading figures in the educational management field today came under Meredydd's influence, including one of the journal's most effective editors, Peter Ribbins, and his colleague Hywel Thomas.

At the same time as BELMAS was becoming established, Ron Glatter, then working with George Baron at the London Institute of Education, was preparing to publish his work on management development for the education service (Glatter 1972). Soon after this volume was published, Glatter became the first Professor of Educational Management in England when he joined the Open University. He was to have a profound effect on the development of the subject in many ways: through his own work; his influence on colleagues such as Tony Bush, the current editor of EMAL; through his support of many of us in other institutions working in the same field; and not least through the establishment of the now highly successful Open University distance learning educational management programmes. The material for the first of these, E321, was published in 1976. Even here, however, the emerging discipline showed how tentative it was about its status: the first unit questioned the appropriateness of applying management theory and practice to educational institutions (Morgan 1976). Nevertheless this was the first significant attempt to link management theory and educational practice, thus overcoming a major weakness in the then current writing in the field which Glatter described as having:

> a strongly prescriptive flavour: the author will advocate a particular management style or technique almost as a panacea for resolving managerial problems but without having adequate theoretical or empirical justification for propounding the solution offered. (Glatter 1977, p. 10)

If London, Birmingham and Milton Keynes were influential centres in the establishment of educational management as an academic discipline, the contribution made in the north of England must not be ignored. The Department of Educational Management at the then Sheffield City Polytechnic, under the leadership of Len Watson, helped to pioneer award-bearing in-service work with its diploma and higher degrees. At the same time similar work – although perhaps more school-based and practical – was going on at Padgate. Later, departments in other colleges, polytechnics and universities followed the example set by these pioneers. Cambridge, Crewe and Alsager, Manchester, Newcastle, Nottingham, Oxford, Warwick and many others established courses. The National Development Centre for School Management Training was established at Bristol University to monitor the growth of Department of Education and Science (DES) funded short courses in school management for heads and deputies. LEAs found ways of creating and supporting management development provision for teachers and heads through institutions such as the Regional Staff College at Dudley in the West Midlands, which were the forerunners of the National College for School Leadership.

It was no coincidence that the development of the academic discipline of educational management took place at the same time as a similar growth in the importance placed on management strategies in schools, as part of the policy thrust to improve both the efficiency and effectiveness of teaching and learning. The 1976 Great Debate on Education may have seemed more a series of closet whispers at the time, but much educational policy in the late 1980s and 1990s can be traced directly to the subsequent Green Paper. By 1977 the management and leadership roles of heads was identified as a major contributing factor to the overall success of schools (DES 1977a). *Better Schools* (DES 1985a) emphasized the need to manage the teaching force effectively and argued that appraisal would make a contribution to this. The plethora of policy documents that bombarded schools, colleges and LEAs in the 1980s is too numerous to analyse here but, as we all know, it culminated in the Education Reform Act (DES 1988a).

The main thrust of this legislative activity was to create a centrally controlled national curriculum that gave children an entitlement to specific curriculum content and enabled direct comparisons to be made between all schools through national assessment (Bell 1992). Organization and management, rather than being vested in LEAs, had been devolved to the schools. Here the responsibility for ensuring that the National Curriculum was taught and tested and for the deployment of resources rested not with teachers, but with governing bodies, on which parents and representatives of the local community were in a majority. The legitimation of these policies was eventually articulated in the White Paper, *Choice and Diversity* (Department for Education [DfE] 1992). These reforms located significant management responsibility with heads and senior staff of schools, introduced new regimes of accountability and inspection through the work of the Office for Standards in Education (Ofsted), and saw the development of the Teacher Training Agency's (TTA) agenda for competence-based training for senior and middle managers in schools, on which the new National Professional Qualification for Headship was based when it was introduced in 1997. In emphasizing management competences the TTA re-opened the debate about the relevance for education of management principles and practices derived from business and commerce, and this has continued through the activities of the National College for School Leadership with its emphasis on the centrality of the headteacher in the leadership of the school.

If, in one sense, the wheel has come full circle, what has changed is the extent to which there is now a direct relationship between national educational policy and leadership and management in individual schools. The interconnectedness of policy and practice, and, at times, the discontinuities between them, are now a major focus for many researchers in the field.

> There was a time when educational policy as policy was taken for granted ... Clearly that is no longer the case. Today, educational policies are the focus of considerable controversy and public contestation ... Educational policy-making has become highly politicised. (Olssen *et al.* 2004, pp. 2–3)

This book focuses on this interconnection between policy and practice, the politicized nature of educational policy and its impact on schools. It establishes a link between past and current policies and identifies ways of responding to such policies and bending them to suit the needs of individual schools and colleges. The book is divided into three parts. Part 1 identifies some key issues in the field of educational management and leadership. Part 2 develops a series of ideas related to leading and managing staff in schools and examines the impact of educational policy at various levels. Part 3 reflects my continued interest in the management of primary schools, a much under-researched area. The first two chapters in this section are a result of my collaboration with David Halpin on an ESRC research project. The final chapter returns to where the book started, with a critique of current educational policy and of the now dominant approach to managing staff in schools. Each part of the book has its own introduction. This spells out the theme of each chapter, expands upon the quotation from Shakespeare's *Macbeth* that I have used to illustrate the theme in the chapter title, and identifies its current relevance.

Part 1: Context and Concepts

Part 1 provides a framework within which the remaining chapters are located. It was argued in the Introduction that education policy is derived from the values that inform the dominant discourses in the socio-political environment. Policy trends emerge based on these discourses that establish a strategic direction for policy, define its organizational principals and determine its operational procedures and practices. This holds good at national, local and institutional levels, as will be illustrated in subsequent chapters. Chapter 1 outlines how the dominant discourses in the socio-political environment have changed since the 1960s and demonstrates that current policy themes and issues can be traced back over time. Thus, 'All our Yesterdays' provides the context for the chapters that follow and identifies the trends that have helped to shape educational policy today and will shape it tomorrow. Chapters 2 and 3 introduce key concepts that have informed much of the research reported here. They are both based on data from the Oakfields School Project, carried out in the late 1980s and early 1990s and funded by the Nuffield Foundation. Chapter 2 explores the concept of school culture and argues that culture is a useful concept for understanding how and why teachers do what they so. Culture is, however, more than simply a product of the interaction between members of the school. Rather it is a product of the values, procedures and practices within the school and its wider environment, and of their contested nature. At Oakfields, the conflict over values and processes was so severe that any teacher might argue that, 'I'll Do, I'll Do, and I'll Do' in order to come to terms with the contested terrain. Chapter 3 starts from the premise that although models of formal organization can apply to schools, such models leave much unexplained. The concept of organizational ambiguity can help develop a deeper understanding of the organizational processes that take place in schools and colleges, although it only offers part of the wider picture. Ambiguity is, however, by its very nature a difficult and somewhat elusive concept. Viewing school organization from the perspective of organizational ambiguity may still leave an observer to say, 'I Have Thee Not, and Yet I See Thee Still' but it has enabled many postgraduate students who are teachers and headteachers to understand their own institutions more fully.

1

All Our Yesterdays: the Development of Educational Policy in England, 1960–2006

Introduction

This chapter explores the four main policy phases through which school management and leadership has passed in the last five decades. These policy phases provided the political context within which all the work in this book was located. Much of what appears here forms a critique of emerging educational policy, based on an analysis of the impact of such policy on the work of those in schools, on an exploration of how staff adapted to policy dictates and changes, and on how policy was and is adapted by heads and teachers at school level to make its requirements both more acceptable and more workable. It will argue that there has been a significant continuity in educational policy over time, such that not only has education policy under the current Labour administration evolved from the policies of the previous Conservative New Right governments of Thatcher and Major, but that the New Right policies themselves were part of a natural evolution from what had gone before. Thus, to see the Education Reform Act (DES 1988a) and the legislation that followed it as a watershed, a revolutionary break with the past, is to misinterpret those policies and to misunderstand what went before. It will also be seen that the current New Labour educational policies have their roots in policies formulated by earlier administrations, and that these New Labour policies are based on serious misconceptions about the nature of schools as organizations and about the value of the research evidence on school effectiveness.

The distinctive pattern of educational policy making in England and Wales was established by the Education Act of 1944. It was a tripartite partnership that provided a national system, locally administered, the organizing principle of which was equal access to educational opportunity for all pupils. The Department of Education and Science made policy which was interpreted at the local level by local education authorities (LEAs) and implemented at school level by headteachers and their staff. National policy was concerned largely with the allocation of resources, the structuring of provision, and the transfer of pupils from one stage of education to another, but not with the curriculum or its assessment. This was almost entirely the province of teachers. Thus schools in England enjoyed a relatively high degree of autonomy as far as the curriculum was concerned. At primary level this included control over the totality of the school curriculum, although this was strongly influenced by the 11+ selection procedures for many children. At secondary level schools made choices about which pupils to enter for external assessment and the forms of that assessment. Duncan Graham, Chief Education Officer of Suffolk and later first chairman of the National Curriculum Council, summed the position up thus:

> When I went to Suffolk in 1979 the thing that shook me most was the feeling that ... chief officers had little to do with the curriculum ... while I could be an honorary member of the curriculum team it was not really my business. (Graham 1993, p. 4)

The Social Democratic Phase 1960–73

The first phase that is central to this analysis (Table 1.1) obviously had its origins in the 1944 Education Act. This phase was characterized by relatively high spending; the expansion of educational provision to meet the needs of a rapidly increasing pupil population; the development of social intervention strategies to tackle pupil under-achievement and a restructuring of the system to abolish pupil selection at age 11 and to replace grammar schools with larger, non-selective comprehensive schools. Throughout this period the system faced a teacher shortage of such proportions that having an adult in front of the class was the main, often the only, management priority in many schools. Little, if any, systematic curriculum planning took place except that required to enable some schools to respond to the demands of external assessment. What was perhaps not recognized by teachers at this time, was just how much autonomy they enjoyed over the curriculum. This may not have amounted to site-based management as it is now understood, but it meant that staff in schools had considerable freedom over what they taught and how they taught it.

The whole system was underpinned by a strong social democratic ethic shared by the major political parties who believed that social inequality should be reduced and that the main way to do this was to improve educational attainment. This ethic, as Kogan notes, was based on the view that:

- the state should act to remedy the effects of the worst inequalities;
- the common good is best constructed and advanced by the exercise of a combination of political policy making and professional expertise;
- the specification of the common good requires rational construction and systematic negotiation and cannot rely on ... market processes. (Kogan 1997, p. 195)

It was a Conservative Minister for Education who wrote:

> The essential point is that all children should have an equal opportunity of acquiring intelligence, and of developing their talents and abilities to the full. (Boyle 1963, p. 1)

Table 1.1 The Social Democratic Phase 1960–73

Emphasis	Strong emphasis on growth and expansion.
School management	Embryonic. Teachers exercised considerable autonomy over the curriculum. Main concern is to have teachers in front of classes.
Priorities	Little clear priority setting.
Resources	No resource management.
Power and influence	Little conflict between interest groups.
Teachers	Aspirations and expectations rising even faster than growth rate.
Motive force	Expansion is the unchallenged motive force. Change brought about largely by state intervention at system level through comprehensivization and funding new initiatives. Collectivism reigns.
Values	Little discussion of values which shape action other than the need to break into the 'circle of deprivation'. Implicitly, education is seen as a major mechanism for social engineering and social improvement.
Equity	Equality of opportunity through equality of access and positive discrimination.
The system	The system is coherent and develops as a whole. Autonomy over the curriculum rests within schools but system autonomy is located at LEA level. Many state initiatives such as Educational Priority Areas are funded.

This was to be achieved though providing equality of opportunity, defined initially as equality of access, and subsequently in terms of positive action. It was this emphasis on equal access that was the motive force for both the abolition of selection and the establishment of intervention strategies, foremost among which were Educational Priority Areas (EPAs), a product of the Plowden Report's concern with the cumulative effects of deprivation (Central Advisory Committee for Education 1967).

EPAs were created to provide a programme of positive discrimination based on a new distribution of educational resources to be used for building, improved staffing, supplementing teachers' salaries and the development of community-based teaching and learning strategies. Grants were awarded to five areas, identified by statistical and political definitions of deprivation, to set up action research projects whose remit was to raise educational standards, to lift teacher morale, to foster home and school links and to assist in giving communities a sense of responsibility (Midwinter 1972).

Although there were only a few projects, their influence was considerable, especially through the community schools movement. The key figures in EPAs sought to locate schools more firmly within their communities, to redefine the nature of schooling and to widen the definition of equity on which it was based in such a way that equality of access, rooted as it was in middle-class values, became subject to scrutiny:

> The goal to be reached is a middle class goal. The whole pressure of social and economic factors demands that schools have this orientation. The standards and ethos of schools are ineluctably of this ilk ... No wonder then that working class children fail ... Whereas it is the norm for middle class children to succeed ... it is the norm for those in EPAs to fail ... the rich potential is left untapped ... Here we reach the core of the dilemma. The school curriculum is, arguably, irrelevant and remote ... (Midwinter 1972, pp. 8–10)

Thus state intervention in education had arrived as a means for achieving both educational and political ends.

It is not surprising, therefore, that state intervention in areas of curriculum and pedagogy can be traced to this period. In March 1960 David Eccles, then Minister of Education, argued in a debate in the House of Commons, that it was to be regretted that education debates were devoted so much to organization and bricks and mortar rather than to the secret garden of the curriculum into which only the initiated might enter (Manzer 1970). He set out to influence both curriculum content and pedagogy. As a direct result, the Schools Council was born in 1963. It embarked on an extensive programme of curriculum development but was constrained by the successful defence by teachers of their control over the curriculum. Consequently, its work could not be placed within an overall national curriculum for all schools and it was not able to insist that its proposals were implemented. Thus, excellent though many of the Schools Council programmes were, the Council could only work by influence and exhortation, which were insufficient to challenge the autonomy that teachers retained over the curriculum (Lawton 1983). This was a situation that many teachers came to regret.

At the same time, the Plowden Report was also playing a significant part in redefining the curriculum. It was this report that established child centredness as the focal point of English primary school teaching, identified learning by discovery as an important element of pedagogy and successfully challenged streaming by ability. These developments had their impact on both teaching and curriculum content as mixed-ability teaching and project-based pedagogy were introduced. These developments were not without their critics. Cox and Dyson (1969) mounted a sustained attack on the social consequences of educational reform as well as on progressive methods and the attainment standards of pupils in both primary and secondary schools. At first these criticisms were dismissed as the work of anti-progressive reactionaries but by 1973 they had became so influential that they were to inform the next major policy phase. The autonomy that teachers had exercised over the curriculum was about to be undermined.

The Resource Constrained Phase 1973–87

The defining agenda for this phase was set out clearly by a Labour Government publication, *Education in Schools: a Consultative Document* (DES 1977b).

The main characteristics of this phase were a growing emphasis on school management, especially the management of resources including teachers; a debate about the nature and purpose of education within which schools were blamed for not producing pupils with appropriate skills and abilities; a decline in the morale of teachers as career opportunities became more limited; increasing state intervention in the curriculum; the targeting of funding; the limiting of equality of opportunity and experiments with alternative funding strategies, including limited forms of site-based management in some LEAs (Table 1.2). It began with the oil crisis in 1973.

This crisis revealed the extent of Britain's relative economic failure, for which education was blamed. In its aftermath, youth unemployment increased significantly. Until the early 1970s school leavers had experienced no difficulty

Table 1.2 The Resource Constrained Phase 1973-87

Emphasis	Emphasis on management, finance and economics.
Priorities	Cost-effectiveness and efficiency set priorities.
School management	Managing the teaching force and experiments with alternative forms of funding, including experiments with site-based management
Resources	Preoccupation with resource management as pupil numbers decline and schools merge or close.
Power and influence	'Who controls resources?'– key question.
Teachers	Aspirations reconsidered. Appraisal introduced. Staff development emerges. Aspirations reconsidered and *career* takes on new meaning – horizontal development.
Motive force	Survival and control over resources are dominant motive forces. Change induced by state, LEA and Manpower Services Commission (MSC) intervention.
Values	Fundamental questions raised about the nature, purpose and control of education. Vocationalism and an emphasis on science and technology emerges. The emergence of the 'Me' generation.
Equity	Equality of opportunity redefined as responding to industry, parental choice restricted through limited and more tightly controlled access.
The system	The system generally contracts as pupil numbers fall. Autonomy moves between central government, quasi-governmental organizations, LEAs and institutions, with the Manpower Services Commission emerging as a key player in providing funding for specific forms of curriculum development. Other than this, intervention withers away.

in obtaining jobs. After the oil crisis, this was no longer the case. Educational attainment of young people became a significant criterion for obtaining (or failing to obtain) employment. Youth unemployment was blamed not on the structural changes in the employment market caused by a rapid decline of labour intensive heavy industry, but on inadequately educated young people and the schools from which they came (Maclure 1997).

The oil crisis also caused the Labour Government to limit spending on education severely at a time when pupil numbers were declining for the first time in twenty years. Many in the education service saw falling pupil numbers as an opportunity to offer a better service to fewer pupils, using the levels of funding that had previously been available. The Callaghan Government took a different view. The resource base declined in line with falling numbers. Instead of moving into a world where they could teach fewer pupils with the same resources, teachers were faced for the first time since 1945 with a declining resource base for education. LEAs were forced to close and merge schools. Many teachers were either made redundant or offered early retirement. In a few months, the main management priority in education at both LEA and school levels changed from encouraging a relatively well-resourced expansion to managing a severe contraction. The education system could no longer cope with new problems by throwing money at them, and for many heads their main management role became that of ensuring the survival of their schools, even if this meant making some staff redundant.

The financing of the education system itself became the main problem. In 1976 the House of Commons Expenditure Committee noted that the DES lacked control over how its money was spent and that it had reduced educational planning to the banalities of resource allocation, not least because it condoned the view that teachers should be allowed to exercise sole control over the curriculum. The Prime Minister, James Callaghan, raised many of the concerns being expressed about education in his speech at Ruskin College (October 1976), one of the defining moments in British educational policy making. He questioned whether the education service in general and schools in particular were providing industrial society with young workers with sufficient training in the basic subjects. As Lawton notes:

> By the end of 1976 it was possible to identify a number of . . . complaints about schools and teachers under the general heading of accountability. First . . . that the enormous education budget should be seen to be giving value for money; second . . . that education ought to pay more attention to the needs of industry; third, parental demands loomed large – particularly in the consideration of the Taylor Committee on the composition of governing bodies of schools. (Lawton 1980, pp. 24-25)

It can be seen, therefore, that equity was being redefined. It was to be less about equality of opportunity and social change and more about responding to parental wishes, to the needs of industry and giving value for money. Key issues began to emerge that were to exercise educational policy makers for the next two decades. These included the structure of the education system, the nature and purpose of education, links between education and industry, teacher autonomy and control over the curriculum, financial control, parental choice and representation on school governing bodies, management and leadership in schools and the introduction of forms of site-based management. These issues, which formed the agenda for the Great Debate, will be addressed in the subsequent chapters of this book.

The Great Debate, launched by the Prime Minister in October 1976, was a series of regional conferences which focused on the Curriculum 5–16; the assessment of standards; the education and training of teachers; and school and working life (DES 1977c). Many of those involved saw the Great Debate as a series of closet whispers and believed that it was neither a debate nor was it very great (Lawton 1980). Its outcome, however, was the publication of a Green Paper *Education in Schools: a Consultative Document* (DES 1977b). This argued that too little attention was being paid to basic skills in the school curriculum and, above all, that education was central to the economic survival of Britain. It also mapped out a much more interventionist approach to education, especially on the curriculum, the vocational relevance of schooling, standards in basic skills and the role of LEAs.

State intervention in the curriculum was pursued in several ways. LEAs were requested to provide information about the curriculum in the schools for which they were responsible (DES 1977c). Documents were published outlining what a school curriculum should contain, not as discussion documents but as embryonic policy statements (DES 1979, 1981). By 1985 the Government was prepared to intervene directly in the secondary school curriculum in a way which could not have been envisaged a decade before. It launched the Technical and Vocational Educational Initiative (TVEI). This project, which eventually affected all schools in England and Wales (Holland 1996) was designed to increase the scientific, technical and work-related aspects of the curriculum, to foster much closer school–industry links and to increase adult (but non-teacher) participation in schools. It was funded through and controlled by the Manpower Services Commission (MSC), a quasi-autonomous subsidiary of the Department for Trade and Industry (DTI). The use of this funding, together with the work of the TVEI projects themselves, was subject to external evaluation. The money was allocated through a bidding process against MSC criteria. This again was the shape of new developments as more and more funding for education was allocated through bidding processes (see Chapter 4).

In parallel with these developments, an increased emphasis on the management of schools was emerging. In 1977 the centrality of management and leadership for the success of schools was already recognized in a study which sought to identify the main features of good schools:

> The schools see themselves as places designated for learning; they take the trouble to make their philosophies explicit ... and to explain them to parents and pupils ... but without exception the most important single factor in the success of these schools is the qualities of leadership of the head. (DES 1977a, section 8)

The centrality of the head's leadership was to emerge as a key theme over the next 20 years. By 1983 it was being argued that:

> Headteachers and other ... staff with management responsibility ... are of crucial importance. Only if they are effective managers of their teaching staffs and the material resources available ... as well as possessing the qualities needed for effective educational leadership, can schools offer their pupils the quality of education which they have the right to expect. (DES 1983, para 83)

This emphasis on resource management and, more especially, on the management of the teaching force was reinforced in *Better Schools* (DES 1985a), which emphasized the need for heads to manage the teaching force effectively and argued that appraisal would make a contribution to this. This was further explored as part of the management responsibility of heads in a later document (DES 1985b). Any attempt to introduce appraisal would mean, of course, that individual professional autonomy would have to be reconsidered in the light of the overall requirements of the schools.

This need to subsume professional autonomy within an institutionally directed framework was also emphasized elsewhere:

> teachers need to work together collectively to produce an atmosphere which encourages children to respond in a positive and responsible fashion ... members of staff work as a team so that they can offer leadership and guidance ... for ... maximum curricular strength and mutual support. (DES 1985c, paras 13–30)

Thus, the need for effective school management had to take priority over teacher autonomy in the classroom. It was becoming clear that if the quality of pupil performance was to improve, schools could no longer be made up of teachers acting independently of each other. Furthermore, heads had to take on the responsibility for:

- formulating the aims of the school;
- reviewing the work and organization of the school;
- evaluating standards of teaching and learning. (DES 1987a, pp. 2–3)

Thus, heads were increasingly expected to play an overtly managerial role unlike that for which they had become heads and for which many of them had been trained (see Chapter 11). At the same time parents and representatives of other lay groups were given greater influence over the management of schools. The 1986 Education Act (DES 1986) increased parental representation on governing bodies and required the governing body of each school to deliver an Annual Report for Parents and to hold an Annual Meeting of parents to discuss that report.

A further managerial responsibility for heads, school finance, was soon to follow as a small number of LEAs introduced site-based management schemes based on financial delegation. Until the early 1980s staff in schools could exercise very little control over their finances. Such control as there was tended to be restricted to the purchase of books and equipment amounting to no more than 3 per cent of the total budget. A small number of LEAs, encouraged by the DES, developed financial delegation much further than this. They gave control over a significant proportion of the budget, including that for staffing, to the schools. In Cambridge, many heads agreed that financial delegation gave them the flexibility to respond directly and promptly to the needs of their schools and their pupils (Downes 1988). In Solihull it was argued that:

> if schools were given the right to spend their budget, as though the money was their own, it would be spent in a way which was more carefully attuned to their needs than if the decisions were made elsewhere. (Humphrey and Thomas 1985, p. 149)

This indeed proved to be the case although only certain selected schools were included in this experiment. Later forms of site-based management owed much to these pioneering schemes.

It can be seen, then, that in a period of resource constraint, the impetus for significant change was generated. The Conservative Government picked up where the Labour one left off and developed policies which were far more interventionist than any that had been seen hitherto. It was no longer the case that educational policy would be constructed through a combination of negotiation and debate between professionals and politicians. Control over education was moving firmly into the political arena. The state would not intervene to remedy the worst effects of inequalities, other definitions of equity had to be found and other mechanisms for the distribution of resources created. It was soon to become clear after the 1987 re-election of the Thatcher Government, that the new definitions of equity and the new resource allocation mechanisms were to be found in the operation of the education marketplace.

The Market Phase 1988–96

The key features of the Market Phase of educational policy in England (quality, diversity, choice, autonomy, accountability) had already begun to emerge before the education act in which they were to become enshrined, the Education Reform Act (DES 1988a). This Act was followed by a series of circulars and more education acts (e.g. DES 1988b, 1991) which together defined the essential characteristics of this phase (Table 1.3). Opportunities were available for growth as those schools defined as successful were encouraged to expand, while those branded failures contracted or closed. Site-based management within a tightly prescribed and monitored National Curriculum framework emerged, responsibility for which was vested in lay governors rather than the educational professionals. The new National Curriculum placed increasing emphasis on science, technology and information technology although many schools had neither the staff nor the equipment to deliver what was required. The curriculum concentrated on basic subjects, formally taught to achieve instrumental outcomes. Equity and social justice in education were subsumed within the philosophy of the education marketplace.

This philosophy was largely derived from the work of right-wing political

Table 1.3 The Market Phase 1988–96

Emphasis	Emphasis on growth in key areas but at expense of others.
Priorities	Priority determined outside schools and LEAs.
School management	Site-based management becoming central to school improvement but subject to rigorous accountability procedures.
Resources	Resources controlled by non-professionals (governors) or those outside the system but managed by heads.
Power and influence	Power shifting away from teachers who are de-professionalized and losing control over the curriculum and its assessment.
Teachers	Career structure provides less vertical mobility but some greater opportunities available, especially for senior staff in secondary schools.
Motive force	The market is the dominant motive force through accountability and choice. Direct state intervention targeted on the curriculum and the drive to raise standards. Change driven by inspection and parental choice supported by deregulation.
Values	Debate about education continues but is mainly located outside the system and focuses on its vocational relevance and the development of technological skills. Individualism predominates.
Equity	Defined in terms of the ability to pay and the access to sufficient resources to exercise choice.
The system	The system fragments. Different forms of institutions are developed to offer choice. Autonomy shifts to schools as state intervention disappears and LEAs become marginalized. Site-based management introduced.

economists such as Friedman and Friedman (1980) and Hayek (1973) who believed that market forces were the most appropriate way of allocating resources and structuring choices in all aspects of human endeavour, including educational policy. This belief was translated into a set of organizational principles for public sector institutions by, among others, Harris (1980), Joseph (1976) and Scruton (1984), the main tenets of which were:

- the absolute liberty of individuals to make choices based on their own self-interest;
- the freedom of individuals to exercise such choices without being subject to coercion from others;

- the freedom to choose being exercised daily through spending choices rather than every five years through the ballot box.

Competition became the motive force for policy implementation. Through such competition, improvement in the nature and quality of service was to be brought about with the family as a unit of economic consumption, its members making choices about products, and public sector institutions behaving as firms seeking to maximize both profits and market share. For this to be achieved in education, budgets had to be devolved to schools and site-based management with site-based responsibility established.

The legitimation of such policies for education was contained in the White Paper, *Choice and Diversity* (DfE 1992) which explicitly addressed the five key themes on which the education policy of the New Right was based. *Quality* was conceptualized in terms of efficient use of resources and teacher and pupil performance. It was to be measured by pupil achievement in tests and examinations compared with the national average performance. The quality of teaching was to be pursued by teacher appraisal and school inspection. Inspections placed particular emphasis on strategic planning, whole school policy in all areas of the curriculum, the link between a school's planning and the day-to-day teaching in school and the grading of teachers' performance by inspectors who observe their teaching. Particular attention was paid to the quality of management of the school. It became clear that headteachers were to be placed at the centre of the inspection process. It was their management skills and leadership styles that were perceived by inspection teams to make the difference between those schools which were successful and those which were failing.

Diversity came partly from the private sector for those who could afford it, or who were fortunate enough to benefit from government-funded assisted places schemes, and partly from new categories of institution which were created, especially grant maintained (GM) primary and secondary schools. The governing bodies of these schools owned their own land and buildings, controlled the totality of their budgets, were the employers of their staff and were responsible for all services. This is true site-based management. GM schools could apply for a change of status becoming, for example, selective rather than comprehensive. Furthermore all schools could choose to specialize in particular curriculum areas and become beacons of excellence, whether or not they had grant maintained status. At the same time, all LEA maintained schools had their budgets largely devolved to them and could therefore identify their own expenditure priorities.

Choice was to be exercised most fundamentally by parents over where and how children were to be educated:

> Parents know best the needs of their children – certainly better than educational theorists or administrators, better even than ... most teachers. (DfE 1992, p. 2)

On this basic assertion much education policy rested in this phase. Choice was increased by requiring schools to admit pupils to the limits of the physical capacity of their buildings, termed open enrolment, thereby enabling parents more easily to move children from one school to another. A school's admissions policy and its capacity were determined by the governing body rather than by the LEA. Parents who transferred their children from one school to another had the ability to influence school budgets since funding followed pupils. Thus, it was in the financial interest of all schools to accept and retain as many children as possible.

With choice then came *autonomy* based on competition fostered by diversity and open enrolment. It was intended to create a climate in which market forces could operate and where some schools would not survive. The market would dictate which schools were to close:

> Where a school is failing, pupil numbers will fall. It will be difficult to attract and retain good quality teachers and the cost of maintaining the premises and disproportionate staffing costs will place an unacceptable burden on the school's budget ... the school will not be able to achieve the high educational standards desired for all pupils. The solution is to remove surplus places and close surplus schools. (DfE 1992, p. 24)

In one sense this is the ultimate test of site-based management, the right to succeed or fail. In England, this autonomy for schools was defined as freedom from the shackles of LEA control, especially those which were Labour controlled (Centre for Policy Studies 1988). Autonomy operated largely through the delegation to school's governing bodies of control over the budget. Resource allocation decisions could be taken in the light of priorities identified in the school development plan which, in turn, was to take into account local needs and parental expectations (see Chapter 10).

With autonomy for schools came greater *accountability* of teachers to governors and of the whole school community to parents, employers and society at large. The mechanisms for holding schools to account – inspections, publishing results, annual reports and meetings – focused on individual schools and those responsible for site-based management, rather than the regional or national structure within which they functioned. Those schools that failed to reach an acceptable standard were deemed by Ofsted to be 'at risk' and, therefore, subject to special measures. An action plan for improvement had to be implemented successfully, often by a replacement headteacher, or the school faced closure. Thus, schools became accountable for the specific delivery of a nationally determined curriculum and were held accountable for their performance in that regard. Where they were deemed to be failing then either the market or the inspection process would provide a remedy.

It can be seen, therefore, that this phase of educational policy, while it has evolved from earlier phases, was about change, about the management of change and about changing the way in which schools were to be managed. The National Curriculum required schools to plan its implementation more thoroughly than was the case hitherto. This resulted in greater teacher participation in curriculum planning and decision making (Bell, Halpin and Neill 1996a). It has also enabled members of the school community to set themselves realistic goals, draw up plans to achieve them, allocate resources, monitor their use, evaluate outcomes and revise objectives in the light of evaluation. This power, however, was not granted to the teachers but to governing bodies and indirectly to parents. Thus, site-based management was defined in terms of the exercise of control over local budgets by governing bodies who had the responsibility for ensuring that resources were allocated in such a way as to ensure that the national curriculum was delivered (see Chapter 6).

At the same time, headteachers were by now both freer than were their predecessors and more constrained (see Chapters 8 and 9). The National Curriculum and Ofsted inspections imposed significant constraints while site-based management gave heads the ability to control resources, created considerable room for manoeuvre and increased the job satisfaction of many heads (Bell, Halpin and Neill 1996a). Great emphasis was placed on the leadership role of the head, almost to the exclusion of all other significant factors. Headteachers carried almost alone the responsibility for school failure. The Chief Inspector of Schools, in particular, took this position. Writing specifically about heads he stated that:

> The weakest schools are invariably the victims of poor management and weak leadership. (Woodhead 1997, p. 8)

Little credence was attached here to differential resourcing, catchment areas or the overall quality of the teaching staff. Conversely:

> It is the leadership provided by the headteacher which is *the* critical factor in raising standards of pupil achievement ... headteachers must have a clear vision of the curriculum ... the strength of personality and interpersonal tact needed to engage with teachers in raising standards; [and] the administrative drive to plan programmes of improvement and see that they were carried through. (Woodhead 1996, pp. 10-11)

Thus, if schools were to take responsibility for their own performance, the individual who shouldered the burden of that responsibility was the headteacher. Little wonder then that fear of failure on the part of some heads has resulted in some schools being subjected to a command and control approach to management which is inappropriate for educational institutions.

The Market Phase of educational policy produced a fragmented structure which emphasized resource management rather than educational values, individual rather than collective responsibility and tolerated the exacerbation of existing inequalities in the name of market forces. The period was not one of decentralization and the end of state intervention, as some might argue. The New Right was centralist and interventionist while, at the same time, devolving power and deregulating. Site-based management in England can best be seen at this time as consisting of significant autonomy within a tight legislative framework, or the McDonald's rather than the Coca Cola approach to franchising. Nevertheless, the New Right believed the legitimacy of government rested on minimizing state intervention. The British New Right during the market phase of policy making advanced the argument that the market was pre-eminent (see Chapter 8). It was not for government to decide or accept responsibility. That was a function of the market. In so arguing the New Right forgot that:

> Governing is like riding a bicycle: you must steer neither too far to one side for too long, nor too far to the other. Instead, the trick of keeping upright and moving forward lies in the deliberate choice of small, adjusted movements from one side to the other. (Etzioni 1997, quoted in Bottery 1998, p. 8)

On Thursday 8 May 1997 the New Right was pushed off its bicycle by the electorate and the Market Phase of education policy appeared to come to an abrupt end.

The Targets Phase 1997 onwards

It is wrong to assume, as many did on the morning of Friday 9 May 1997, that New Labour would abandon in their entirety the policies of the New Right. Indeed, in the arena of educational policy, many of those New Right policies which were most disliked by educational professionals have been retained and even enhanced while others, thought to be moribund, have been revisited (Table 1.4). This is not to say, however, that the New Right and New Labour are the same. This is far from the case. Tony Blair, the incoming Prime Minister, referred to the New Labour policies as the Third Way, a combination of business focused policies designed to foster enterprise and policies intended to re-establish social welfare. He placed education at the centre of the Third Way because it impacts on both the economic and the social welfare dimensions of life. Educational policies will be designed to produce a work force which is literate, numerate and has information and communication technology skills because:

> Learning is the key to prosperity – for each of us as individuals as well as for the nation as a whole. Investment in human capital will be the foundation of success in the knowledge-based global economy. We need a well-educated, well-equipped labour force … As well as securing our economic future, learning … helps make ours a civilised society, develops the spiritual side of our lives and promotes active citizenship. Learning enables people to play a full part in their community. It strengthens the family, the neighbourhood and consequently the nation. (Department for Education and Employment [DfEE] 1998a, p. 7)

The New Labour approach to all policy making, including that for education:

> rests on the premise that government at the centre not only can, but should, remake society to fit an *a priori* grand design. (Marquand 1998, p. 21)

Intervention in education is back. New policies and new approaches have been introduced, many of them driven by performance targets established by the government but to be achieved by those in schools and colleges. This is to

Table 1.4 The Targets Phase 1997 onwards

Emphasis	Greater accountability and an improvement in pupil performance reinforced by setting targets and inspecting pupil achievement.
Priorities	Achieving excellence through government defined targets for literacy and numeracy and improving work skills.
School management	Central to achieving targets – the return of the Hero Innovator who creates the effective school, but site-based management remains as a key strategy.
Resources	Managed internally but with increasing central control and direction.
Power and influence	Some internal autonomy but performance targets and strategies to achieve them identified centrally.
Teachers	Formal systems for professional development are established at all levels, including pre-promotion qualifications.
Motive force	The legacy of the market is still evident but target setting and 'naming and shaming' used.
Values	Debate about fundamental issues continues and moves into a discourse about delivery and organization rather than content. Vocationalism and the importance of IT and other work skills emphasized. A return to the notion of citizenship emerging.
Equity	Defined in terms of achieving specific attainment targets for all pupils.
The system	Fragmentation addressed by the re-emergence of LEAs as key players in delivering government policy, by the return of state intervention and by centrally funded co-operative developments such as Educational Action Zones based on bidding for funding against externally driven, needs-based criteria.

be a crusade to overcome social disadvantage and improve economic performance, as the Secretary of State for Education points out in his introduction to the White Paper *Excellence in Schools* (DfEE 1997a).

> To overcome economic and social disadvantage and to make opportunity a reality ... To compete in the global economy ... We must overcome the spiral of disadvantage ... I ask you to join us in making the crusade for higher standards a reality in every classroom and every household in the country. (DfEE 1997a, pp. 3–4)

It is a crusade to deliver excellence: 'There is nothing more important to the Government than raising the standards children achieve in schools. The White Paper *Excellence in Schools* committed us to exacting targets ... Our vision is of excellence for all' (DfEE 1998b, p. 4). The theme of achieving excellence through setting targets continued to shape the educational policy agenda into the Labour administration's second term. The new strategy for primary education, introduced in 2003, was to: 'Use tests, targets and tables to help every child develop his or her potential, help the school to improve and the public to understand the progress of the pupils and the performance of the school' (Department for Education and Science [DfES] 2003, p. 5).

Education, therefore, remains at the centre of New Labour's economic and social agenda. It is to provide the impetus for economic growth. It will enable individuals to gain access to qualifications that will make them employable, productive citizens and will thus restore the social cohesion that was lost during the New Right's flirtation with pure individualism. This was all too important to be left to the market yet many elements of the New Right education policy remain.

At the same time, a raft of New Labour education policies were introduced:

> The Government's aim is to build a world-class education system by taking excellence wherever it is found and spreading it widely ... We have moved beyond the sterile debates about school structures. *What matters is what works.* We will let excellence flourish with a light touch from the centre. We want good schools to thrive by taking more responsibility for their own affairs under the leadership of effective headteachers. But when schools fail we will intervene promptly to protect the prospects of the pupils. *Pressure and support will go hand in hand.* (Blair 1998, p. 30, my emphases)

This is the key to understanding the new phase of educational policy making. It is based on retaining a degree of autonomy for schools, but with that comes the responsibility to deliver excellence by meeting prescribed targets. It is a pragmatic strategy which can and will incorporate ideas from a range of ideological perspectives and implement them through both pressure and support.

Much would rest upon the shoulders of headteachers who were to receive much of the credit for success and take responsibility for failure:

> The leadership qualities and management skills of the headteacher are a major factor contributing to a school's performance. When a school is put into special measures, one of the factors leading to this decision is often poor leadership ... In many cases the headteacher leaves the school. (Ofsted 1998a, p. 4)

Furthermore, the role of headteachers was to become even more demanding in the future:

The vision for learning set out in this White Paper will demand the highest qualities of leadership and management from headteachers. The quality of the heads can often make a difference between the success or failure of schools. Good heads can transform a school; poor heads can block progress and achievement. It is essential that we have measures in place to strengthen the skills of all new and serving heads. We need to ensure that in future all those appointed as headteachers for the first time hold a professional qualification which demonstrates that they have the leadership skills necessary to motivate staff and pupils and to manage a school. (DfEE 1997a, p. 46)

No concept of shared or distributed leadership can be found here. Heads are central to the government's strategy. In order to ensure that they are fit for purpose a new hurdle in the race for headship has been introduced, the National Professional Qualification for Headship (NPQH), which is now mandatory. A further qualification for experienced heads and one for middle managers in schools has also been introduced under the aegis of the National College for School Leadership (NCSL). Once they have been prepared and assessed as suitable, heads have to lead and manage their school's improvement by using pupil data to set targets for even better performance while being subject to inspection and the publication of inspection reports:

From September 1998, each school will be required to have challenging targets for improvement. The use in school of reliable and consistent performance analysis enables ... headteachers to monitor the performance of classroom teachers. (DfEE 1997b, p. 26)

Thus, it is no longer sufficient for heads to have a sound knowledge of the curriculum, be outstanding teachers and good leaders and site-based managers, they must also have the appropriate qualification and subscribe to the ethos of the school effectiveness movement, for that is the source from which New Labour's target-driven approach to raising standards and improving quality is derived.

Barber makes this clear in a most influential book, *The Learning Game*, endorsed by Tony Blair as 'provocative and timely, illuminating and optimistic' (Barber 1996, front cover). Barber argues that schools should either be improving or successful or both and that where intervention takes place, this should be in inverse proportion to success. Thus: 'The general assumption ... is that most schools have within them the capacity to improve ... as long as national government provides a sensible policy and funding framework' (Barber 1996, p. 149).

Headship then has moved away from professional leadership or even the management of market forces, although both sets of tasks remain as part of the head's responsibilities. Those responsibilities, however, are now more firmly focused on the search for enhanced school success through explicit measures of institutional and individual performance to be delivered through site-based management (see Chapter 6). In other words, headship is crucial to the government's crusade for school improvement. This encapsulates the New

Labour approach to its educational policy. Nevertheless, this policy still retains significant elements of New Right strategy.

If we return to the five themes of the New Right White Paper *Choice and Diversity: a New Framework for Schools* (DfE 1992), and consider them from the New Labour perspective, we find that all the themes can still be identified, albeit in modified forms, and the policies to implement them are still largely recognizable. The centrepiece of New Right policy, the National Curriculum, remains intact although for primary schools, at least, there is a greater emphasis on literacy, numeracy and information and communication technology (ICT) at the expense of art, drama, music and the creative arts generally. The emphasis on *quality* remains although the focus is now on raising standards and achieving excellence. Furthermore, the standards that are to be achieved are now expressed in terms of targets. These will be set for all schools in conjunction with their LEAs, but must move towards those set nationally. These targets are that by 2002, 80 per cent of pupils aged 11 will attain the standard in English expected for their age group: that is the average standard for the age group. In mathematics, 75 per cent of 11-year-olds will achieve the standard expected for their age group. Targets are also to be set to reduce exclusion and truancy by 30 per cent, provide nursery education for all four-year-olds through the National Childcare Strategy, to ensure that no child under the age of seven is taught in a class of more than 30 and to connect every school to the Internet.

Teachers are not to be left on their own, or to the mercy of the market, to ensure that they meet targets set for their schools. Already, detailed guidelines have been given for setting and achieving targets. Heads and their staff are urged to adopt a five-stage cycle for setting targets for school improvement which requires that the school:

> *Stage 1: analyses its current performance* – looking critically at pupils' current achievements is an essential first step towards improvement.
> *Stage 2: compares its results with those of similar schools* – by comparing current and previous results, and those from similar schools, a school can better judge performance.
> *Stage 3: sets itself clear and measurable targets* – with good information, a school can set itself realistic and challenging targets for improvement.
> *Stage 4: revises its development plan to highlight action to achieve the targets* – Once it has set its targets, the school must then take determined action to improve.
> *Stage 5: takes action, reviews success, and starts the cycle again* – A school must monitor and evaluate its actions in terms of improved pupil performance. (after DfEE 1997b, p. 7)

Even more detailed guidelines on this approach to school improvement were given in *School Evaluation Matters* (Ofsted 1998b), which poses a series of questions designed to elicit data on the strengths and weaknesses of schools and concludes by recommending that schools adopt the Business Excellence Model, arguing that: 'The best industrial models for performance review . . . are consistent with the OfSTED Inspection Framework' (Ofsted 1998b, p. 21).

New Labour is not only clear about the broad approaches that it wishes to be adopted in schools. It is also clear about the detailed strategies to be deployed in all schools in specific curriculum areas. There is a National Literacy Strategy which sets out detailed teaching objectives to enable children to become fully literate and gives guidance on the implementation of the Literacy Hour which all primary schools are required to adopt (DfEE 1998c). This is meant to provide a practical structure which will enable teaching objectives to be achieved and the national targets for literacy to be attained. This is the first time that any government in the UK has instructed teachers in the detail of what to teach, how to teach it and how long to devote to it.

The National Numeracy Strategy (DfEE 1998d) appeared a few months later. This was a product of the work of a task force chaired by a leading figure in the school effectiveness movement who had already made an impact under the previous government with his work on the benefits of class teaching of mathematics in Taiwan. Summer Numeracy Schools and homework clubs in both primary and secondary schools were by now commonplace in order to help children to cope with the work required from them under the government's new guidance on minimum levels of homework. Furthermore, intense pressure was now being exerted on teachers to adopt a wider view of their own role and for many others to take an active part in providing learning opportunities for children. In *Extending Opportunity: a National Framework for Study Support* (DfEE 1997c) more than twenty different ways were detailed to enable young people to have access to a range of activities in addition to normal classroom teaching and learning. These included after-school study support centres, breakfast clubs, Saturday study sessions, Summer University, links with professional football clubs to promote literacy and numeracy, peer tutoring, mentoring by business people and community service. Site-based managers were to be responsible for much of this. In a most fundamental way, therefore, government intervention had penetrated beyond the curriculum.

Much of this intervention was intended to raise standards by directly improving or supporting the performance of teachers. Ofsted inspections also played a key role in this under the New Right by observing and commenting upon, but not directly identifying and reporting on the teachers that inspectors observed. Not only could this part of the inspection be included in the report but any teacher whose performance fell below the acceptable standard had to be named and, it was claimed: 'We will deal speedily and fairly to remove teachers not up to the job' (Blair 1998, p. 34).

For the first time the arrangements for appraisal were included in the inspection schedule, thereby ensuring that far more attention would be paid to teacher appraisal than had recently been the case. The abandoned New Right policy of paying more to good classroom practitioners was revived and implemented by New Labour and the appraisal of teacher performance based on individual performance targets became linked to pay and promotion (DfES 2005). Progression through an incremental pay scale, while not abolished, has become less rewarding for the basic scale teacher. Threshold Assessment has now been introduced by which teachers have to demonstrate, partly through performance review, partly through a portfolio of evidence and partly through an assessment by an external assessor, that they are fit to progress on to the next stage of the pay scale (DfEE 2000a, Mahoney *et al.* 2004). This increase in target setting and performance appraisal does not mean, however, that *diversity* has been entirely rejected, although its emphasis has also changed, focusing much more on difference within a centrally and locally controlled framework which encourages site-based management. The private sector still offers choice for those who can afford it but the Assisted Places Scheme has been wound up because it is believed to drain resources away from public education. It was claimed that over £260 million would be released by 2001 which was to be used to reduce class sizes and improve primary school accommodation (Blair 1998). City Technology Colleges were being left to wither on the vine. Beacon schools, providing examples of best practice, were identified and funded, while grant maintained schools returned to the LEA fold within a new school framework, Foundation schools, which, like GM schools, could employ their own staff and own their own premises. Most other schools retained their existing status with LEA controlled schools becoming community schools within which the LEA employs staff and owns the premises. Diversity was to be fostered within community schools by strengthening arrangements for site-based management through financial delegation in order to ensure that schools have the greatest possible proportion of relevant funding delegated to them. Similarly, *choice* has acquired a different emphasis while remaining a policy theme, not least because it was widely believed that the professional classes were more able to exercise choice than other social groups (Hirsch 1997). The marketplace continued to operate but as a controlled rather than a free market. A code of practice for admissions was produced and an independent adjudicator on school organization and admissions appointed and parents were given greater representation on both school governing bodies and LEA committees where many decisions about admissions are taken.

The trappings of both autonomy and accountability are still much in evidence. *Autonomy* through site-based management and the delegation of powers to school governing bodies was to be enhanced. Resource allocation decisions are still to be taken by governing bodies in the light of the targets that schools set within overall national targets. There was, in primary schools, a much greater national emphasis on deploying resources to reduce class sizes, dispelling a favourite New Right myth that class size and pupil performance were independent variables. Furthermore, autonomy was no longer defined as freedom from the shackles of LEAs. LEAs, now subject to their own Ofsted inspections and target setting, have a role to play in helping their schools to achieve high standards but within a site-based management framework. The penalty for failing LEAs is now similar to that of schools, being placed in special measures and having power removed. Thus *accountability* has spread to LEAs. As far as schools are concerned, all of the elements of accountability that provided the impetus for the education market remain. Results will still be published; league tables will still be produced but will provide more detail and will have a value-added element; increasingly rigorous inspections by Ofsted continue. In 2004 a new approach to inspection was announced based on a self-evaluation review. This is not a self-evaluation but a review of steps taken to evaluate school performance and of targets set and actions implemented as a result of those evaluations (MacBeath 2006). Ofsted's judgements, however, became even more telling since the Secretary of State's 'Fresh Start' idea was incorporated into Ofsted strategy. This is where a school which is significantly underachieving is immediately closed, perhaps over an extended summer break, and a new school opened with a new staff and a new governing body thereby making the threat of extinction the ultimate sanction for failing site-based managers. Some of the key features of the education marketplace, therefore, remain intact or have been strengthened.

Nevertheless, there are significant differences between the education policy of the Labour Government since 1997 and that which preceded it. Policy is no longer driven by market forces alone. It is located within the context of school improvement which is articulated through a centrally determined set of targets, rather than operating only through fear of failure and threat of closure, although both the fear and the threat remain (see Chapter 12). LEAs are reinstated as partners in the enterprise of achieving excellence. Support, guidance and resources linked to specific targets must be made available by LEAs to schools. LEAs now have a duty to ensure that their work helps to raise standards in schools. They will be required to prepare an Educational Development Plan, in consultation with their schools, to promote school improvement and to help schools to reach their individual performance targets. Some resource allocation is linked to competition for pupil numbers while competitive bidding for funding against specific criteria has been extended. The most significant example of this was the Education Action Zone (EAZ) policy.

Education Action Zones evolved from the Educational Priority Areas of the 1960s which focused on improving pupil performance in basic subjects in deprived areas. The new EAZs were to provide opportunities for action where currently approaches were not working quickly enough to raise standards in both urban and rural areas of deprivation: 'Each of the zones will be in areas of relative disadvantage. Many will also be in areas where educational perform-ance is well below average' (Adamson 1998, p. 1).

EAZs typically involved two or three secondary schools and their feeder primary schools. They were led by a Forum which provided an action plan as part of the bid for the EAZ. This plan might include an application to the government to modify the National Curriculum or to operate outside the national pay and conditions arrangements for teachers. Money was allocated by a competitive bidding process based on submissions which included a clear statement of the level of disadvantage being addressed and the roles to be played by LEAs, schools and other partners from industry and commerce in establishing ways to raise standards. The strategies recommended include many of those identified in *Extending Opportunity* (DfEE 1997c). These strategies, and EAZs themselves, have been criticized by leaders of teachers' unions because they are interpreted as seeking to undermine teachers' conditions of service, especially working hours and holiday entitlements. Nevertheless, when the first 25 were announced they were described as:

> a radical initiative to raise standards in England's most deprived areas. The zones mobilise public and private partnerships at local level to improve schools. All of them have business partners, ranging from Blackburn Rovers in Blackburn to Rolls Royce in South Tyneside ... Every EAZ has ambitious targets to raise achievement. Innovation in teaching and learning methods is the key to the policy: including super

teachers, curriculum changes to give priority to literacy and numeracy, and all year round schooling. (Blair 1998, p. 34)

To the extent that they focused on disadvantage, EAZs were EPAs with a much stronger managerial thrust and a more clearly defined set of performance criteria (Bell and Stevenson 2006). To the extent that they depended for their success on partnerships with industry and commerce, they harked back to TVEI. They were firmly located within an educational policy framework derived from the school-effectiveness movement and were intended to have a far-reaching impact on the work of teachers in schools and classrooms.

Conclusion

Thus, government intervention in education has taken on a new form. It impacts on the classroom as much as on the LEA and the wider administrative structure. It is both broad in its scope and detailed in its application. It is concerned with achieving specific and measurable performance targets against which everyone and everything in education will be judged. This phase of educational policy making, therefore, appears to be strongly post-Fordian (Bottery 1998). Policy making and implementation strategy is becoming increasing centralized. Specific criteria for success and the targets against which success is measured are determined by central policy makers while a variety of providers are encouraged to compete against those criteria. The agenda focuses on raising standards but the standards to be attained are determined centrally. The responsibility for achieving those standards is clearly defined. In schools it rests with the headteacher, but schools must receive specific support from LEAs. Equity is now defined in terms of meeting those standards while social justice will be expressed in terms of fostering civic virtues such as employability and productiveness. Direct competition is no longer a necessary virtue but neither is it an unnecessary evil. School autonomy remains an integral part of this policy. Schools that are meeting the defined standards or are striving to improve will retain their autonomy. Those that are believed to be failing will lose their autonomy.

Thus, the modality of state control has shifted from: 'The detailed prescription of how schools should operate to the setting and monitoring of performance targets they have to meet' (Whitty 2005, p. v). This pattern of state control, however, has its origins in the education policies that were developed in the 1960s and 1970s. The concern about the extent to which policy makers at both national and local levels were excluded from decision making about the curriculum and an increasing determination by those policy makers to hold teachers to account for what they did both emerged as policy issues in those decades.

2

I'll Do, I'll Do, and I'll Do: Organizational Culture, Schools and Teachers' Work

Introduction

Schools are a product of their history, environments and the changes within them that have an impact on the ways in which teachers' work is defined and carried out. Underpinning what teachers do is a range of values and beliefs that are a product of past and contemporary events (Beynon 1985). These values and beliefs combine to form organizational cultures within which teachers' work is legitimated. The actions of teachers, in turn, help to give meaning to aspects of those cultures. This chapter analyses the forging of a new organizational culture over a period of three years in the late 1980s in one school, Oakfields, created by the closure and amalgamation of three institutions whose staff had different and, to some extent, incompatible professional cultures. It is, therefore, about cultural transformation and the role played in that transformation by the headteacher. It identifies the different organizational cultures of three schools in one small town and examines, through a series of critical incidents, the clash of cultures that had to be managed as a new institution was formed from the three constituent parts as a result of an amalgamation. Such amalgamations were common towards the end of the Resource Constrained phase of educational policy as LEAs struggled to meet the demands placed upon them within very restricted budgets. Managing this amalgamation presented the headteacher responsible for the new institution with a challenging set of leadership issues that had to be confronted in order to establish the cultural identity of the new school and to transform the institution into something more than the sum of its constituent parts.

Data on Oakfields School was collected by interviews with 53 staff, through questionnaires distributed to all staff with a 45 per cent response rate, and by observation of key meetings, documentary analysis and teaching in the school. The main part of the research took place in the year following the amalgamation but follow-up interviews with ten members of staff took place in the subsequent year (see Bell 1994a for a fuller account of how this research was conducted). Information about the cultures of the three schools was collected during the interviews by asking teachers about their perceptions of the school from which they came, and about the other two schools. The researcher, who had worked in each school, was able to use local knowledge where it was confirmed by other data. The information collected in these ways was remarkably consistent. The concept of organizational culture is particularly helpful in understanding the attitudes and behaviour of the teachers in the new school and how and why they responded to the difficult situation in which they found themselves. This chapter will examine how the residual cultural elements from three different institutions interacted with the predominant culture of the new school during the first year of its existence to influence the nature of school work and the relationships between teachers and the new organization.

The concept of organizational culture

The use of the concept of culture in social scientific research generally and in educational research in particular is not new. There is, however, no agreement on the precise definition or even use of the term although Taylor formulated what is widely recognized as the classic definition. He stated that, 'culture ... is that complex whole which includes knowledge, belief, art, morals, law, custom and any other capabilities and habits acquired by man as a member of society' (Taylor 1971, p. 1).

Perhaps the most extensive examination of culture was made by Kroeber and Kluckhohn (1952), who suggested that the essential core of culture consists of traditional ideas and their attached values. The nature and extent to which culture influences behaviour, or is defined by it, may depend on how far the values on which the culture is based are embedded in a society and on the extent to which they are professedly or actually followed by its members. Culture in this sense, therefore, consists of sets of values that help individuals construct the reality of organizational life. From this point of view an organization is a precarious web of interpretations and meanings through which individuals and groups establish and sustain a semblance of order in their daily interactions (Morgan 1989). The values and beliefs that predominate within the culture of any organization give shape to it and help to define its main purposes and how it functions.

Organizations each have their own distinctive sets of shared values, beliefs and behaviours that make up their unique culture. This culture is a socially constructed reality that is shaped by historical circumstances and created and sustained through many kinds of social processes, images, symbolic actions, rituals and use of language. Organizational culture rests, therefore on shared meanings that, in turn, are based on common values and norms that legitimate various patterns of social behaviour and help to reinforce and perpetuate them within the organization. Within each organization people can select from a wide range of purposes, motivations and behaviours. They may emphasize some actions, minimize the importance of others and exclude yet others as the culture of the organization. This was certainly the case in Oakfields School.

Organizational culture and schools

The interest in organizational culture as it relates to schools is not new. Waller (1932) established the importance of culture, beliefs, rituals, ceremonies and values for the school as a social organization. Nias *et al.* (1992) recognized that the organizational culture consists of rules of behaviour that guide interaction between those who subscribe to a set of beliefs and values. In schools, an organizational culture grows and is sustained by human discourse. Torrington and Weightman (1989) point out that such a culture is the glue that binds the institution together. It is 'living, growing and vital, able to strengthen and support the efforts of those who use it and will frustrate the efforts of those who ignore it' (Torrington and Weightman 1989, p. 19).

Thus, as Fullan and Hargreaves (1992) point out, a school's organizational culture influences the ways in which things are done and how members of the organization relate to each other. It reflects the subjective side of school organization that enables the school to survive with a distinctive identity (Neville 1995). This organizational culture, therefore, is revealed through the actions of its members rather than through formal documentation or public utterances.

A useful distinction has been made between generic and genetic cultures (Prosser 1992). Generic culture enshrines the fundamental high priority values and beliefs of the school while genetic culture incorporates distinctive processes and ways of doing things that reflect generic values. Generic culture, Prosser argues, is far more difficult to change than its genetic counterpart. This study concentrates on the struggles within one school to establish its own generic culture and to develop appropriate genetic elements. It is possible that, since a school's generic culture may be taken for granted, significant elements of it may be known without being understood (Torrington and Weightman 1989). In the case of a newly formed school such elements tend to be identified and articulated through critical incidents which challenge core values. Where a school does not have a well-established culture, critical incidents may form an important part of the process of defining and embedding it.

The three schools

As Duigan (1987) has observed, life in organizations such as schools is often uncertain and complex. Members of those organizations are confronted with dynamic situations consisting of complicated systems of changing problems that interact with each other. Decisions within schools are often constrained by factors over which staff have no control. Thus schools operate in a turbulent environment characterized by instability and unpredictability. Schools are not able to disregard the pressures emanating from their external environment, nor are they necessarily able to buffer themselves against the unforeseen by gaining control over the source of the uncertainty. As will be argued in Chapter 3, decision making in schools may not be rational or necessarily appropriate to the circumstances as perceived by all members of the organization. This may create a situation in which staff experience varying degrees of attachment to the school as its nature fluctuates and as issues emerge and are resolved or shelved.

This was the case with the three schools in this case study. Pupil numbers were falling, schools had surplus places and too many teachers, and the economic situation at both national and local levels required that savings should be made in locally provided services such as education. In the light of these pressures the Local Education Authority decided to reorganize secondary education. A number of possible plans were considered. The option preferred by local politicians and educational administrators was to close three schools, two of which shared the same campus, amalgamate them and open a new school on the shared campus. This had the advantage of enabling the LEA to close one more of its small and relatively inefficient high schools on the outskirts of the town and to sell the land for development. It also left the selective schools largely untouched and avoided the problems associated with trying to restructure church schools. The plan would have administrative benefit and remove the inconvenience of having two schools with the same name but with different headteachers on the same site.

As might be expected, the impact of the plans on the three schools was considerable. In each school the prevailing culture was very different. The staff of the high school, Loxley, prided themselves on working in a small organization within which they could get to know pupils well and provide for their individual needs. This school had a strong tradition of special education and of working effectively with children from racial minorities. Its staff regarded themselves as secondary school teachers, that is not teachers of academic subjects, and saw their prime role as meeting the educational needs of non-academic pupils. The school was not particularly successful in public examinations. The staff thought of themselves as a caring group, although corporal punishment, which was still legal at that time, was used. It was, in many ways, a paternalistic institution in which decisions were taken in the best interests of pupils but without their active involvement. The headteacher had been at the school for a long time. His management style can best be described as *laissez-faire*. He allowed his staff to get on with their jobs without interference from him.

The Loxley High School community responded to the threat of closure by highlighting the main differences between itself and the other two schools. A public campaign against closure was mounted by senior staff and parents. It was claimed that a unique type of educational provision would be lost if the school closed and that the proposed new school would be entirely unsuitable for pupils from Loxley. This argument depended for its force on the creation of a stereotypical view of the other two schools and the ways in which the interests of pupils from non-selective schools and those from ethnic minorities would be ignored in an institution dominated by staff and pupils from the selective parts of the bilateral schools. Bilateral schools accepted two types of pupils, those who passed the 11+ examination for selective education and those who did not. These children were normally treated as entirely discrete groups within one institution.

The staff of the two bilateral schools felt that the education they offered was being caricatured by the high-school staff. In their different ways, however, the staff of each school were heavily influenced by their perceptions of the cultures in the other schools. Although the bilateral schools shared a campus and were in two halves of the same building, they were different in many ways. The boys' school, Barford, was regarded by the staff of the other two schools as very traditional in its approach to teaching and learning. It was hierarchical, tightly, perhaps inflexibly, organized and rigid discipline was enforced by a deputy headmaster of very long standing in the school. It was an authoritarian school with a tradition of valuing high academic standards, especially in science, and significant sporting achievements. It had specific and detailed codes of behaviour reinforced by corporal punishment and an extensive detention system, operated by staff and prefects. It was hierarchic in structure. As one teacher explained it, the school was dominated by a strong team at the top, in which all the senior staff was male and which operated on the basis of seniority and length of service as two significant criteria for staff promotion, good examination results being a third.

The belief in seniority as a criterion for preferment was so strong that the majority of the staff at Barford confidently expected that their headmaster would become the head of the new school because the head of Loxley, by far the longest serving of the three heads, was retiring and their man, who was in his second headship, had been at Barford far longer than the female headteacher who was in her first headship at the girls' school. It was anticipated, therefore, by the staff of Barford that the new school would become a mirror image of their school. As a result, the proposals received tacit support except insofar as it was possible to identify in the girls' school well-qualified staff with a good record of achieving notable public examination results. Here there might be conflict over jobs, since it was known that the new school would not require all the staff who taught in the three schools. Staff of the high school were largely discounted by those of the boys' school in this regard. The possibility that preference might be given to staff of the girls' school was recognized by the boys' school staff, although the prevailing view in the school was that their girls' school counterparts were weak on discipline and too progressive in their approach to teaching and learning to achieve high academic standards.

The staff of the girls' school, Lowchurch, thought their school to be a much more liberal institution than the more rigidly organized and traditional boys' school. Their headteacher, who had been in post almost three years, was supported by a senior management team consisting of a male and a female deputy. The predominant management style was participative and, at times, collegial. The school had a reputation for valuing individuals and having a flexible approach to teaching and learning, especially in the arts subjects. Its prospectus placed great emphasis on fostering self-discipline and independence in its pupils and on encouraging them to take responsibility for their own progress. Its pastoral arrangements were an important and well-developed part of the curriculum. Lowchurch staff saw this as a great strength and believed that their colleagues in the boys' school lacked many of the skills necessary to foster self-discipline in pupils and to cope with the challenges of teaching mixed classes rather than groups of boys. Although a number of individuals were vociferous in their criticism of the processes and decision-making procedures the Lowchurch staff were, perhaps, the least opposed to the amalgamation collectively. This was due, in part, to the attempts made by the head and her senior staff to set up a support system for the staff. This enabled them to enhance their qualifications and gain further experience by job exchanges and sharing responsibilities, thus preparing for the changes. It also enabled them to apply with confidence for new positions either within the new school or elsewhere. No such system existed in the other two schools.

Each of the three headteachers had been aware for almost two years prior to the event that their schools were likely to be merged. The head of the high school took little part in discussions on the merger and did little to promote the interests of his staff. This was left to a very able female deputy and a senior and long-established head of faculty. The other two heads made it known from the outset that they were interested in the headship of the new Oakfields School. The headmaster of Barford shared the expectations of his staff that, as the senior man, he would be appointed. He set about making his own school an even more tightly managed institution with an even greater emphasis on academic achievement and sport, a model of what the new school might become. His approach to the impending change was described as, 'Do as before but more so.' The head of Lowchurch adopted a somewhat different approach. She had been given the impression at her interview for her current post that if the merger took place then the new school, which would be mixed sex and have pupils of mixed academic ability, would need to look less like a traditional grammar school and more like a comprehensive school with a reasonable concern for academic attainment but with a strong pastoral structure. She took this to mean that if she made a success of the headship of the girls' school then she would be a very strong candidate for the new post. As a result she set up a small planning group from within her senior staff to plan what the new school might look like.

In the event, the head of Lowchurch was appointed headteacher of Oakfields. The staff of Loxley High School were somewhat relieved because they could see roles for themselves in a pastoral structure which they anticipated would be part of the new school. The staff of the boys' school and its headmaster were devastated. They let it be known publicly that they feared that academic standards and discipline in the new school would decline. A group, based around the senior deputy, began tacitly to oppose the creation of the new school by trying to influence parents and local politicians and by leaking stories to the press. One such leak concerned the cost of an initial planning residential weekend that was organized for senior and middle management at the new school. The local press produced banner headlines about the cost of a 'luxury weekend' and suggested that the money might be better spent on much-needed science equipment. The weekend was cancelled.

It can be seen, therefore, that each of the three schools that were to make up the new institution had very different cultures (see Table 2.1) and that these differences were also recognized by staff in the other two schools. The organizational cultures which prevailed in each school helped to determine the perception of the other institutions and played a significant part in shaping the attitudes of teachers towards the impending amalgamation. Once the amalgamation had taken place and Oakfields School established, aspects of each culture, the fundamental high priority values from which the identity of each school was derived, re-emerged as powerful sub-cultures of resistance in the micro-political processes through which the staff of Oakfields set about the task of creating and defining the essential features of the new school. The Loxley High School staff's concern for the pastoral development of pupils, the Barford teachers' belief in the pre-eminence of high academic standards based on success in public examinations, and their Lowchurch colleagues' emphasis

Table 2.1 Characteristics of the three constituent schools and the newly formed school

	Loxley	**Barford**	**Lowchurch**	**Oakfields**
Pupils	Unsuccessful at 11+, boys and girls with some ethnic minorities, no sixth form	Boys only, mainly white, selective with sixth form, plus those unsuccessful at 11+	Girls only with a few from ethnic minorities, selective with sixth form, plus those unsuccessful at 11+	Boys and girls with some ethnic minorities, all ability range with sixth form
Teaching staff	Male and female, mainly non-graduate	Male, mainly graduate	Female with some male, mainly graduate	Male and female, graduate and non-graduate
Teaching and learning style	Based on pupil need but fairly traditional with a strong emphasis on special educational needs and the needs of minority groups	Extremely traditional with streaming and an expectation of high academic standards especially in science subjects	Flexible but with an emphasis on pupils taking responsibility for their own learning. An expectation of high academic standards especially in arts subjects	Flexible with an emphasis on pupils taking responsibility for their own learning and special needs. High standards expected across all subjects
Pastoral care	Based on good teacher–pupil relationships, small group work, knowing pupils well and caring for them but with some corporal punishment	Based on rigid discipline, a strong code of behaviour reinforced by corporal punishment	Based on pupil self-discipline and the development of independence	Based on independence and self-discipline with good pupil–teacher relationships
Management style	*Laissez-faire*, staff left to plan own work	Authoritarian, rigid and based on seniority and length of service	Collegial and participative	Collegial and participative

on pupil self-motivation and self-determination each proved to be powerful sets of generic cultural values from which different staff groups derived strong genetic beliefs about ways of doing things and about which work-related activities were appropriate for teachers in the new school. The sub-cultures which coalesced around these sets of values were sufficiently distinct to approximate, at least for a time, to what Hargreaves (1992) calls 'Balkanization'. At the same time the newly appointed head recognized that, as Gronn (1996) suggests, the defining of a school's values means shaping its enduring institutional character.

Loxley and Barford schools had existed in their present form with more or less the same structure and culture since the LEA had embarked on a process of reorganization to introduce non-selective education in two of its four areas in the early 1970s. Although selective education was retained in the area in which Loxley and Barford schools were located, some organizational changes also took place there to establish these two schools in the form in which they existed at the time of the amalgamation. Lowchurch School also dated back to the same period as the other two institutions but had undergone significant changes in both its culture and its structure, initiated by its newly appointed headteacher over the three years prior to the amalgamation. It was largely this culture that was to be introduced to Oakfields School.

The new school vision

Organizational cultures are built through the everyday business of school life but formal leaders play a central role in developing and articulating those cultures through a commitment to the organization's basic purpose (Duigan 1987). These formal leaders often become the heroes and heroines whose thoughts and actions Deal (1988) identified as being so important in shaping school culture. At Oakfields the newly appointed head was to become the main heroine about whom stories would be told and around whom several influential organizational myths would centre. She had a clear vision of what she wanted the school to be. The main elements of this vision were: a style based on the development of a culture of collaboration; relationships based on independence and individual autonomy rather than on a dependence of the pupil on the teacher; discipline based on self-control rather than through enforcement supported by sanctions; and the development of teaching and learning processes which would enable the child to enter the world after formal education as an active participant and a responsible contributor to it, capable of as much independence as possible.

On the basis of this vision the head's first priority was to create a school where all members of it were treated with equal respect. Almost all the staff professed to accept the school's aims and to recognize the importance of developing individual autonomy in pupils. There were, however, some conflicts about how the vision might be realized, which stemmed from differing views about what teachers should do and which strategies were effective in different situations. This chapter illustrates those conflicts through an analysis of three critical incidents that were central to the development of the generic culture of Oakfields School.

Negotiating the organizational culture of Oakfields School: three critical incidents

Discipline in the school

The head wished to base discipline in the school on pupil autonomy, responsibility and self-discipline in accordance with the school's expressed aims. She abolished corporal punishment and instituted a system of reporting on pupil progress in cases of difficulty with academic performance or behaviour, much to the dismay of many of the staff from Barford and some from Loxley. They anticipated that general order and discipline in the school would suffer. Furthermore, they found themselves in a situation in which activities that had previously been widely accepted and which had been a significant factor in defining professional competence were now no longer legitimate. In essence, these teachers felt de-skilled and placed at risk by this new policy and many of them had neither the capacity, the inclination nor the necessary skills to develop alternative strategies with which to relate to their pupils, influence their behaviour and foster their learning.

It soon became evident that one member of the senior team, although a good administrator, had some difficulty in coping with disruptive pupils. As a result he was heavily criticized by some of his colleagues, especially those from Barford where he had been the junior deputy head. His credibility, and that of the whole senior management team, suffered in spite of the most efficient way in which he solved a number of complex organizational problems. Being a good disciplinarian remains a more accepted criterion for professional status in teaching than being a good administrator. The majority of teachers, however, believed that pupils should be encouraged to develop self-discipline. In the event, some teachers did encounter discipline problems once the sanction of corporal punishment was withdrawn, but most did not. A significant group followed the new approach with reluctance while a very few continued to practice corporal punishment covertly until one long-established member of the boy's school was disciplined and eventually dismissed for this. Discussion in the staffroom about class control was, for a time, very animated. Key figures from the Lowchurch staff, supported by a group of teachers from the high school with pastoral and special needs responsibilities, did act as forceful advocates for an approach based on pupil self-awareness and self-discipline. Appropriate teacher activities here included discussion with pupils, involving pupils in setting standards of behaviour and in taking responsibility for their own space in the school. Procedures based on these values became the accepted pattern of dealing with disciplinary matters by the end of the second year of Oakfields's existence.

This situation illustrates how powerful generic values can shape attitudes towards professional practice. As Davies (1990) shows, a uniform feature of different cultures within schools is a concern with the teachers' need to control a large cohort of sometimes unwilling participants. In Oakfields, differences in values and beliefs among the staff based on past experience meant that groups of teachers formed conflicting views about which strategies for managing pupil behaviour were workable. Furthermore, some teachers demonstrated that the generic elements of the cultures from their previous schools were extremely resistant to change even where the genetic elements were modified reluctantly. Eventually some members of staff did change although others did not. Many of this latter group eventually left the school.

Pupil access to buildings

A similar and related conflict emerged over pupil access to the school. The staff of both Loxley High School and Barford believed that a decision to allow pupils open access to the buildings at lunchtimes was a mistake. Pupils, in their view, could not be trusted to be in school unsupervised and lunchtime supervision of pupils was not part of a teacher's day-to-day responsibility. This view was supported by horror stories of what had happened in other schools where pupils were allowed unlimited access to the building. In the event, vandalism and violent behaviour did increase. Considerable pressure was exerted on the senior management team by the staff as a whole to 'be seen about the building at break times' and to accept responsibility for their own policy. This was regarded by some teachers as an essential part of the work of senior managers in the school. It was agreed that they would be available if needed. The head already walked the building at breaks to enable her to meet pupils. This came to be one the school's rituals. Her senior colleagues followed suit while arguing that it was a waste of time and not appropriate for them to do.

In spite of these difficulties, however, open access remained the school policy. Teachers began to take advantage of it to develop work with pupils and to use the time to solve some timetabling problems, especially for pupils taking public examinations. This became so important to many teachers and pupils that the success of the open access policy was later to be cited as evidence of the effective establishment of an organizational culture based on pupil self-discipline and control. Over time, working with pupils on this basis became the established and accepted practice at Oakfields School. A key aspect of the generic organizational culture at Oakfields School had been established and elements of the old cultures abolished. This helped to define those legitimate working relationships between teachers and pupils which were to form part of the genetic culture.

Registration

The senior management team organized the school day in such a way that an afternoon registration period with the form tutor was omitted from the timetable. This was due to the difficulties of incorporating the demands of the General Certificate of Secondary Education (GCSE) into the timetable. Registration was to be carried out by whoever happened to be teaching the class in the first period after lunch and absences reported by sending a pink form to the school office. It was clear that some staff, teaching at the extremities of the building, would not return their pink slips until the end of afternoon school so absences could not be followed up until the next day. This was a radical departure from the usual approach to school organization. Those with a dependency-control view of pupils predicted that truancy would increase while others argued that pupils would act responsibly. Again the generic culture of the schools from which teachers came tended to be the determining factor in predicting their initial responses to this issue.

It was soon evident that the new approach to registration had considerable limitations. The working arrangements for afternoon registration, which resulted from pressures on the new organization, were not effective. Many teachers did not know the pupils well enough to carry out registration quickly or accurately. Others, under pressure to get lessons started, simply forgot to take the register and attempted to do this some days later. Pink slips were not processed with sufficient speed to enable meaningful checks to be made. Truancy, in the form of opting out of specific lessons or missing afternoon school, did increase. Examples came to light of pupils attending morning registration and then leaving school for the rest of the day.

The head resorted to exhortations to teachers through the Staff Bulletin to ensure that they carried out the appropriate procedures. Members of the senior management team took the view that the system was not ideal, but it could work if staff co-operated. Evidence to the contrary was discounted and those who criticized the system most vociferously were regarded by some senior staff, although not the head, as villains rather than victims of a situation. Changes could not be made to these procedures without bringing into question the legitimacy of a major generic element of the school culture as it was defined by senior staff.

The system, although flawed, remained in operation throughout the first year of the school's existence, in spite of considerable pressure from all quarters to have it modified. At the start of the second year, afternoon registration by form tutors was reintroduced. Since the generic culture of Oakfields School was being challenged it was only possible to respond to this by, at best, making changes to the genetic culture on the basis of organizational expediency. This was achieved by the headteacher who asserted that the removal of the split-site arrangement created time to enable form tutors to carry out afternoon registration. In fact the use of two sites had very little bearing on the registration system or the timetabling problems that had precipitated it.

These three critical incidents show that some features of the daily life of a school exemplify some of its important values and become critical in the process of defining the nature of its organizational culture. Appropriate ways of working with pupils, of monitoring pupil attendance at school and of supervising them at various times during the school day were all significant issues that helped to define what teachers should do and how teachers saw themselves in the first year of Oakfields School's existence. The precise nature of the values on which these interactions are predicated often only become clear through processes of challenge and conflict.

Leadership and organizational culture

In each of these critical defining incidents, the head had a pivotal role in creating and sustaining a significant aspect of the school's organizational culture. She had a senior management team consisting of three deputies and a senior teacher over whose appointment she had no control. At least two of this team would not have been of her choosing. She was also supported by a group of very able middle managers over whose appointment she had been able to exert considerable influence. Much time was spent by the head developing, supporting and encouraging this group who, between them, had responsibility for all the main departments in the school through a faculty system. They were either faculty heads or heads of large departments within a faculty. They came to identify themselves as a coherent group and worked as such, recognizing, before many of their colleagues, that working practices within and between departments had to be changed if the new school was to operate effectively. They termed themselves 'The Snowman Group' because the head gave each of them a coffee mug with the picture of a snowman on it as a Christmas gift at the end of Oakfields' first term. They formed a powerful group within the school, espousing, articulating and supporting those values on which the new organizational culture rested. They all held positions which enabled them to play an active role in establishing this culture.

Through this group the culture of collaboration was established at two levels. Staff within the departments were encouraged to become involved in decision making and helped to take responsibility for the work within the department beyond that required for their own classroom activities. At the same time, departments were encouraged to collaborate within faculties, and faculties to co-operate with each other. This extension of responsibility and collaboration did not prove to be easy, especially as participation and collaboration had not been a significant feature of two of the constituent schools. As a consequence of this some teachers did not regard it as part of their job to become involved in school or even departmental-level decision-making processes.

A small but significant number of teachers, especially among the boys' school staff, avoided taking part in any school-level decision making, arguing that their function was to teach a subject and that senior management were paid to run the school. Others took a similar stance in their departments, concentrating on their own classroom work while resisting any involvement in the wider work of the department. Senior and middle managers had to work hard to overcome this reluctance. They were helped by the decision taken by the head to review all teaching methods, syllabuses and resources. This review was to provide a challenge to many aspects of the genetic culture that teachers had brought with them from Barford and Loxley Schools.

The head, in a middle-management meeting, reminded her Snowman Group that traditional approaches to teaching were no longer entirely appropriate. Pupil involvement in lessons increased their attention span and helped to develop skills for project work on which much of the GCSE assessment was based. The group was then asked to identify strategies within their own departments for developing and reinforcing such pedagogy and to identify the support that would be needed. Much of this support, such as in-house and external in-service training, was then forthcoming. These strategies provided many teachers with the confidence to develop or extend new forms of teaching. At the same time, stories about the successful use of pupil-based teaching and learning, common understandings, shared meanings and informal support networks were all established. The myths and legends through which the culture of collaboration at Oakfields was to be strengthened were emerging. Thus, the middle management at Oakfields, encouraged and supported by the head as cultural leader, were important in establishing a key element of the school's generic organizational culture on which a new genetic culture involving different teaching and learning styles was to be based.

Much of the teaching in Loxley High School, in Barford and, to a lesser extent, in the science area of Lowchurch had produced a relationship of dependence between pupils and teachers rather than one based on independence and autonomy that Oakfields was trying to establish. Staff in the English, craft, design and technology (CDT), science and humanities departments particularly responded by becoming involved in a heated debate about educational means and ends, about teaching styles and about the nature and extent of their own responsibilities beyond the classroom. Many of the Barford staff, in particular, felt that they were being de-skilled by this change over which they had little or no control because their previous emphasis on formal class teaching was being undermined. Some Loxley staff, already under pressure by what they perceived to be the need to establish their credibility as teachers of academic subjects, also felt threatened. Such changes in pedagogy are difficult to implement and relatively easy for teachers to resist if they so choose. As Dreeben (1973) has pointed out, schools do not have lines of communication along which policy can be transmitted and implemented. Teaching and learning in classrooms are primarily determined by notions of what count as appropriate activities which, in turn, are based upon values and beliefs derived from training and past experience of what worked and what was rewarded. Hence teachers from Loxley and Barford tended to have different views from the majority of their Lowchurch colleagues.

The staff were also encouraged to move towards a culture of collaboration by the timetabling of as many meetings and working parties as possible during school hours. The effect of this was to give greater legitimacy and primacy to these activities. At the same time, subjects had been grouped into faculties to enable staff to collaborate and to give children a greater sense of curriculum coherence. In CDT this proved very successful with teachers of art, fabrics, metalwork and drama combining their subjects in an interesting way. In the humanities, however, a teacher who had been in charge of economics at Barford remarked, 'The history and geography areas are going their own ways. I teach economics but this does not seem to impinge on the other two subjects.' A physics teacher claimed that the juxtaposition of periods of physics and chemistry would lead to confusion in the minds of pupils. These situations were not easily resolved. Collaboration was not well established across all subjects. The subject-based tradition in which most British secondary school teachers are trained mitigates against this. The cultural legacy from their former schools tended to reinforce individualism and autonomy, especially for those staff from Loxley who felt defensive about their subject expertise and for teachers from Barford whose subjects were often in competition to gain the best examination results. Some teachers continued to isolate themselves from their colleagues, from departments or from the whole school. As Davies (1990) points out, such isolation is a common experience among teachers. What is not often recognized, however, is that teachers choose to be isolated in order to shield themselves from changes about which they feel uncomfortable. By the end of the first year the attempts by the head and her middle management team to establish the culture of collaboration had succeeded to the extent that staff acknowledged that they had opportunities to be involved in decision-making processes and influence decisions if they so desired. The expectation that they would participate was widely recognized as legitimate.

Conclusion

The organizational culture of the new institution which was influenced by the turbulent environment within which the school was created was complex, fluid and not easy to manage. It is evident that Oakfields did have an organizational culture based on core values. It is also clear, however, that these values and beliefs were not universally accepted, applied or interpreted in a uniform way and were contested by significant groups of staff. This was, in part, a product of the history of Oakfields, its three constituent schools and the processes of amalgamation. The organizational culture at Oakfields was clearly defined and articulated by the head and many of her senior and middle-management staff. The challenges that were made to it often stemmed from those who were steeped in the residual cultures of the constituent schools. As Beynon (1985) has pointed out, underneath the apparently settled face of a secondary school there are likely to be conflicts between antagonistic teacher groups with very different historical traditions and training. Such cultural differences produced a variety of views about the nature and extent of teachers' work in the new school. Conflicts about both the generic and the genetic elements of the organizational culture of Oakfields School often focused on the work that teachers were expected to do. Such conflicts, although tense and difficult to manage, helped to crystallize the essential features of the organizational culture of Oakfields School and to involve a large number of staff in debating seminal issues about what it means to be a teacher.

Such conflicts over basic values, and the different approaches to teaching and managing that derived from them, were a significant feature of the first year of the school's existence. These values influenced both the definition of appropriate work and the working practices of all of the staff and pupils in the school. Key opinion leaders played crucial roles in the events that helped to shape the school's organizational culture and formed the informal networks within which the culture was formed and transmitted. The head of this school, like many others, found herself involved in conflict over the core values that formed the generic culture of the organization and about how those core values would be implemented within the school's genetic culture. She found herself acting as the main cultural leader within the school, based on her formulation and articulation of the beliefs and values of the new school, the authority which she derived from her role and the support that she received from key staff in management positions. Her clear view of the values of the school and the organizational culture which derived from those values helped her and many members of her staff to cope with and give meaning to the difficult process of school amalgamation. As a result, she was able to evaluate systems and practices in the light of the school's culture and encourage others to do the same. She sought, through her own actions and through those of her supporters, to modify the behaviour of others in such a way as to make that behaviour compatible with the culture of collaboration.

In the context of school amalgamations, therefore, cultural leadership implies transformational activity, that is, the capacity to shape events so as to alter their course. Although this may not always produce conflict, those involved in such transformations may find themselves in conflict where the desired outcomes, in this case establishing a culture of collaboration, are incompatible with outcomes perceived by others as appropriate. The head of Oakfields, like most other heads (Ribbins and Marland 1994), recognized the value of motivating colleagues and of consultation and delegation. She motivated many of her staff by articulating her vision of the school and establishing a shared sense of purpose and direction. This also enabled her to influence the thinking of key groups within the school and to manage the amalgamation by providing clear leadership and delegating powers to clearly identified and trusted followers, such as the Snowman Group. This group in particular took on the day-to-day tasks of bringing about the necessary transformations, especially in the formation of policies related to teaching and learning. At the same time the head sought continually to promote and interpret the essential features of the school's culture, particularly as it impacted on wider management issues, and to communicate with the whole staff and consult widely as she managed the change process. As Bass and Avolio (1993) point out, effective transformational leadership requires inspiration, stimulation and followers who identify with the aspirations of the leader. The head of Oakfields took on this role in order, in Dimmock's (1995) phrase, to build the new culture. Within that culture teachers found themselves having to come to terms with a redefinition of what it means to be a teacher as a result of working in a new institution formed by amalgamation. This experience was similar to that faced by many teachers at this time whose schools were closing or being amalgamated. As an increasing number of policy changes and new initiatives have been introduced to which teachers have been required to respond, the culture of many schools has been reshaped by outside pressure. By understanding how and why the staff of Oakfields School responded as they did to their situation, it is possible to develop a better understanding of the leadership and management strategies that are necessary to enable teachers and pupils to cope in the face of rapid and extensive change.

3

I Have Thee Not, and Yet I See Thee Still: the School as an Ambiguous Organization

Introduction

In traditional models, the features attributed to schools as organizations are clear goals, identifiable personnel, a relevant and explicit technology and relationships based on positional rather than personal factors. These structural features are thought to produce consistency, predictability and stability. Taken together, the extent to which a school's organization is thought to exhibit these characteristics indicates something about the nature of its authority and control structures. If an organization is found to be unpredictable, or thought to be irrational in its decision making, then those who are subjected to this unpredictability or irrationality are aggrieved because such events are unexpected in the context of a formal organization. Similarly, when some sections of an organization fail to respond to the demands of other parts in the expected way, a degree of tension is created between the sections and perhaps between their members. This is as true of schools as it is of any other form of organization. The expectations and the assumptions on which they are based may, however, rest on an unrealistic notion of the nature of schools as organizations, which tends not to be reflected in much of the literature.

In the first detailed British analysis of the literature on schools as organizations, Banks (1976) began her discussion with Etzioni's definition which identifies the central feature of any organization as being a structure designed to pursue specific goals (Etzioni 1964). She reinforced the Parsonian position that it is the primacy of goal orientation that provides the main feature for distinguishing organizations from other social structures (Parsons 1964). Thus basic to the idea of any organization, whether it is a school, a prison or a large corporation, is the idea of a means–end relationship between the formal arrangements of the organization and its goals. Organizations themselves – including schools – are assumed to have a relatively high level of predictability, stability and consistency. From this it follows that such factors as the division of labour, power and communication in the school are deliberately planned to facilitate the achievement of the school's goals. This focus on goals tends to suggest that schools are highly effective goal-seeking organizations. Yet schools can certainly be regarded as operating adequately even when official goals are not reflected in the real state of the school. Frequently, attempts to identify the organizational goals of schools produce an analysis of such a high level of abstraction as to defy specification (e.g. Shipman 1985). This may be the result of wide variations in goals between schools, the differences between schools themselves and the difficulty in obtaining any real consensus about what the goals of schools are and ought to be, let alone how they might be achieved. Perhaps, therefore, the analysis of schools as organizations should reflect this situation and recognize the essentially problematic nature of goals in the organizational structure of the school.

If the identification of goals is regarded as one essential factor in understanding organizational characteristics, then the nature of the structures designed to achieve them is equally important. The classical approach to an analysis of these structures has involved the application of the Weberian concept of bureaucracy, which can be seen as an organizational response to an increase in the size and complexity of units of administration. Swift (1969) identified these characteristics as:

A rational arrangement of offices providing certain means for adminis- tration and control over office holders' actions. Officials enter the bureaucracy expecting security, specialization, salary and seniority based on achievement and qualifications ... The rights, duties and qualifications of the officials are carefully defined so they are replaceable with minimum disruption to the organization. Offices will be arranged hierarchically to facilitate demarcation of responsibility. (Swift 1969, p. 32)

Burgess (1986) notes that all schools have a hierarchy of position and a formal structure of authority. The intended consequences of these character- istics are impersonality and uniformity of practice. The complex nature of the activities carried out by schools demands, it is argued, both the efficiency and the rationality claimed for this form of organization. In order to achieve its goals, the school's activities must be regulated by an impartially applied, consistent system of abstract rules, the duties of members of staff must be officially prescribed, a division of labour maintained, and a hierarchy of authority established, resulting in a clear delineation of status and function between the various positions. Reid (1978) suggested that everyday experi- ence of schools confirms that they do indeed exhibit many of the character- istics contained in the original Weberian formulation, while Packwood (1989) drew attention to the extent to which the authority of the headteacher is derived from the hierarchical and bureaucratic nature of school organization. Hummel and Nagle (1975) claim that formal organizations such as schools are:

characterised by rationality and efficiency ... and freedom from conflict. Rationality ... the capacity for objective, intellectual action ... leads to increased efficiency in the allocation and use of available resources: and because each component ... has clearly defined functions to perform and its own unique role to play in the total organization, there is minimal room for conflict. (Hummel and Nagle 1975, p. 245)

In so arguing, such writers have tended to be somewhat uncritical in their application of formal organizational models to schools. They attempt to analyse what goes on in schools as though both the activity and its institutional setting existed independently of the larger society, insulated from it and uninfluenced by it. They tend to ignore the findings of case studies on the structure and culture of schools which support the view that schools create, through their own organizational framework, many of the problems of disorder and non-involvement which they experience (Hargreaves 1967; Lacey 1970). The tensions which might be produced within a school by emphasis on an impersonal application of rules are serious enough to merit more detailed consideration than they often receive in this type of analysis.

Under the influence of this relatively uncritical analysis, schools have tended to be regarded as stable, predictable institutions within which officeholders apply agreed rules and procedures in a consistent, impartial manner. By implication it is thought that the membership of the school can easily be identified or, as the systems approach might have it, the boundaries clearly defined (Sugarman, 1975). This, in turn, indicates that the relationship between members is clear, specific and based on a thoroughly understood technology for achieving desired goals. Relationships with the external environment are assumed to be stable and predictable, or, where this is not the case, can be coped with by the application of the relevant rules and procedures; contingency theory, however, suggests that perhaps a more complex process than this is sometimes as work (Glatter *et al.* 1997).

On the evidence derived from this type of analysis an observer might expect, for example, that decisions formulated in schools would be the results of a logical and rational process in which those eligible to participate did so, and that the importance of the decision to be taken would be the fundamental determinant of the priority attributed to it by the potential decision makers. In some ways this could be a less than accurate analysis of what is actually happening. It may also be positively misleading since it is predicated on the assumption that schools have more control over factors such as the environment within which they operate than perhaps is the case.

The school as an ambiguous organization

A view of organizations which attributes to them orderliness and rationality may be extremely attractive, especially to those working in schools. It promises consistency, predictability and a stable and secure framework within which to work. There is, however, increasing evidence that at least some organizations are not always like this. Cyert and March (1963) suggested that the overall rational pattern of behaviour in organizations, based on a set of commonly held goals, was frequently modified by a large number of departmental, rather than organizational, interests. Experience in schools leads to the belief that this is equally true of departments and groups in schools. This position is frequently reinforced by appeals to the notion of professional autonomy as a justification for departures from agreed procedures or institutional goals.

As a result of this and similar factors, individuals often discover that they work in schools which are organizationally more complex, less stable and less understandable than they have previously assumed, or that the management literature might suggest. Perhaps it needs to be recognized more explicitly that organizations, including schools, sometimes operate in a complex and unstable environment over which they exert only modest control, and that is capable of producing effects which penetrate the strongest and most selective of boundaries. In some countries, schools are directly subject to the free range of market forces which create severe problems for some industrial organizations. In most others, schools are now unable to disregard pressures emanating from their wider environment (Gewirtz *et al.* 1995, Levačić 1995). They are no longer able to respond to the uncertainty which such pressures often bring by attempting to buffer themselves against the unforeseen, or by gaining control over the source of the uncertainty and thus restoring stability. The external pressures are, in many cases, too strong for that. It was not possible, for example, for most schools in England and Wales to use either of these techniques to counteract the effect of the introduction of market forces and competition for pupil numbers. As money followed pupils, schools were subjected to pressures on their income and expenditure as they attempted to meet the demands from national and local governments, parents and other stakeholders (Foskett 1998). Similarly, schools were not able effectively to respond to external criticism of the content, methods and objectives of education which came from parents, politicians and industrialists. These and other similar pressures have created a situation in which the internal organization of the school has begun to resemble what has been called organizational ambiguity (Cohen, March and Olsen 1972).

As Bush (1995) has pointed out:

> Ambiguity models assume that turbulence and unpredictability are dominant features of organizations. There is no clarity over the objectives of the institutions and their processes are not properly understood. Participation in policy making is fluid as members opt in and out of decision opportunities. (Bush 1995, p. 111)

The ambiguous organization is an organization with a structure that is partly determined by external pressures and partly a product of the nature of the organization itself. It is ambiguous in the sense that the relationship between goals, members and technology is not as clearly functional as conventional organization theory indicates that it will be. Cohen *et al.* (1972) suggest that much organizational activity can best be understood as being characterized by unclear goals, unclear technology and fluid membership since such characteristics, it is argued, may be instrumental in creating a set of internal responses to perceived ambiguities. Cohen and March (1974) argued that many of the 42 college principals in their Carnegie Commission on Higher Education study were frequently required to take decisions in situations in which considerable ambiguity surrounded goals, technology and participants. This work was followed by a series of case studies on such disparate areas of educational decision making as the selection of a dean for an American university, desegregation decisions in San Francisco, the reorganization of the University of Oslo and a study of a Danish Technical University (March and

Olson 1979). Such work has begun to provide a theoretical framework within which it might be possible to re-examine the organization of schools.

As March and Olson (1979) show, the external demands made on educational institutions from a wide variety of sources often conflict with rapid and extreme policy change, especially at a time of limited and even declining resources. The environment in which the three constituent institutions of Oakfields School found themselves, in the previous chapter, was turbulent in several different ways. Each school had too few pupils and was over-staffed. It was clear that the LEA would close at least one of them. The newly formed Oakfields School found itself in a similarly turbulent environment since the LEA had already stated that the school would have to shed substantial numbers of staff in the first five years of its existence (Bell 1989a). It might also lose its sixth form. It was obvious that members of the Oakfields staff had little opportunity to exert any influence over decisions emanating from this turbulent environment.

This, together with the different views about the nature and content of education which already existed within Oakfields and the teaching profession more generally, produced a situation in which it is not very clear what the goals of the school were or should be. Different members of the school perceived different goals, or attributed different priorities to the same goals, or even were unable to define goals that had any operational meaning. Thus while it is commonly expected that those who work in schools should have some overall purpose, it is likely that the organizational context of many schools actually renders this either impossible or very difficult. Hence schools face an ambiguity of purpose, the result of which is that the achievement of goals which are educational in any real sense has ceased to be central to the functioning of the school. Furthermore, it has often been found difficult to specify a constant set of educational goals. In Oakfields School it was noted that there was a series of some what different and sometimes conflicting statements about the goals of the school (Bell 1989a). These statements tended to change over time and even varied between different parts of the school organization. They were frequently stated in terms which are notoriously difficult to translate into action and, while goals may be imputed to schools by observing the behaviour of a range of people within them, this imputation itself tends to be as ambiguous, since it is extremely difficult to obtain general agreement on it.

At times, goals may actually be in conflict. Improving pupil achievement may be unachievable in a climate where efficiency and cost-effectiveness is also a goal (see Chapter 7). Thus husbanding scarce resources in the face of market forces tends to have priority over the facilitation of learning; uncertainty generated by failure to recruit pupil numbers overshadows much of the work done with existing pupils, and a common sense of direction is frequently not evident in the teaching which does take place. The debate at Oakfields about how far the school should facilitate self-directed learning and self-discipline as opposed to teacher-directed learning and discipline by staff control almost inevitably created a situation in which no common purpose could be established and goals remained both contested and ambiguous.

Given, then, that the educational goals are ambiguous and may well not occupy a focal position in school life, the way in which schools attempt to fulfil these goals is equally unclear. Even when the goals are expressed in the most general of terms related to the facilitating of learning, different educational and political ideologies may lead teachers to approach their tasks in a number of ways. More fundamentally, however, teachers may be unsure about the technology which they deploy in terms of their pedagogy and its relationship to the content of what is being taught, the outcomes to be achieved, and the modes of assessment to be adopted. The precise relationship between means and ends is often unclear and teachers are often uncertain about exactly what it is they are required to do: 'Teachers ... do not know enough about subject matter, they do not know enough about how to teach, and they do not know enough about how to understand and influence the conditions around them' (Fullan 1993, p. 68). Teachers in Oakfields School were unsure about what it was they wanted their pupils to learn, about what it was the pupils had learned about and how, if at all, learning had actually taken place (Bell 1989a). The learning process was inadequately understood and therefore pupils may not always have been learning effectively. Furthermore, there was disagreement about the basic structuring of learning. Here the dispute was about how a particular end could and should be achieved. Some science teachers, for example, argued that for the content and related skills of their subject to be taught, their subject had to be allocated double periods. Furthermore, adjacent periods of, say, physics and chemistry could not be timetabled because the pupils would become confused (Bell 1989a). At the same time, however, the headteachers was trying to ensure that all staff encouraged pupils to see the interconnectedness of different subjects.

The basic technology available in schools is often not understood because its purposes are only vaguely recognized. In such a situation new teachers do not so much acquire the skills of teaching as learn how to conform to the normative and formal structures in order to reduce the demands made upon them by the organization to acceptable proportions. Since the related technology is so unclear the processes of teaching and learning are clouded in ambiguity. This produces a range of situations between teachers, and between teachers and pupils, within which rules and procedures cannot be operated with bureaucratic consistency, impartiality and predictability because the various parties involved do not perceive with any degree of clarity what is expected of them and what may justifiably be expected of others.

This is equally true of interdepartmental relationships inside schools. In some departments at Oakfields, especially those teaching science and technology subjects, it was felt that the required changes were either too difficult to implement or were not producing the expected improvements in pupil performances. Teachers in the same department interpreted the content, pedagogy and desired outcomes of their teaching in different ways. In the humanities department the departmental head noted that teachers of history and geography were going their own ways while economics impinged on neither subject area. Some teachers were using a 1950s textbook, others taught though modern worksheets and one senior teacher continued to use the notes he had prepared when he first started teaching (Bell 1989a). The staff in those departments reacted to organizational ambiguity by attempting to operate their departments as semi-autonomous units within the larger school in an effort to shut out other teachers who, they felt, might be unduly critical of their 'failures'. This happened in spite of the fact that it was pointed out that the goal of improving the overall standard of pupil performance and the technology used – the implementation of mixed-ability teaching – were not directly connected in a causal relationship. Such general failure to understand the technology on which schools are based results, therefore, not only in an inability to make the most of it but also in the attribution of expectations to the technology which that technology is too diffuse and weak to fulfil. This situation, when not appreciated, may produce unfortunate consequences for the school's internal and external relationships.

It is often the case in schools such as Oakfields that their goals and processes are either not really understood by members or are contested by those members. Such schools operate on the basis of procedures such as trial and error, learning from the accidents of past experience and pragmatic inventions of necessity. This situation itself may be unidentified, with the result that some schools manage to operate as if the technology were clear. The participants have notions about cause-and-effect relationships in educational activity, which are used to make judgements about those activities and to take decisions about the nature and direction of changes. When situations arise which are not easily accounted for within this framework, such situations are regarded as abnormal. This can lead to the creation or reinforcement of boundaries between schools and the wider community as teachers fall back to a defensive position, from which they perhaps use their claim to professional autonomy to fight off demands for accountability. Thus, because those within schools do not fully understand their own technology and so do not appreciate its weakness, they may be in danger of attempting to turn schools into increasingly closed institutions which try to shut out parents and other interested parties.

This situation is exacerbated by the very nature of school membership which, in an ambiguous organization struggling to cope with environmental turbulence, is often in a fluid state or loosely coupled. Members move in and out of decision-making situations: 'The participants in the organization vary among themselves in the amount of time and effort they devote to the organization' (Cohen and March 1974, p. 3). Loose coupling, therefore, suggests impermanence, dissolvability and a fluctuating commitment on the part of the members of the organization (Weick 1976). In Oakfields School this was true in the sense that the school consisted of groups of pupils and teachers, all of whom made a wide range of demands on the organization. By their very nature, schools gain and lose large numbers of pupils each year. They may also experience a high turnover in teaching staff or even find it difficult to recruit staff with required skills. The interests of this changing group, and their ensuing demands, are not predetermined and therefore the best ways to meet these demands are not always predictable. Schools are thus open to a wide variety of possible demands and influences, which may affect their activities. The recent developments in school accountability have resulted in another form of fluidity in the membership of some schools (see Chapters 9 and 10). Membership of the school community is no longer confined to teachers and pupils. Governors, parents and other stakeholders are all part of the school. These groups, however, opt in and out of their membership. Parents tend to opt in to the school community to represent the interests of their children but opt out at other times (Bird and Bell 1999). Similarly, school governors are in some respects members of the school community but in others, are either excluded or exclude themselves from aspects of its life and work (see Chapter 9). As schools seek more community involvement, their membership might also include local pensioners, youth groups, sports clubs and a whole variety of other members of the public at large as well as groups and individuals who have a formal, if imprecise relationship with the school. At any one time it may prove extremely difficult to say who belongs to the school and who does not, or to be precise about the nature of that membership. Hence membership is loosely coupled in the sense that the strength and degree of permanence of the bonds that attach many individuals to the school community vary over time.

Membership of the school is also fluid in the sense of the extent to which individuals are willing and able to participate in its activities. This is determined by the extent to which members of the school community are willing to devote time and energy to aspects of the work of the school. This, in turn, may be dependent on other demands being made on those members, since the level and extent of the commitment of members of the school community can be changed by events in their personal lives. Similarly, the nature of the tasks or the issues to be addressed will influence the degree to which members become involved in the school. The importance attached by individuals or groups to particular activities or decision arenas, or by the immediacy or otherwise of particular events, will influence the extent to which they are willing to invest time and energy in their membership of the school. Commitment may also be influenced by the characteristics of the school itself, in the sense that it is often easier to become involved in some aspects of school life than in others. Thus, for any individual, the level of commitment to membership of the school may change, both over time and according to the nature of the activity itself. In this way schools are peopled by participants who wander in and out of the work of the school. The notion of membership is thus ambiguous and therefore it becomes extremely difficult to attribute responsibility to a particular member of the school for some areas of the schools activities while, over other areas, there exist considerable conflicts of interest.

When these characteristics are found in any organization, including schools, then the predominant ethos within that organization is unpredictability (Turner 1977). The more traditional forms of organizational analysis will, therefore, tend to confuse rather than clarify, and conceal more than they reveal, because they emphasize predictability and stability, focusing on the formal nature of the organization at the expense of it ambiguous aspects. It may, for example, not be apparent from an analysis that concentrates on the formal aspects of management and leadership that if the school is regarded as an unpredictable organization existing within a turbulent environment, then specific skills are required by those working in the school (March and Olson 1979). Individuals must be highly adaptive, creative and flexible in order to react to constantly changing situations which cannot be predicted. They will need to have full discretion and full delegated powers from their superiors in order to cope with such situations. It is likely that the decisions made by such an individual will be short term and made in an attempt to respond to immediate demands and, as such, may be subject to rapid modification. For such responses to be understood, the traditional notion of the school as a hierarchical decision-making structure with a horizontal division into departments and a vertical division into authority levels needs to be abandoned. Such a conceptualization is unsuitable for the analysis of an ambiguous organization. The fundamental importance of unclear technology, fluid membership and the problematic nature and position of educational goals has to be accorded due recognition in any sociology of the school.

Ambiguous schools and organizational choice

The more traditional models of the school as an organization provide a particular set of expectations about how schools function and, in particular, about how decisions are taken: 'Formal models assume that problems arise, possible solutions are formulated and the most appropriate solution is chosen. The preferred option is then implemented and subjected to evaluation in due course' (Bush 1995, p. 115).

In a situation of an unclear technology, fluid membership and problematic goals this procedure cannot be followed, because of the lack of clarity or agreement about goals. The taking of decisions and the solution of the problems cannot be based on some notion of common goals to be implemented by the application of a known and understood set of techniques: 'Proponents of the ambiguity model claim that this logical sequence rarely occurs in practice. Rather the lack of agreed goals means that decisions have no clear focus. Problems, solutions and participants interact and choices somehow emerge' (Bush 1995, p. 116).

In conditions of ambiguity there are no set criteria for making the choices between problems and solutions that the formal model posits. The process is much more random. Decisions are outcomes of the interaction between four main components of the decision-making process:

1. *Problems* ... the concerns of people inside and outside the organization ... and they may not be resolved when choices are made;
2. *Solutions* ... somebody's product. A computer is not just a solution to a problem ... it is an answer looking for a question ... you often do not know what the question is ... until you know the answer;
3. *Participants* ... come and go ... every entrance is an exit somewhere else, the distribution of entrances depends on the attributes of the choice being left as much as it does on the attributes of the new choice;
4. *Choice opportunities* ... occasions when an organization is expected to produce ... a decision. (Cohen and March 1974, p. 82)

In an ambiguous organization the ideal solution and its related problem may not be linked. If, for example, the problem with which the school is concerned is to raise standards, there may be a whole range of possible solutions to that problem. The one adopted may depend more on the amount of time and energy devoted to its solution or on some partially understood notion of the relationship between learning and teaching, than on any concept of the 'ideal' solution. The area of unpredictability refers mainly to the way in which these factors are combined rather than to their long- or short-term feasibility. The possibility must be recognized of seeing patterns in the apparently unpredictable and disordered processes of making choices when goals are unclear, technology is uncertain and the cast of participants changes over time. This, in turn, will show that not only has this ambiguity an identifiable structure of its own, but that this should be the focus of concern for the study of the school as an organization. In any organization in which it is not always possible to base decision making on some perception of common goals, decisions will be taken in some other way (Cohen and March 1974). The ideal solution and the problem may be happily united but this is not likely to be the usual outcome. Neither will a series of such decisions necessarily be consistent with each other since there is no common point of reference. Decisions are more likely to be made by 'flight' or by 'oversight' (Cohen *et al.* 1972).

In Oakfields School there was a major concern with attempting to raise standards, but there was also a range of problems related to pedagogy, teaching style, pupil discipline and the administration of afternoon registration, some of which were related to the question of standards and some of which were not (Bell 1989a). Some staff were unwilling to teach in particular ways, use particular materials or group children according to certain criteria. Timetabling presented a serious difficulty because of a shortage of staff in specialist areas and because of the conflicting demands being made by different departments. Raising standards was, therefore, only one of a number of problems confronting a similar set of people at the same time. As a result, solutions were chosen and attached to problems in such a way that implementation was problematic and, in any case, the solution to be implemented did not address the substantive problem. Nevertheless these inappropriate solutions remained in effect until some more attractive choice came along (flight). Cohen and March (1974) argue that the failed solution is likely to remain in operation much longer than if the criteria of rational planning had been applied. This is because both the solution, and the problem which it was meant to solve, have become linked in the ambiguous environment of the ambiguous organization. They will remain linked until sufficient people have sufficient time to examine other possible solutions to that problem. Similarly, the choice of solution to the problem of how to raise standards, whether successful or not, may have been made without concern for other problems which exist at the same time (decision by oversight). This would mean that the latter would be ignored in an attempt to solve the former. The result might be that a whole range of other solutions attach themselves to the problem of raising standards, although the choice of solution was made without reference to these other problems. For instance, the introduction of mixed-ability teaching, arrangements for students to have free access to school buildings and afternoon self-registration all came into this category.

Table 3.1 A comparison of the characteristics of bureaucracy and an ambiguous organization

Dimension	Bureaucracy	Ambiguity
Dominant values	Stability, predictability, consistency, fairness	Randomness, playfulness and loosely sectional
Goals	Derived at institutional level from shared, accepted rules reinforced by leaders	Unclear, ambiguous, contested, constructed as *ex post* rationalization
Level at which goals are set	Institutional and rule based	Unclear but reinterpreted at a variety of levels
Rules and norms	Precedent and rule interpretation based on rationality	Segmented, inconsistent and based on episodic participation in decisions
Belief about means–ends	Shared acceptance of routines	Unclear, ambiguous, decisions not goal-related
Technology	Rule bound and impersonal	Ill-defined and poorly understood
Power and control	Based on rule and the hierarchy of office	Decentralized and shifting, not associated with formal organizational structure
Structure	Hierarchical	Problematic and possibly shifting
Process	Set by senior staff and bound by rules	Unpredictable and may vary by sub-unit
Membership	Fixed by rules	Fluid and loosely coupled
Patterns of communication	Through routines defined by rules and procedures	Haphazard collection and use of information
Decision process	Procedural rationality through office and embodied in standard operating procedures	*Ad hoc*, issue-centred and often based on flight or oversight
Decisions	Interpretation of rules and previous decisions but may be imposed through rule interpretation	Not linked to intention, a result of a loose association of people, problems and solutions
External links	Closed or open	Source of uncertainty and turbulence

Source: after Bush 1995, p. 147 and Bell 2006, p. 1.

Conclusion

As Bush (1995) notes, the ambiguity model has much to offer, but it has to be assessed alongside the formal organizational model. Table 3.1 exemplifies the differences between bureaucracy, the most pervasive model of formal organization and organizational ambiguity.

Once the implications of the differences between formal and ambiguous organizational forms are recognized then the importance of decision-making processes such as flight and oversight are clear. The whole approach to such processes as decision making needs to be re-examined in the light of this analysis. It is clear that ambiguity of this type does have an identifiable pattern. It is also clear that sometimes the attempt to solve a particular problem serves purposes other than seeking answers to immediate problems. Having identified the nature of these methods of making choices, it is possible to develop a model of the school which not only embraces the recognition of such ambiguous tendencies but which does not place undue emphasis on order, stability, practicability and rationality and which can provide practical guidelines for those working in schools. For example, it might enable schools to discover ways of coping with some of the more ambiguous social problems, problems for which there are no clear solutions and to which schools are increasingly being asked to provide responses.

More widely, once it is recognized how schools like Oakfields actually respond to the situations in which they find themselves and over which they have little control, it is clear that the traditional model of the school is not helpful in understanding how such schools function. The notion of the school as a hierarchical decision-making structure based on vertical authority levels and with a horizontal division into departments needs to be abandoned because such a conceptualization is inappropriate for the analysis of organizations attempting to cope with the turbulence that emanates from an unstable and unpredictable environment. Once the fundamental importance has been established of unclear technology, the problematic nature of educational goals and the loosely coupled membership then the possibility emerges of identifying patterns of behaviour in apparently unpredictable and disorderly processes.

Part 2: Leading and Managing Staff in Schools

This section of the book explores some of the themes that have emerged in educational management and leadership since the 1960s and which are current in the contemporary arenas of policy and practice. These include accountability, autonomy and performance management; the imperative to ensure that educational institutions are economic, effective and efficient; control over curriculum, pedagogy and assessment; and the increasing importance of middle managers and leaders in schools. Chapter 4 opens the section with an analysis of one of the most important attempts by government in the 1980s to influence the shape of the curriculum, increase the status of scientific, technical and vocational work in schools and to develop closer links between the school curriculum and the needs of industry and commerce. TVEI has had far-reaching consequences for education in schools and colleges and its impact is evident in current educational policy and practice. It provided the first example of a significant shift in the organization and leadership in schools, especially at middle-management level. It pioneered the role of school co-ordinator, which has now become an integral part of the management structure of most educational institutions. At the time, the importance of this 'cloudy messenger' was only recognized by a few people, but the development of this role heralded the creation of other similar roles in other government-initiated programmes which have sought to change content and pedagogy in the school curriculum. Chapter 5 continues the theme of new middle-management roles, arguing that the role of school co-ordinator has now taken on a wider and more significant aspect, that of middle leadership. Middle leadership is distinct from middle management, a term reserved here for the more traditional role of head of department. Middle leadership is more often cross-curricular and school-wide. In some ways this role is like a 'walking shadow', casting an influence in many parts of the institution, often without being clearly defined. Chapter 6 explores how schools are required to 'perform in measure' in order to balance the demands of accountability and autonomy. It argues that the current emphasis on pupil attainment and performance management, especially in the context of self-managing schools, may have important implications for headteachers and teacher professional identities, and for the extent to which equity and social justice might be facilitated by schooling. In this final chapter in the section, issues of professional identity and professionalism are considered from the perspective of the pressure on schools to be effective, efficient and economic at one and the same time.

4

The Cloudy Messenger: a New Role in Schools – the Case of the TVEI Co-ordinator

Introduction

The Technical and Vocational Educational Initiative (TVEI) was one of the major curriculum and organizational innovations implemented during the Resource Constrained Phase of educational policy (see Chapter 1). In fact, it marked the beginning of the transition between that policy phase and the next, the Market Phase. TVEI was a five-year project sponsored by the Manpower Services Commission (MSC), a quasi-autonomous governmental organization set up to improve education and training, funded not by the DES but by the Department for Trade and Industry. This represented an attempt by central government to become much more closely involved in the school curriculum by largely bypassing the LEA, a strategy that was to become extremely common within a few years (Gleeson 1987). TVEI represented both strong central control and devolved local autonomy, another pattern that was to become very familiar in education.

TVEI was introduced in 1983 and was designed to enable pupils and students to acquire a range of key skills and understandings linked to work experience and the world of work more generally. Its wider agenda, however, was to raise the status of science, technology and vocational subjects in the school curriculum, to develop equal opportunity within schools and to make schooling more relevant to the needs of industry and commerce:

> In essence the project may be viewed as an attempt at a major innovation to stimulate curriculum development and to introduce new approaches to teaching and learning through a limited life project ... TVEI has its roots in wider historical debates about the nature of schooling itself, not least regarding the ways in which schools should respond to industry's needs. (Gleeson 1987, p. 2)

All LEAs were entitled to bid for TVEI projects for their schools. The rewards were considerable, up to £400,000 for some LEAs. The bids had to demonstrate how the proposed projects might:

> provide a four-year curricula designed to prepare students for particular aspects of employment ... and include initiative, problem-solving abilities and ... give a balance between general, technical and vocational elements of programmes varying according to students' individual needs ... while relating the technical and vocational elements to potential employment opportunities and including arrangements for assessment. (McCulloch 1987, pp. 26–7)

Funding could be used to provide new buildings and equipment, to support curriculum development and provide materials, to develop new forms of assessment, to provide extra teaching and support staff, to finance school visits and to support cross-school collaboration. Each project had to have a clearly defined management structure. This included a project co-ordinator working at LEA level across the participating schools and colleges who was responsible for the day-to-day management of the project, and school co-ordinators in each institution involved in the project, who were responsible for the running of the project in their schools. The project co-ordinator and the school co-ordinators had to meet regularly and report to a management committee which met at least twice yearly in many projects. This consisted of all co-ordinators, senior LEA representatives, representatives of industry and commerce, especially those providing work placements or supporting programmes, and the local evaluators. These initiatives were supported by TVEI Related In-Service Training (TRIST) programmes, which were intended to spread and replicate the curriculum materials and teaching styles developed as part of the TVEI projects.

TVEI projects, with their emphasis on cross-curriculum collaboration within schools, school co-operation and organized and supported work experience and assessment through portfolios, required a new form of management at school level; the very nature of TVEI projects was a significant element in shaping the nature of the resulting posts. These TVEI co-ordinators were responsible for the academic and pastoral work of the students following the programme, for the day-to-day organization of courses, for work experience, careers guidance, the provision of profiles for students and for co-ordinating cross-institution co-operation.

By the end of the academic year 1985/86 most of the 104 local education authorities in England and Wales had some form of TVEI courses operating in at least some of their secondary schools, with the notable exception of the Inner London Education Authority (McCulloch 1987). Some projects were based on complex consortia arrangements while others consisted of school-based modules with a relatively low degree of inter-school co-operation. All of the projects, however, had to conform to the criteria established by the Manpower Services Commission for TVEI. TVEI proposals had to be innovative within the strict terms of the MSC's conceptualization of appropriate curriculum development for the 14–18 age group. They had to be cohesive in the sense that learning was a developmental process. They had to be cost-effective, and contain opportunities for a variety of cross-institutional collaboration. They had to be manageable, both within the school and within the LEA and, finally, they had to be capable of replication without the input of the resources which the MSC provided through its TVEI Unit for the initial courses.

It can be seen from these criteria that the MSC was attempting to develop a specific view of good educational practice. The courses had to be integrated in the sense that they should transcend traditional subject boundaries and also encourage initiative, problem-solving abilities, and other aspects of personal development. A deeper understanding of the economics of late twentieth-century industrial society had to be engendered by the courses, which aimed to emphasize a positive view of commerce and industry. Pupils should be given experience of the 'world of work', and courses should have a strong, but not exclusive, vocational element which should be fostered through the course content, through the provision of work experience, and through the involvement of representatives of local industry in the planning of programmes. It has been claimed by its proponents that TVEI introduced another way of thinking to the world of education. When the notions of good practice which were embodied in the criteria for programmes are examined, this statement can be seen to have some force.

The context of local evaluation

The data which forms the basis for the argument in this chapter was drawn largely from the local evaluation exercise on the TVEI programme in one West Midlands Local Education Authority, 'Addleton'. The same team were involved in four other evaluations – one in a Midlands county, 'Centralshire', another in a county in mid-Wales, 'Midshire', a third in a Black Country town, 'Walls End' and a fourth in a Midlands city, 'Ranley' (Merson and Bell 1987). The data has, therefore, to be interpreted in the light of the methodological context within which local evaluation of TVEI projects had to operate. This context was determined by three main factors: firstly, the totality of TVEI evaluation; secondly, the nature and extent of local evaluation; and thirdly, the relationship between evaluation, research and policy making.

The national evaluation

The national evaluation of the TVEI programme consisted of three main strands. Firstly, there was an initiative-wide programme of monitoring and evaluation, directly mounted and funded by the MSC over the life of the initiative. This involved two main sub-programmes, curriculum change development based on a longitudinal study of a group of students, teachers, schools and a comparative analysis of different groups of students, teachers, schools and TVEI projects to explore the content, organization, teaching and learning process, assessment, guidance and counselling within TVEI programmes (Gleeson 1987). The second strand of the national evaluation consisted of a number of action-based studies aimed at influencing progressive developments and promoting good practice. Closely allied to these was the third strand, the establishment of four TVEI databases, a financial, an operational, a curriculum and a statistical database. It was within the context of this national evaluation that a local evaluation team had to operate. There were considerable problems of overlap, and duplication between the survey studies planned by the National Foundation for Educational Research for the initiative-wide evaluation, and those planned for some LEA evaluations. The evaluation division of the TVEI Unit provided detailed guidelines for local evaluation exercises to avoid unnecessary duplication, but the nature of the national evaluation was so extensive and detailed that some overlap was almost inevitable (Gleeson 1987).

Local evaluation of TVEI

The National Steering Group (MSC 1983) suggested that the overall aims of the independent studies of each LEA project should be:

1. to enable each LEA to have regular independent feedback concerning its own projects;
2. to enable an independent assessment of each project as an entity, which could be widely disseminated;
3. to give further insight into the particular features and implications of individual LEA projects;
4. to support the Initiative-wide Evaluation and the National Special Studies.

Local evaluators were exhorted to concentrate on curriculum content and organization, the pupils themselves, the teachers, the schools and the LEAs, the impact on industry, trade unions, parents and the wider community. At the same time, it was suggested that LEAs would want to ensure that this work did not duplicate other studies, and that it could be carried out on 1 per cent of the LEA's total TVEI budget. The effect of all this was for LEAs to expect more of local evaluations at both authority and school level than they could possibly deliver. Evaluators could not cover the four areas to be evaluated in any detail, let alone concentrate on particular aspects of individual schemes. Furthermore, evaluation studies were to be based on rigorous methods of investigation, incorporating, for example, cohort and longitudinal studies, in-depth interviews, group discussion, observational methods and action research. Such methods could be supplemented by large-scale surveys of students, teachers, employers and parents, statistical data, applicable documentation and relevant factual evidence such as educational records and student profiles. This proved impossible for most relatively small-scale local evaluations.

The importance of local evaluation proposals always have been clear to those people responsible for writing the proposals, at the time of writing. Negotiations about specific details of the evaluation activity came to play an increasingly significant part in drawing up the evaluation contract. At least one group who conducted the evaluation of four different projects developed an acute awareness of what could be done within the standard local evaluation budget. Two principles were followed. Firstly, the emphasis of the evaluation was qualitative rather than quantitative. Secondly, the evaluation programme had to be formative in the sense that the evaluators were expected to contribute regular feedback on TVEI as it was being implemented. The evaluators were also required to identify in-service training needs and to provide in-service work for the LEA. Thus the work of the evaluator had a direct impact on policy making and implementation (Merson and Bell 1987, Merson and Bell 1988; Bell and Hodge 1990).

Evaluation, research and policy making

The evaluators of the Addleton TVEI project tended to approach their work from a qualitative research perspective and attempted to collect data which reflected the understandings of those involved in the various aspects of the projects, and subjected that data to various forms of analysis which were then shared with participants (Merson and Bell 1987). Data was collected in a variety of ways including:

- termly meetings with the project co-ordinator;
- termly meetings with each school co-ordinator;
- observations of a sample of TVEI lessons;
- surveys of all TVEI teachers;
- in-depth studies of a small group of teachers;
- in-depth studies of school co-ordinators;
- in-depth studies of particular aspects of the project;
- focus group discussions with TVEI students;
- twice yearly interviews with headteachers/college principals;
- analysis of financial data;
- analysis of assessment data;
- analysis of teaching materials;
- attendance at steering group meetings.

This evaluation took place over a five-year period and it attempted to evaluate the principal aspects of the project, especially curriculum content and the modular structure of the courses; the management of TVEI within a consortium arrangement and within the institutions themselves; the definition and achievement of good practice within TVEI, in terms of teaching and learning styles; teaching relationships; and the planning and development of the curriculum. This work was supplemented by a series of short intensive studies, which attempted in-depth evaluation of particular aspects of the project. These studies covered profiling and work experience, personal and social development, special educational needs and people's attitudes to the conception of TVEI. Thus it can be seen that this local evaluation project was almost a mirror image of a part of the national project. Overlap and duplication was impossible to avoid if LEAs were to be given the kind of feedback that they required.

It was recognized that the evaluation process involved judgemental activity which was different in kind from the analytical process which is normally associated with research. In spite of this, however, the direct attribution of 'praise' for those aspects of the project which have come to be regarded as

singularly successful or 'blame' for those particularly fraught with difficulty was avoided. As Beckhofer (1974) has suggested, the research process proved to be a messy interaction between the empirical and conceptual worlds, with the processes of deduction, induction, and analysis occurring more or less simultaneously. Furthermore, the evaluation, at various times, adopted each of the three different positions which, it has been argued by Shipman (1985), normally exemplify the relationship between research and policy. He suggested that research workers or, in this case, evaluators, may wish either intentionally to influence policy, or to develop a substantive or formal theory, based on the analysis of data, or simply to collect data as a first stage in the analytical process. This last position Shipman describes as 'just doing research'.

So what were the findings? Even where explicit criteria existed, and where objectives were clearly stated, they were in practice open to a range of interpretations and they could even be ignored. The evaluation, therefore, had to take into account not only the stated criteria, and the objectives for this particular project which were derived from them, but also the local, school-based interpretations of the criteria. It also had to examine the extent to which practice in schools reflected these criteria, or was an unintended consequence of attempts to meet them. It was found that practice refined policy fairly drastically in some cases. The resignation of TVEI co-ordinators and the difficulty of obtaining work experience and publicly accredited examinations meant, for example, that policy and related practice emerged as diffuse and incremental. Practice became loosely coupled with policy as those involved sought ways of coping with a particular crisis. The evaluation evidence had to compete with other evidence as people strove to make sense of different situations. The reactions of those teachers involved in the project, as well as those not involved, were based on an understandably selective view of evidence. For example, where the fourth- and fifth-year option provision of a non-TVEI department in one school was cut as a result of falling rolls, resulting in the redeployment of one teacher in that department, the blame for this situation was placed firmly on the TVEI project within that school. In fact it was probable that a similar redeployment would have taken place whether or not the school had a TVEI option. There was also considerable disagreement about the nature, purpose and value of one of the key management roles in this TVEI project, that of school co-ordinator.

The school co-ordinators in one TVEI project

The post of school co-ordinator

School co-ordinators held one of the key posts in the whole TVEI monolith. They were responsible for the day-to-day organization and teaching of courses, for arranging work experience, careers guidance and provision of profiles for pupils on the courses, for liaising with teachers of TVEI pupils in the home institution, and helping to co-ordinate the cross-institutional elements of the projects. Many school co-ordinators had also written large parts of the course for their own school, and had to write examination proposals for those courses. The actual responsibilities of the school co-ordinator tended to be defined at LEA rather than national level, and consequently there existed a range of different approaches to school co-ordination. Contrary to the then current educational myth, the MSC did not impose a universal pattern of administration on the TVEI programme. It provided a general framework within which projects must operate, but left significant parts of the administration and management of the initiatives to local negotiation. The role of the school co-ordinators is an interesting example of how a position which all projects had in common evolved in different ways and revealed significant features of both local and national organization.

In the National Guidelines for TVEI projects, minimal attention was paid to the role of school co-ordinator (MSC 1983). There was little or no task description and no role definition. The guidelines and criteria were drawn up with the intention of providing a framework for managing a complex project, but they did not pay attention to the implications of having a school co-ordinator. From the criteria, it can be seen that TVEI was about curriculum development, changing teacher–pupil attitudes, changing learning and teaching strategy, and about relevance, cohesion and progression (MSC 1981). School co-ordinators needed to be concerned with all these aspects of the projects within which they were working. In order to do this they needed to have sufficient status to carry weight within their own institution, because it must be recognized that schools are essentially hierarchical; status is equated with salary, and status is almost always necessary to achieve change.

School co-ordinators also had to operate within the LEA itself. This emerged in the way in which TVEI submissions were written. Some LEAs had the submission written by inspectors and advisors in the office, with schools hardly being consulted at all, and the final proposals almost being imposed upon them. Other submissions were written by headteachers or by heads and teachers responsible for the courses. All submissions, however, posed an implicit question for school co-ordinators. That is, what should co-ordinators do? Should their activity be concerned with curriculum development, pastoral care of pupils, administration of courses, or should they merely be clerical assistants? Part of the answer could be found in the submission, but the real process of role definition took place within the schools as school co-ordinators attempted to implement the proposals embodied in the LEA submissions to the MSC (Merson and Bell 1987, Merson and Bell 1988; Bell and Hodge 1990).

In Midshire, for example, school co-ordinators who held scale-3 posts were given responsibility for the development of profiling and for counselling TVEI pupils (Bell and Hodge 1990). Here school co-ordinators had no curriculum development role whatsoever, and were only concerned with these limited pastoral elements of the project. In Centralshire, the heads worked closely together and recognized that co-ordinators must work closely with headteachers. The heads were able to operate across the whole school, and believed that this was also necessary for school co-ordinators. It was a logical progression from this that the heads themselves did the co-ordinating for the first year of the project. After the first year, headteachers chose deputy headteachers to be co-ordinators, and to continue the whole-school approach to the TVEI project in that particular LEA (Merson and Bell 1987). In Walls End, the school co-ordinators were appointed without any form of job description, and without any indication of what the tasks to be undertaken were. After their appointment, they were asked to draw up a job description, and, as a result, five different roles emerged (Merson and Bell 1988). In this LEA, the co-ordinators all acted in slightly different ways in their own schools. There was, therefore, a certain dynamic associated with the creation of the role of TVEI school co-ordinator, which existed over and above the initial LEA submission to the TVEI Unit of the MSC. This dynamic was associated with ways in which the LEA, the project director and the headteachers perceived the TVEI project within their own particular LEAs.

School co-ordinators: a negotiated role

In Addleton TVEI projects, the headteachers of the seven participating schools and the project director co-operated on writing a job description for the school co-ordinator before applications were invited. This job description stated that the school co-ordinator would be directly responsible to the headteacher and, where appropriate, the project director. This in itself was unusual since it is rare for a teacher within a school to be responsible to someone operating outside the school, in this case the project director. The headteachers concerned agreed to this division of responsibility. It was a measure of the extent to which the heads themselves could co-operate, as well as the extent to which the project director was able to work with the headteachers, that there were no major difficulties with this aspect of the co-ordinator's role. It was particularly notable given the extent to which school co-ordinators had to work outside the school to attend meetings with the project director and others during school time, when cover was made extremely difficult by union action (Merson and Bell 1987).

The job description stated that the school co-ordinator would be expected to:

1. Organize procedures for the TVEI section of the option system and liaise with the teacher in charge of third-year options:
2. Be responsible for supplying information concerning transport of students to and from other schools, liaising with other co-ordinators when necessary;
3. Counsel students regularly;
4. Liaise with teachers of TVEI students in their own schools, with other co-ordinators and with parents of the pupils in their own schools;
5. Collate information and progress and complete other TVEI records;
6. Provide information about TVEI to colleagues;
7. Co-ordinate arrangements for work experience, careers guidance and residential courses in accordance with school policy;
8. Attend meetings and undertake INSET for the project;
9. Undertake other duties as requested by the headteacher in connection with the school's TVEI project. (Bell 1985)

In Addleton, the role of the school co-ordinator as seen from the job description was a combination of administration, liaison work and pastoral work. There was also an element of in-service work as part of the dissemination of project material and ideas. For all this a scale-2 post was to be awarded, that is one pay point above the basic scale for teachers at that time.

In fact, the awarding of a scale-2 post as mentioned in the job description was misleading, because all the co-ordinators who were appointed already held a position of responsibility within the school. The pay point available for the post of TVEI school co-ordinator, therefore, was added to existing scale points, so most co-ordinators held scale-3 posts. When the co-ordinators were appointed, it soon became clear that at least some of them already had curriculum development responsibility for TVEI courses within their own schools, since four of them were involved in the planning and the teaching of their options (Merson and Bell 1987). The three others did not actually teach the TVEI elements, but were available at the time that the options were running, in order to counsel and guide pupils, and to work with colleagues. Thus, as soon as the school co-ordinators were identified, two processes appear to have been at work. Firstly, the identification of school co-ordinator led to extra responsibilities being added to the job description because of the people appointed in particular schools. Secondly, a process of differentiation appears to have started, such that what began as a similar post, based on the same job description, soon began to develop different aspects in different institutions. These parallel processes of extension and differentiation continued because at least three of the co-ordinators had changed by the end of the academic year 1984/85, one being given full-time secondment, and two resigning due to pressure of work.

Variations and similarities in roles

The co-ordinators themselves were from a range of different backgrounds, and had a variety of experience (Merson and Bell 1987). The school co-ordinators collectively and individually had substantial teaching experience, but only two had any industrial or commercial experience. Four of the co-ordinators were working in areas which did not relate to their own subject qualifications, and two of these co-ordinators did not teach TVEI studies, they only administered the programme (see Table 4.1). They all, by the nature of their appointment, carried other major administrative responsibility within their schools. This then highlighted two major problems for school co-ordinators. The first, matching of qualifications to teaching subject, is an acknowledged problem in secondary schools, and TVEI, in presenting novel curriculum areas, heightened this problem. Secondly, heavy professional demands arising from developing new teaching and learning materials were made upon school co-ordinators, even if they were responsible only for the administration of courses. The burden of co-ordination, plus other major administrative responsibilities within the school, together with their different backgrounds and experiences, proved to be a central concern for co-ordinators, and exerted a significant influence over how their roles developed.

Another variation in the school co-ordinator's role was the distribution of work, and the amount of time available for co-ordinating activities. The co-

Table 4.1 Characteristics of TVEI school co-ordinators in Addleton LEA

	Co-ordinator status	Co-ordinator role	Subject area	Focus of TVEI programme
School A	Head of department	Admin but no TVEI teaching	Non-TVEI related	Manufacturing
School B	Deputy head	Admin but no TVEI teaching	TVEI-related	Childcare/technology
School C	Head of department	Admin and TVEI teaching	TVEI-related	General
School D	Deputy head	Admin but no TVEI teaching	Non-TVEI related	Technology
School E	Scale 2	Admin and TVEI teaching	Non-TVEI related	General
School F	Head of department	Admin and TVEI teaching	Non-TVEI related	General
School G	Scale 2	Admin and TVEI teaching	TVEI-related	Catering

ordinators argued that the time available for TVEI duties ranges from 35 minutes to 210 minutes each week, while the average time was just below two hours (Merson and Bell 1987). This compared favourably with the initial staffing for the project which was calculated on the assumption that 80 minutes would be available for each co-ordinator for TVEI administration. TVEI co-ordinators themselves argued that there should be a move towards a more equitable distribution of administration time among the co-ordinators and that there should be additional time, say 40 minutes for each co-ordinator, for curriculum development meetings. They also believed that all co-ordinators should be released from other major departmental responsibilities, since these placed a major strain on co-ordinators and put them in a difficult organizational position within their own institution. At the same time, co-ordinators also felt constrained by the pace of the introduction of TVEI. The speed of the launch was noticeable in terms of the co-ordinators' lack of preparatory training for the new and complex role. In some cases buildings were still being modified late into the autumn term in which the projects were due to start, essential equipment was still arriving and in many cases teaching materials had to be developed and adapted as the courses were progressing.

Apart from particular co-ordinating and monitoring functions, school co-ordinators found that they had to deal with many other extra claims on their time, including developing curriculum materials, organizing delivery of equipment and dealing with interested visitors as well as meeting a range of evaluators. A number of them believed that they were becoming isolated within their own institutions. This was partly because of the hostility which

TVEI encountered from some teachers in some schools, which was usually due to specific local circumstances, and partly because of the demands of assessments, evaluation, and explanation of TVEI which required that school co-ordinators spent a great deal of their time working with TVEI material. There was, however, a variation between school co-ordinators in Addleton in their status within the school organization, two being deputy headteachers, three scale-3 heads of department, and two teachers on scale 2.

Co-ordinators themselves were aware of this. A number felt that they should have immediate access to the headteacher, because they were not always informed in curriculum development work within the school generally, and could not represent the TVEI perspective within the school committee structure. In School B, for example, the school co-ordinator was a member of the school senior management team. He reported to that team in much the same way as its other members. In School A, the co-ordinator liaised with the deputy headteacher, wrote reports and provided minutes of meetings for the headteacher. This school also had regular meetings between the head and the co-ordinator on a fortnightly basis. These were supplemented, as in any other school, with the steering group meetings.

In School C the TVEI co-ordinator was regarded as simply another department head whose work was constantly under review. The co-ordinator was responsible for the academic and pastoral development of the pupils following the TVEI course and he reported to the headmaster the same way as the other heads of department (Bell 1985). It is clear, however, that in this school, as in most others, more was required of the co-ordinator than was required of heads of non-TVEI departments. This was partly because of the demands of the project itself, partly because more information had to be provided for outside agencies, and partly because there was a great deal more money to be spent.

The co-ordinator in School D was a member of the senior management team, although there was no requirement to make reports to the team. The co-ordinator held informal discussions with the headteacher as and when they were required, although it was not clear who decided what these requirements were. This informal method was adopted in several other schools, partly to ensure that unnecessary meetings were not held, and partly to give both the headteacher and the co-ordinators maximum flexibility. It was difficult for an external evaluator to make specific comments about where a co-ordinator should be required to fit in the formal management of any school. What was important was that both the headteacher and the co-ordinator understood exactly what the channels of communication were, and when they should be used.

There was a lack of understanding over this matter in at least some of the schools, and this generated anxiety among the co-ordinators themselves. The anxiety was exacerbated by the need of co-ordinators to accept responsibility for co-ordinating activities between schools, not just within a single school. The consortium arrangement in this LEA was such that pupils moved from one school to another in order to take an appropriate option. This required co-ordinating the timetable, making transport arrangements, and transmitting information between schools. The co-ordinator also had a responsibility to the project as well as to the school, and this required that he worked closely with the project director, and with the other school co-ordinators (Bell 1985). This external aspect of the role placed considerable demands on the school co-ordinators, both in terms of time and of the skills they needed in order to do the job successfully. Because of the strains of carrying out these responsibilities, several school co-ordinators found themselves faced with one of the classic dilemmas of management. That is, how to reconcile the competing claims of those activities which are necessary to ensure that the school functions smoothly on a day-to-day basis, and those activities which are necessary in order to make an innovation successful. The routine activities tended, on the whole, to be associated with the non-TVEI area of responsibility carried by the school co-ordinators, while the activities concerned with managing innovation tended to be related to TVEI work. This meant that school co-ordinators were faced with difficult choices. Different co-ordinators made different choices in these circumstances and this is a further feature of how the role of school co-ordinator developed and how differentiation occurred between holders of the same position in different schools.

Conclusion: identity and clarity

TVEI co-ordinators appeared to have established a fairly strong group identity, which articulated itself through an agreement on their own training needs. This was the result of an in-service day provided by the evaluators at the instigation of the project director (Merson and Bell 1987). These needs included training in the efficient use of secretarial time and in more general office skills. Much of TVEI was concerned with curriculum course development and the school co-ordinators felt that they required skills in these areas, not least because they were increasingly required to disseminate TVEI material and knowledge, both within their own schools and within the Local Education Authority. Several co-ordinators felt that they did not have the counselling skills relevant to the pastoral work they were expected to do, while others felt that management skills were lacking in their particular case. They also identified a need to be trained in the effective use of their own time, although it was quite clear that the time allocated in some schools for the co-ordinators to carry out their TVEI duties was simply inadequate.

Similarly, since co-ordinators were expected to monitor and evaluate the courses within their own schools, they required training in monitoring and evaluation skills. Much of the TVEI work was carried out through regular meetings. For the organization to have effective meetings was highlighted as one of the areas in which school co-ordinators required further training. They also recognized that the process of creating a group identity through regular meetings, some of which had a specific purpose and others of which were troubleshooting and problem-solving, grew in importance as the project progressed. It is clear that an increasing burden was placed on the internal organization of schools in order to ensure that those people training TVEI courses could meet together regularly to discuss those courses and their future development.

There could be no doubt that there was a singular lack of clarity about the role of the school co-ordinator within Addleton for the entire duration of the project. Expectations embodied in the job descriptions were built into the work which the co-ordinators did, but these expectations were added to and developed in a variety of different ways which were not anticipated either when the LEA submission to the MSC was written, or subsequently as the co-ordinators began to work in their schools. The role continued to evolve as the pressures changed, and as the place of TVEI and those working with it became more firmly established within the school (Gleeson 1987). Role differentiation between school co-ordinators continued to occur on the basis of different schools' situations, different sets of skills and abilities which the school co-ordinators had, changes in the group of school co-ordinators, and the extent to which individual co-ordinators were able to meet or fend off demands made upon them within their own schools and across the TVEI project within the LEA.

In spite of the difficulties that they encountered most of the school co-ordinators used their TVEI experience to continue with successful careers in schools. Three eventually became headteachers. One became a university lecturer and another an LEA advisor. One remained a head of department while the seventh left teaching to take up a career in industry, in a company used by that school for its industrial placements. As for TVEI itself, it was the forerunner of many developments in education policy. It established the importance of co-ordination which was to be continued in the implementation of the National Literacy and Numeracy Strategies and elsewhere in schools. It opened the way for further developments in middle management in schools (see Chapter 5). It heralded the introduction of bidding by schools for key aspects of educational funding and showed how LEAs could be marginalized in the administration of school-based curriculum development. Thus it paved the way for City Technology Colleges and other forms of autonomous school organization. It influenced the content of National Curriculum that was to follow in 1988 and demonstrated for the first time how an educational initiative could be implemented quickly, a model adapted for the rapid introduction of the National Curriculum. Above all, it established that the agencies of central government could influence the content and the pedagogy of the school curriculum.

5

A Walking Shadow: the Emergence of Middle Leadership in Schools and Colleges

Introduction

Middle managers in all educational institutions have the responsibility for balancing and co-ordinating the whole curriculum for either specified groups of pupils or students, or for the entire pupil or student body. Traditionally, this work has been carried out by heads of department and heads of year. Since the 1988 Education Reform Act (DES 1988a), however, middle-management roles in schools and colleges have broadened and extended to include more institution-wide responsibilities and more explicit staff management and leadership functions. This expanded role is based on the school co-ordinator model established by TVEI from 1983 onwards (see Chapter 4) and is termed middle leadership in this chapter. It may involve ensuring that cross-curriculum themes and issues, such as special educational needs, teacher professional development and personal, social and moral development are adequately addressed, that literacy, numeracy or school-improvement strategies are implemented, that the core institutional values and aims inform both teaching and learning. Middle leaders are now also involved in making judgements about performance of their colleagues (see Chapter 6). As Southworth and Conner (1999) put it, middle leaders:

> have to develop the skills of working with colleagues, create the work groups, teams and manage their meetings so that they accomplish their agreed tasks, establish systems of communication and plan and monitor them, create and sustain dialogues about teaching and the improvement of practice. (Southworth and Conner 1999, p. 12)

This often requires middle leaders to work with other middle managers such as subject leaders, heads of departments and colleagues with cross-curriculum or pastoral responsibility. The extent to which this is the case, the impact that it has on the functions of the middle leader and the skills required to carry out those functions depends, to a large extent, on the nature of the curriculum itself.

The middle leader and the curriculum

Lumby (2001) notes that the essential defining element of any curriculum is the content of what is taught, the subject area within which teaching and learning are located. Where subject boundaries are discrete and impermeable, the essential decision making at this level is likely to rest with subject specialists, but where boundaries are permeable and subjects loosely defined, middle leaders will have a significant role to play. Middlewood and Burton (2001) explore Wragg's (1997) cubic curriculum, the three dimensions of which are the subject taught, cross-curricular themes, and the forms of teaching and learning deployed. Here, the role of the middle leader is to mediate between the three aspects of the curriculum and to seek to ensure that the learned experience of pupils is coherent, since Wragg's cubic curriculum appears to be based on the assumption that, while subjects may be important, they will not be so tightly defined or dominant as to preclude cross-curricular elements. Middlewood and Burton (2001) go on to reformulate this cubic curriculum to emphasize three curriculum levels, that which is acquired, that which is taught and that which is resourced. They identify a hierarchy of perspectives that begins with a vision about the purpose of education and leads on to strategies for achieving that vision and an organizational structure to operationalize those strategies. Middle leaders may have a variety of roles to play within such a framework. It is possible, however, for a curriculum designed within this framework to incorporate a range of different beliefs about the essential nature and purpose of education. This, in turn, will help to shape the ways in which middle leaders carry out their responsibilities.

It has been argued (Egan 1999) that most education systems and the curricula that they deliver have, in the Western world at least, been shaped by three main sets of ideas. The first is that education is and should be a process of induction to the norms and values of society. The curriculum will reflect such notions of social utility and will select and differentiate as well as socialize children into adult roles. Here the middle leader will have a central role to play in articulating the significant norms and values, in contributing to the processes of selection and differentiation and communicating with a variety of audiences. The second is that education is a process of seeking the truth through the accumulation of high-level disciplined knowledge based on critical analysis of conventional wisdom. The curriculum will be shaped by a pursuit of such knowledge and will differentiate students according to their ability to cope with a critical, analytical search for truth. Here the middle leader may be marginalized in the face of a strong subject-knowledge-based emphasis to the curriculum, but may contribute to the development of analytical skills and critical thinking. The third is that the educative process is one of spontaneous natural development. Here the curriculum will support and facilitate this natural process and ensure that children reach their maximum potential. The middle leader, like other teachers, becomes a facilitator and a monitor of progress whose main function is to allow pupils to find their own path through the educative process.

Egan (1999) claims that nearly all modern conceptualizations of education, from the most radical to the most conservative, are constructed from these three ideas. It is assumed that schools should socialize children adequately, that they should achieve academically commensurate with their abilities and that the individual potential of each student should be developed. Yet these ideas are fundamentally incompatible. If education is a naturally occurring developmental process then children should be isolated from the norms and values of any society for as long as possible to allow that process to take place untainted by the belief systems of a particular society or social group. If students are to attain skills of critical analysis, this will lead them to challenge existing values and conventional wisdom, yet if schools are to socialize children these beliefs must be accepted by those same children. These tensions may impact on the work of teachers in a variety of roles, but for middle leaders who have the responsibility of making a coherent whole of the entire curriculum, they cause particular problems.

Egan (1999) goes on to argue that the curriculum should be restructured around five different sets of understandings in order to minimize these tensions and contradictions:

> Somatic - understanding the world through physical interaction with it;
> Mythic - understanding the world through the use of oral language to categorize and conceptualize it;
> Romantic - understanding the world through the use of literacy to transcend the immediate;
> Philosophic - understanding the world through the development of general schemata;
> Ironic - understanding the world through a sense of identity, place and belonging.

Such a subject-free curriculum would pose considerable challenges for middle leaders but, as yet, no education system has moved very far in this direction. What this brief consideration of Egan's (1999) attempt to reformulate the curriculum demonstrates, however, is that middle leadership as a form of middle management cannot be understood independently of the educational context within which the middle leader is located.

Skills, competences and middle leadership

Although curricula based on Egan's (1999) fivefold model of understanding have not yet been developed, significant attempts have been made to explore the possibility of curricula based on, or incorporating, core skills or generic competences. Marsh (1997) notes that examples of such curricula can be found in Australia, Britain, the Netherlands, New Zealand, Norway and Switzerland, although both the definition and incorporation of these skills into the curriculum has taken different forms. For example, in New Zealand the National Curriculum incorporates seven essential skills: communication, problem solving, numeracy, self-management, social and co-operative skills, work and study skills, physical skills. All pupils are to acquire these skills as part of their compulsory education. In Australia the delivery of key skills was targeted at students in further education, and covered language and communication, mathematics, cultural understanding, problem solving and personal and interpersonal skills (Finn 1991). These were extended to incorporate collecting, analysing and organizing data, planning and organizing activities, and working with others and in teams (Mayer 1992). In both countries concern was expressed about the extent to which transferability of skills was taking place and about how this might be managed. It soon became apparent that the learning process needed to be managed by teachers working across the skill areas who could take an overview of the development of all students. In South Australia, for example, this was done through competence portfolios, the development of which was supported and monitored by what might be termed a middle leader.

In Britain these developments followed a number of different patterns. Harwood (1992) points out that middle management in a broad, non-subject or pastoral care sense is a relatively new concept in British education: 'The concept has been applied increasingly since the mid-1980s to describe leadership roles in the context of cross-curricular initiatives such as ... Supported Self Study, Records of Achievement and associated in-service Education and Training' (Harwood 1992, p. 17).

One of the earliest attempts to incorporate key skills into the work of both schools and colleges in a planned and coherent way was in the administrative structure of TVEI (see Chapter 4). As Tomlinson (1986) reported, involvement in TVEI meant that teachers had to develop new skills, learning had to become more active and experiential, and new forms of assessment based on profiles and criteria had to be designed. Above all, Tomlinson (1986) argued, new forms of school organization had to evolve as schools became more responsive to the needs of pupils, less constrained by traditional subject boundaries and timetables, and where they needed to co-operate more effectively with each other and the wider community. Within schools and colleges these new approaches to the curriculum and the related new forms of organization were managed by a new type of teacher, a TVEI co-ordinator or middle leader. This was the first time that a role had been established in British schools that was entirely separate from either the academic or pastoral structures, but still central to both the academic and pastoral development of pupils. It was a new role and one which still exemplifies many of the difficulties that face those who have middle or cross-curriculum functions within secondary schools and colleges today. It was the forerunner of many of the posts that involve middle leadership. These middle-leader posts, like that of the TVEI co-ordinator, are partly shaped by the curriculum context and school-management structure within which they are located and are partly a product of negotiation based on expectations and an understanding of what is possible.

Middle leadership in primary schools

In primary schools significant new middle-leadership roles have been established such as the Special Needs Co-ordinators (SENCO), Professional Development Co-ordinators, Literacy and Numeracy Co-ordinators and Key Stage Co-ordinators. To these can be added teachers with responsibility for the cross-curricular themes and issues that permeate the National Curriculum, including Personal, Social and Health Education (PSHE), Spiritual, Moral, Social and Cultural (SMSC) development, information and communication technology (ICT), welfare, environmental education and citizenship. In primary schools the demands of a highly prescriptive National Curriculum has already generated a fundamental change in school organization through an increased emphasis on subject expertise and pupil performance, especially in literacy and numeracy, that has led to an increasing reliance on subject co-ordinators (Alexander *et al.* 1992). Although Campbell (1985) has argued that it is possible to identify a broader rationale for this role that is based on collegiality and to identify good practice based on teacher collaboration and expertise, it is now evident that the National Curriculum has been instrumental in firmly establishing the need for co-ordinators. This is largely because the National Curriculum in Britain is the archetype of a centre-periphery model of curriculum development that assumes that the exemplary curriculum product will be faithfully replicated in all schools (Hacker and Rowe 1998). Even though, as Richards (1998) points out, it was capable of being domesticated to suit particular purposes in individual schools, the National Curriculum is subject-focused yet with some increasingly powerful cross-curriculum themes. In order to be managed effectively such a curriculum requires both subject and cross-curriculum leadership, both of which will require generic leadership and management skills in order to: 'provide professional leadership and management for a subject (or area of work) to secure high-quality teaching, effective use of resources and improved standards of learning and achievement for all pupils' (TTA 1998, p. 4).

This is what is required of middle leaders in primary schools. There are, however, a number of ways that middle leaders in primary schools may interpret or implement their role. Osborn and Black (1994) identify four possible models:

1. resource gatekeepers where middle leaders manage resources and offer help if requested so to do;
2. planning and resource facilitators who plays an active role in planning the implementation and development of their area of responsibility and disseminate ideas and materials;
3. consultants who meet regularly with colleagues to shape good practice and implement school policy;
4. critical friends who may spend some time working alongside colleagues in their classrooms, acting as catalysts, encouraging and supporting new ideas and approaches.

It is clear that the growing emphasis on skills and competences and on monitoring both pupil and teacher performance will shift the nature of the middle-leader role away from the reactive aspects of resource management towards the proactive-consultant and critical-friend functions. Lawn (1991) claims that: 'Teaching has been redefined as a supervisory task, operating within a team of teachers ... work is related to the overall development plan or whole-school management policy' (Lawn 1991, p. 72). Ofsted (1999) emphasized this trend when it recommended that teachers' work should be managed more effectively and that middle and subject leaders should become more involved in the reviewing, monitoring, evaluating and appraising of the work of their colleagues.

The interim evaluation of the implementation of the National Literacy Strategy in primary schools, which requires all schools to have Literacy Advisors appointed to manage the strategy across stages and subjects, notes that in order for middle leaders to be effective two things are necessary: 'Provision of non-contact time to enable the co-ordinator to monitor and evaluate lessons and planning, giving the co-ordinator a leading role in audit and action planning' (Ofsted 1999, pp. 8–9).

Thus, the success of middle leaders in primary schools depends on two crucial factors: the extent to which non-contact time is allocated to incumbents to allow them to develop their role and status, and the degree to which middle leaders are located or incorporated within the senior management structure of their schools. As Campbell (1989) pointed out, even before the full implementation of the National Curriculum and the raft of policies that followed it in the UK, policy changes have undoubtedly increased the workload of primary teachers. It has proved extremely difficult for most primary teachers to be allocated the appropriate time to carry out their normal duties, let alone shoulder the additional management burdens that middle and subject leadership brought with them. Moore (1992) showed that four years after the publication of the National Curriculum, only 12 per cent of primary schools were able to provide a regular amount of non-contact time for some teachers with co-ordination responsibility. In many schools the issue of time allocation remains a prime determining factor in the construction of the middle leaders' role.

To some extent this issue has been addressed in recent changes in teachers' conditions of service (DfES 2005), which also introduced a new form of middle-leadership, teaching and learning-responsibility payments (TLRs), which, while relevant across both primary and secondary schools, are of particular importance for primary schools. For TLRs to be awarded:

25.3 Before awarding a TLR the relevant body must be satisfied that the teacher's duties include a significant responsibility that is not required of all classroom teachers and that –

    (a) is focused on teaching and learning;

    (b) requires the exercise of a teacher's professional skills and judgement;

    (c) requires the teacher to lead, manage and develop a subject or curriculum area; or to lead and manage pupil development across the curriculum;

    (d) has an impact on the educational progress of pupils other than the teacher's assigned classes or groups of pupils; and

    (e) involves leading, developing and enhancing the teaching practice of other staff.

25.4. In addition, before awarding a TLR1, the relevant body must be satisfied that the significant responsibility referred to in paragraph 25.3 includes line management responsibility for a significant number of people. (DfES 2005, p. 46)

Again, the role of middle leader has been extended and broadened to include an even wider range of responsibilities, all of which must be understood within the overall context of the management of schools. As Harwood (1992) notes, existing and planned management styles and practices in any particular school can create or exacerbate difficulties for middle leaders, while O'Neill (1997) argues that:

> Individual schools need to redefine a role for the co-ordinator which builds on the values of the school, an awareness of what is desirable and attainable ... and a clearer understanding of the cost of co-ordination. Co-ordinators can only change and develop classroom practice with the active consent of colleagues. (O'Neill 1997, p. 31)

Where a management style based on individualism exists, O'Neill (1997) claims that the professional isolation and experiences of working alone make it difficult, if not impossible, for middle leaders to operate effectively. In the style that he terms 'Balkanization', O'Neill (1997) suggests that while there may be disputes over territory, expertise and resources, middle leaders may be able to work with specific groups. Where comfortable collaboration exists, limited advice and help may be offered by middle leaders but in contrived collegiality there may be considerable middle-leader activity but little tangible outcome. Thus, preconditions for effective middle leadership in primary schools will include openness, trust, a clearly articulated set of aims, a willingness to give and receive advice and an organizational structure that allows, supports and encourages the necessary professional interchanges that are required for such middle leadership to be of value.

Middle leadership in secondary schools

In secondary schools similar factors appear to be operating, but the management structure is more complex. The size of most secondary schools means that more formal structures, usually based on subject departments, are used as a basis for allocating resources and for organizing staff, resources and pupils. Hannay and Ross (1999) suggest, with particular reference to secondary schools in Canada, 'The power of the taken-for-granted middle management departmental structure cannot be underestimated as it has defined teachers' roles, interaction patterns, knowledge considered of worth and learning opportunities offered to students' (Hannay and Ross 1999, p. 356).

There is also a clearer division of responsibility between middle and senior managers. As Busher and Harris (1999) have identified in their study of middle managers in secondary schools, the distinction between middle and senior management is that while the latter are responsible for overall school policy, the former are operationally responsible for overseeing and developing the work of their colleagues. Much of this involves a brokering role based on the translation of school policies into classroom practice. The difficulties inherent in this situation are not merely a function of size. The increasingly complex curriculum, the emphasis on subject-specific teaching, learning and related patterns of assessment, combined with a growth in cross-curricula initiatives, have forced secondary schools to rely on complex middle-leadership structures. Coleman *et al.* (1995) argue that the changes in curriculum content have raised critical organizational issues for schools, such as managing the arrangements for post-16 provision, which, in turn, will have implications for other areas of school management. Consequently it is important for secondary schools to have a management structure that recognizes the importance of the coherence of the educative experience for all pupils. Such a whole-school approach, within which middle leaders have an important role to play, will have two distinct dimensions:

> A lateral view in the sense that it looks across the whole curriculum, to identify the totality of the learning that the curriculum offers [and] ... a longitudinal view in the sense that it adds continuity and progression in the student's learning experience, and searches out the gaps and the repetition that the subject-centred approach inevitably produces. (Duffy 1988, pp. 116–17)

The National Curriculum has not eradicated this lack of coherence. If anything, it has been exacerbated (Ribbins and Marland 1994). As a result, the role of the middle leader, while becoming more difficult, is even more essential because each subject in the National Curriculum was developed separately so, as one head points out: 'The crucial issue ... is the necessity for somebody to look at the curriculum as a whole' (Ribbins and Marland 1994, pp. 57–8).

Nevertheless, there are key factors that inhibit the performance of middle leaders, similar to those in primary schools: time available to do the work, and the matter of the status and position of middle leaders within the management structure:

> Co-ordinators share certain difficulties with heads of faculty, including limited contact time, but their relatively low status in many schools makes their role even more difficult. The impact of cross-curriculum activity in schools is likely to be limited by such weaknesses. (Coleman, Middlewood and Bush 1995, p. 31)

At the same time, for many middle leaders, role definition remains weak with no formal recognition of function or responsibility. It has proved difficult for them to recruit colleagues to provide support and the low status of middle leaders has produced extremely limited outcomes (Coleman, Middleton and Bush 1995). This situation was made worse in many schools because middle leaders did not have access to the support structure provided for many of their colleagues through their membership of a subject department. In a study of Information Technology co-ordinators, Owen (1992) found that co-ordinators in his study had limited time to fulfil their role, had weak formal status within their schools and were perceived as having a lower status than subject-based leaders. Owen concluded that:

> Where the role incumbent has low status and restricted curriculum experience then delegating the production of policy ... becomes fraught with danger. The degree of danger is increased if organizational factors, such as little designated time for strategic planning, lack of ... support and resource are also evident. (Owen 1992, p. 39)

In pastoral care, the traditional location of much middle-management work in secondary schools, the situation is remarkably similar. Harrison (1998) reports that there exist a number of areas of conflict that impact on the contemporary pastoral domain. These include:

- a lack of shared understanding as to the nature and purpose of pastoral provision;
- a lack of confidence in the pastoral domain on the part of many teachers;
- inappropriate management structures for effective pastoral care;
- inadequate support for pastoral care.

The subject-focused nature of the National Curriculum in Britain has tended to devalue this form of cross-curricular provision in many secondary schools and has created a situation in which many pastoral managers are reactive rather than proactive in providing support for pupils and colleagues. This is largely because they have been marginalized both by recent developments in curriculum content and organization and by an increasingly subject-focused management structure in many schools driven by the emphasis on the publication of examination results. A similar situation exists in Singapore where: 'the preoccupation with providing a good academic education and securing excellent results in the national examinations has tended to eclipse the guidance and caring aspect of education' (Salim and Chua 1994, p. 76). Once established, however, it was noted how the pastoral-care systems enhanced the teaching and learning processes even in the most academically focused schools. Nevertheless, as in British schools, pressures of time and inappropriate management structures inhibited the extent to which pastoral middle leaders could fulfil their roles (Ong and Chia 1994).

This situation appears to be continuing in many schools in Britain, even for new middle leader roles. By September 2000 all secondary schools were required to have appointed a Literacy Advisor to manage the implementation of the National Literacy Strategy at Key Stage 3. It is evident from a pilot study that teachers appointed to those posts were being drawn from relatively junior members of staff or from staff with very limited relevant expertise. They were not being located centrally within the management structure of the school nor were they recognized by colleagues in subject departments, including English departments, as having a significant role in cross-curriculum matters (Weston 2000). Thus the situation in which the literacy advisors or middle leaders in the schools in this pilot study found themselves is very similar, especially in regard to their status within the school's management structure, to that of the co-ordinators in the earlier research project. Nevertheless, Megahy (1998) can still argue that the way forward in secondary education is staff to be appointed: 'To be responsible for the whole curriculum experience on offer to a particular group of pupils, information on their individual progress, and proposals for action to bring about improvement' (Megahy 1998, p. 46).

Middle leadership in further education

In post-compulsory education settings in Britain both the curriculum and college organization have been subject to even more radical change than has been the case in the primary and secondary sectors. The further education sector is complex with an emphasis on vocational training (DTI 1994). It comprises over 400 tertiary, sixth form, agricultural, arts and performing arts colleges and other specialist institutions (Lumby 1995). The introduction of new patterns of funding, an earlier adoption of modular courses than either the higher education or the compulsory sectors, new vocational and skills-based courses and qualifications and the increasing recognition of the importance of lifelong learning have all served to reshape further education. Specific curriculum developments have also been important. The specification of modules as units of teaching and learning, the use of learning outcomes to define learning and the development of units of credit have all had a singular impact on the work of further education colleges. The increased flexibility and choice that these developments have brought emphasize the importance of effective curriculum management generally and middle leadership in particular (Robertson 1995).

A learner-centred curriculum leads to a situation in which students make more of their own choices. This, in turn, must lead to new relationships between students and tutors and, in turn, to new approaches to curriculum management. Middle leaders and other middle managers, therefore, are now required to recognize the importance of core skills, guidance and counselling and not the delivery of subjects as central to their work (Lumby 1995). As with middle leaders in other sectors, having the time to carry out their duties is important since the tasks to be achieved are extremely time-consuming. The management challenges for middle leaders might be summarized as developing the skills necessary to manage student–tutor partnerships, to manage student use of resources and to manage the new student learning pathways (Nash 1995). This implies changes in both the organizational structure of colleges and a shift in the power relationships that underpin those structures.

Middle leaders who work in colleges that have moved away from the traditional hierarchical and bureaucratic structures are better placed to function effectively than those who do not. They are more able to co-ordinate curriculum development and student support across layers of hierarchy but may, as Lumby (1995) has noted, face the problem of having responsibility without authority. Lumby (1995) goes on to argue that in order to fulfil this complex and demanding role, middle leaders in further education need to undertake the following tasks:

- curriculum planning, including:
  - identify and organizing the delivery of key skills;
  - developing flexible learning pathways;
  - evaluation and quality assurance;
- administrative support, including:
  - co-ordinating admissions, guidance and support systems;
  - liaising with industrial and other partners in the learning process;
  - managing physical and staff resources;
- implementation, including:
  - ensuring that flexible learning pathways are available;
  - developing and sustaining a team approach to teaching and learning;
  - monitoring student and staff progress. (after Lumby 1995, p. 5)

In further education, then, as with the other sectors, the role of middle leadership is shaped both by the nature of the curriculum and the organizational structure of the individual college. It is a complex role that demands specific skills to meet the challenges that it presents.

Effective middle leadership

Effective middle leadership depends on a number of interrelated factors. For the individual middle leader, training has widely been acknowledged as important. As long ago as 1975, the Bullock Report recommended that all middle leaders with responsibility for language and literacy should receive regular training. By 1999 Ofsted noted that in-school training should be high profile and properly resourced, and was still commenting on the need for training for the same group of teachers, the National Literacy Project Literacy Advisors, noting that: 'Many co-ordinators reported that they also need help to develop their training skills and the skills to manage change' (Ofsted 1999, p. 9).

Tan (1994) noted the importance of training for pastoral middle leaders in Singapore. An innovative role required an innovative approach to training:

> In order to meet the demands of training a great number of pastoral care-givers [we] experimented with two non-traditional approaches ... Since pastoral care and career guidance in the Singapore context adopts a whole-school approach, we were convinced that the most effective way to prepare front-line care givers would be to conduct school-based in-services courses for the staff of pilot schools ... In addition ... we also conducted ... campus-based, school-focused in-service courses. (Tan 1994, pp. 200–1)

Training is undoubtedly important but it needs to recognize the extent to which the challenges of middle leadership are now different from those which faced middle leaders hitherto: 'The job has changed from modelling desired behaviours and attitudes into leadership, strategy, deployment and negotiation ... This is a much more daunting role' (Waters 1996, p. 5). In order to meet the demands of middle leadership the incumbents of those posts need a clear understanding of what is expected of them. This may be transmitted partly through training and partly through experience. Middle leaders will be expected:

> to apply professional knowledge, understanding, skills, attributes and the most appropriate leadership style ... However, leadership is not about the application of separate or specific knowledge, skills or attributes to a specific task, but rather about the integration of the most appropriate knowledge, skills and attributes to a task or set of tasks in a given context or situation. (Field, Holden and Lawlor 2000, p. 9)

The main focus of any middle leader's role will be to support and improve pupil learning. This will be achieved by contributing to policy making, working with colleagues, deploying resources effectively, monitoring and evaluating performance and progress and managing change. There are five different but related activities that middle leaders must undertake if they are to be effective. These are:

- orientation - reviewing the current strengths and weaknesses in their area of responsibility;
- elicitation - considering views of colleagues about how the middle leader should operate, what needs to be done and identifying what skills are required;
- intervention - acquiring new skills, refining strategies, tactics and approaches;
- review - reflecting on progress, monitoring what has been achieved and what needs further attention;
- application - tackling new aspects of the post using acquired skills and learning. (After Bell and Ritchie 1999, p. 22)

These activities cannot take place in a vacuum. It is clear that certain approaches to school organization are more likely to produce effective cross-curriculum management than others. Cheng (2000) notes the importance of organizational structures that allow for teacher involvement in implementing curriculum change and developing cross-curricular approaches in Hong Kong. Lee and Dimmock (1999) confirm, in the Hong Kong context, that teacher collaboration must be meaningful, principals and senior administrators need to engage fully in planning across the curriculum and whole-school policies must be formulated if effective middle management is to be secured. Thus, some types of management structures are more likely than others to facilitate and support good practice for middle leaders. Such structures tend to have common elements. They will be: 'organizations in which face-to-face relationships dominate ... in which people routinely interact around common problems of practice and ... that focus on the results of their work for students rather than on the working conditions of professionals' (Elmore 1996, p. 20).

In Norway it has been concluded that in order to support cross-middle initiatives, the most important thing a headteacher can do is to foster a climate in which such activity is considered to be important (Midthassel *et al.* 2000). However, as Maes *et al.* (1999) warn on the basis of their study of a series of cross-curricular initiatives in several European countries: 'It is not yet clear how participation in decision making, school-based management and strategies enhancing teacher empowerment enhances teacher expertise and ultimately student performance' (Maes *et al.* 1999, p. 665).

Nevertheless, middle leaders, if they are to be effective, need to be located within a management structure that creates a collegial and collaborative culture and allows middle leaders to be empowered and to empower others. Lo (1999) has shown, on the basis of an analysis of a curriculum innovation in Hong Kong, key elements similar to those found in British and European schools which foster the work of middle leaders. These include participation in decision making and in school committees in an open and highly supportive climate in which the relationships were based on low directiveness and high collegiality on the part of the principal. Middle leadership is further enhanced where teachers as a group are motivated and the head is concerned with teacher professional development (Lo 1999).

It should not be assumed, however, that these elements are relevant in all cultures. In Thailand, for example, where there is considerable emphasis on the need to change the nature of the school curriculum to develop problem-solving and other analytical skills (Charoenwongsak 1998), fundamental cultural norms influence how such changes might be managed. The apparent lack of sincerity in the governmental rhetoric that exhorts Thai educators to change, the lack of a clarity and sincerity of purpose for educational reform and the lack of certainty over what is to be achieved, all mitigate against such changes (Hallinger *et al.* 2000). Curriculum change here is driven by exhortation which relies on compliance from Thai teachers who, when instructed to change by educational administrators in this highly centralized system:

> will politely accept their orders and try to 'do it' – *within the scope of their capabilities*. Such polite acquiescence does not, however, begin to suggest that change has been implemented ... the monitoring of reform seldom goes beyond the use of check lists. Supervisors perform what principals refer to as 'hit and run' missions to check on implementation at site level ... the system is satisfied that change has taken place ... What we describe here is a shared mythology of change. Participants at each level ... are doing *what is expected of them* and all agree that everyone has done what was asked. Yet, change fails to occur. (Hallinger *et al.* 2000, pp. 218–19)

For this situation to be avoided in British schools middle leadership and management in all schools must be inextricably linked at all levels. At its most strategic, management involves formulating a vision for the school based on strongly held values about the aims and purposes of education and their application to specific institutions and translating this into action. Middle leadership involves the articulation of this vision and its communication to others. If management at the strategic level involves translating the vision into broad aims and long-term plans, then it is at the organizational level that the strategic view is converted into medium-term objectives supported by the allocation of appropriate resources and the delegation of responsibility for decision making, implementation, review and evaluation. Here, the middle leader has a crucial role to play in planning, implementing, monitoring and evaluating the work of colleagues across the curriculum. In turn, the implementation of these medium-term plans requires them to be further sub-divided into the totality of the delegated tasks that have to be carried out. At the operational level, therefore, resources are utilized, tasks completed, activities co-ordinated and monitored. Middle leaders need to be involved in this operationalization of policy on a day-to-day basis. The three levels of management must work in harmony towards a common purpose, especially if middle leadership is to work effectively. This will not happen if all members of the school community do not share the vision and if values are not largely communal. Each level of management depends on the other two. To emphasize one and ignore the others is fundamentally to misunderstand the nature of educational management.

Headteachers and principals cannot manage schools and colleges alone nor can they carry the burden of motivating others to achieve objectives and complete tasks without significant support from colleagues. Here middle leaders have a crucial role to play but, for them to succeed, schools and colleges must move towards inclusive forms of management and leadership. In Canada it has been argued that:

> middle management leadership is gradually shifting from a hierarchical model . . . to a perspective based on collaboration and teacher leadership . . . The middle management model based on whole-school functions and processes is contributing to cultural change and is impacting the learning opportunities offered to students. (Hannay and Ross 1999, p. 346)

As Busher and Harris (1999) point out, this implies a transactional leadership role by which working agreements are secured with departmental colleagues about how to achieve school goals. A transformational approach to leadership will also be required to enable middle leaders successfully to manage the many changes that will be necessary. Here middle leaders will be involved in setting directions, developing people, fostering shared decision making and building relationships within the school community. This will require a considerable shift in the power relationships in schools and colleges as middle leaders further develop their expertise.

6

We Will Perform in Measure: Accountability, Performance and School-based Management

Introduction

Educational institutions are now, more than ever before, required to produce students with the appropriate skills and capabilities to match national priorities (Bell 2004a). Education also has an important role to play in developing national identity, social cohesion and social justice. In order to meet these demanding challenges, significant changes have taken place in many education systems over the last two decades, not the least of which has been the introduction of a range of measures designed to hold educational institutions to account for the contribution that they make towards meeting national priorities through the performance of their students. As Scott (1989) has pointed out, many governments are now increasingly exercising their right to determine the broad character of the schools and colleges which they support, to ensure that educational institutions contribute fully to economic development and other goals established by governments for the nation state. This right on the part of government derives from the extent to which education, being largely supported by public funds, must be accountable for the best possible use of those funds.

It is possible to trace the development of accountability in state education through at least three stages. The first is the establishment of state regulation of education in the sense of defining the parameters of provision such as the start and length of compulsory schooling. Here the accountability on the part of the state was for the adequacy of provision, and for educators it was largely to their profession and professional colleagues. This type of accountability was largely located within the Partnership and Social Democratic Phases of educational policy. As policy moved into its Resource Constrained phase, accountability came to be based on the direct regulation of that provision by determining curriculum content and, in many cases, pedagogy. Here the state was beginning to take some responsibility and hold educators to account for the content of what was taught and the outcomes of that teaching. Finally, through the Market Phase and into the Target Phase the state has moved towards the direct regulation of the outcomes of education by holding institutions accountable for student learning.

Both the concepts and the mechanisms for accountability as they relate to education have moved a considerable distance from that posited by Sockett

(1980), who argued that accountability had both a simple and a complex meaning. At its most basic it is to hold someone to account, which implies being obliged to deliver an account as well as being able to do so. In its more complex form accountability has also come to mean responsibility for adherence to codes of practice, rather than outcome. This traditional form of accountability is based on a commitment to students and other stakeholders and allows accountability to be exercised outside the immediate context of politics and the market (Scott 1989).

> Professionals are judged by other professionals: they are accountable to their peers ... Legal and contractual accountabilities exist and can be used in extremes, but they are not what secures proper performance. Commitment to pupils and their parents, to the outcomes of training, to best practice and to ethical standards are more effective here. (Burgess 1992, p. 7)

In the climate of the twenty-first century, however, the concept of professional accountability may be criticized by some for its inward, provider-dominated focus in contrast to the consumer stance espoused by governments in many countries. 'The time has long gone when isolated, unaccountable professionals made curriculum and pedagogical decisions alone, without reference to the outside world ... Teachers in the modern world need to accept accountability' (DfEE 1998a, para 13).

Following the development of both neo-liberal and neo-conservative education policies in the 1980s and 1990s, accountability has taken a different form. Neo-liberalism emphasized individualism, free markets, competition, and authoritarian but minimal forms of government. The mechanism of the market was to supersede government order and supply and demand became the main regulatory mechanism for the distribution of scarce resources and for holding educational institutions to account. Neo-conservatism advocated adherence to traditional values and institutions and rejected equity and social justice as an acceptable basis for educational policy. Here, accountability mechanisms focused on performance management (Leithwood *et al.* 2002). Now, educational institutions and the individuals working within them are held accountable for student performance and for the contribution to national priorities or performance targets. Accountability, therefore, is more likely to be as Kogan (1986) describes, a process by which schools, colleges and their staff are: 'liable to review and [to] the application of sanctions if their actions fail to satisfy those with whom they are in an accountability relationship' (Kogan 1986, p. 25).

Thus, accountability might be seen as: 'the submission of the institution or individual to a form of external audit [and] its capacity to account for its or their performance ... accountability is imposed from outside' (Scott 1989, p. 17). As Coleman and Earley (2005) point out, such accountability can be seen as a counterpoint to greater freedom at institutional level, since demands on schools are increased to justify how this greater freedom is used to enhance pupil performance. There is an inherent tension here for teachers who have to operate as professionals within an organizational framework since their professional control over the content of what they teach and the pedagogy they choose to deploy is often challenged . A measure of autonomy is required for practitioners to be effective while the school remains accountable for their performance. Is it possible to establish a balance which ensures that guidelines concerning performance can be applied while a degree of professional autonomy is retained? Edwards (1991) notes that accountability leads to control, while autonomy and choice foster the release of human potential; the central issue here, however, is about the forms that the accountability mechanisms take and the impact of their application. Leithwood *et al.* (2002) suggest that there are four different approaches that have been adopted to accountability by New Right governments. These are market approaches, management approaches, decentralization and professional control through site-base management. The common thread that binds these approaches together is: 'A belief that schools are unresponsive, bureaucratic, and monopolist ... Such organizations are assumed ... to have little need to be responsive to pressure from their clients because they are not likely to lose them' (Leithwood 2001, p. 47).

Perhaps in response to this, accountability has come to rest heavily on the inspection of educational institutions, the development of state-wide curricula and the publication of comparative data on the performance of schools and colleges. This data is intended to engender competition between institutions and to facilitate parental choice or, in other words, to ensure that market forces operate within education. Such developments have often been accompanied by increased central control of the curriculum, the development of more powerful inspectorates, the rigorous appraisal of teachers and the emergence of a performance culture based on centrally determined targets. What is involved here is a simultaneous process of centralization and decentralization. The curriculum, pedagogy, standards of performance, measurement of outcomes and, in some cases, the pedagogy to be deployed, have been centralized. The management of resources, student recruitment and responsibility for managing the workforce and its remodelling have been delegated to schools. Many central governments have increased their ability to set the policy agenda and to define the aims, purposes and outcomes of education, often at the expense of professionals within education services, both teachers and regional administrators. The introduction of choice and the operation of market forces in education have tended to move power away from the providers of education in favour of consumers. Within schools, performance management has strengthened the operational power of head-teachers and senior staff in schools, that is the power to influence how the service is delivered and to hold to account those within schools who are responsible for that delivery. This exercise of accountability through operational power finds its most complete expression in school-based management or self-managing schools.

Self-managing schools

As Caldwell (2002) points out, self-managing schools may benefit from site-based management but they are not necessarily autonomous schools. Autonomy implies a degree of independence that is not provided within education systems in which central control is exercised over curriculum content, pedagogy and outcomes. Schools can be considered self-managed when: 'there has been decentralized a significant amount of authority and responsibility to make decisions related to the allocation of resources within a centrally determined framework of goals, policies, standards and account-abilities' (Caldwell 2002, p. 35).

Karstanje (1999) warns, however, that while decentralization may shorten the distance between the policy makers in the government and the policy implementers in the schools and colleges, it may not mean that the institutions gain more autonomy. Such autonomy may shift to the regional level and make little difference to schools. Deregulation, however, does lead to an increase in institutional autonomy if the effect of the deregulatory process is to shift the locus of decision making to the institution. Deregulation: 'will give ... schools greater freedom and less central control. New freedoms ... will enable them to meet the needs of pupils and parents more effectively' (Blair 2001, p. 44, quoted in Caldwell 2002, p. 36).

The rhetoric that underpins school-based management is that decisions concerning institutions within the education system should be made by those inside schools and colleges rather than by national or regional officials, because those on the ground are best able to make the best decisions about appropriate provision of education and the allocation of resources. Newland (1995) cites the example of South America where, he argues, most countries are administered by a structure the most outstanding characteristic of which is: 'the high degree of centralisation ... all decisions relating to educational matters [are] taken by ... civil servants ... and the teaching institutions fall under their control' (Newland 1995, p. 103, quoted in Bush 2002, p. 10). Consequently, educational programmes are too uniform, there are serious inefficiencies and it is difficult to remove incompetent teachers. It is argued that self-managing schools avoid these and similar difficulties. By devolving more responsibilities to self-managing schools, greater effectiveness through greater flexibility and more efficient deployment of resources can be achieved (Caldwell and Spinks 1998; Bush 2002). This will produce: 'The confident, well-managed school running its own budget, setting its own targets and accountable for its performance' (DfES 2001a, p. 63).

In Hong Kong, school-based management was also intended to raise standards:

> The School Management Initiative (SMI), embarked upon in Hong Kong in March 1991, is a major restructuring of the operations of secondary and primary schools, with the belief that greater self-management can enhance school performance. With self-management, schools are more free to address their own problems, and in order to manage changes and routines in a controlled manner, systematic and effective planning is important and highly desirable. (Wong *et al.* 1998, p. 67)

Similarly, the Schools Excellence Model (SEM) in Singapore was specifically intended to improve student performance. It is based on devolving power over some aspects of resourcing and pedagogy to the institutional level, but within a tight national quality framework based on competition between schools: 'once people in the school setting are motivated and sensitized to the drive for excellence ... then organizational excellence will be eventually achieved, thereby schools will become agents for continuous improvement and innovation' (Mok 2003, p. 357). This model is based on self-assessment and the development of internal accountability mechanisms that can enable the school to respond to the national quality framework. The SEM schools do have powers devolved to them, but they are not in any way autonomous since in every aspect of what they do, they are held to account by the government. The elements of target setting and performance management become integral to the mechanisms for holding schools to account. The devolution of budgets to schools and the establishment of self-managing schools introduces another set of elements into the accountability and choice arena. This aspect of school-based management rests on the application to education of the values of the market: competition and choice. Consequently, accountability mechanisms are also based on these values. In self-managing schools, therefore, these mechanisms can be seen to take four different but related forms: accountability for student performance, accountability for resource management, dispersed accountability and accountability for teacher performance. The argument here is that self-management places on the school the responsibility for the achievements of its students. Decisions about the deployment of resources to sustain and improve student performance are taken at school level. Such decision making and the identification of the outcomes to be achieved should be taken in conjunction with parents, governors and other stakeholders. The responsibility for these decisions, therefore, is dispersed among the school community although the teachers shoulder the main burden.

Accountability and student performance

With the apparent freedom that self-managing schools enjoy, however, comes accountability. In England and Wales, for example, self-managing schools, while able to set their own targets, have now become accountable for their own performance within an established national accountability framework (DfES 2001a). As Bullock and Thomas (1997) point out, the main thrust of deregulation in England was to give schools control over spending priorities while, at the same time, reducing autonomy over what was taught:

> The autonomy of schools has been enhanced in the area of control over human and physical resources but control over deciding what is taught has been reduced by the national curriculum. Accountability has been altered and the role of the professional challenged. (Bullock and Thomas 1997, p. 52)

They note that a similar pattern can be found in Chile, China, Poland, Uganda and the USA. In many Australian states, schools have had devolved to them the responsibility for utilities, buildings, flexible staff establishments and appointments, but this has been associated with greater centralization of both curriculum and assessment, while in New Zealand: 'Accountability has been strengthened by performance monitoring against charter objectives established by the school and the government. The efficiency of the change depends on the "market" benefits being generated. The impact of the reforms may threaten equity' (Bullock and Thomas 1997, p. 54). At the same time, those within the schools are accountable to government and stakeholders for the management of resources to achieve those outputs. Under a system of school-based management, accountability for student achievement rests squarely with the individual school. Such accountability is usually based on the assumption that the curriculum consists of a series of specific outcomes and the pedagogy to achieve them: 'Outcomes remain the focus, but they are now constituted as targets and benchmarks, rather than just comparisons with other institutions' (Fergusson 2000, p. 208).

Once this framework of targets is established, it then becomes the function of the teacher to use the pedagogy to ensure that the outcomes are achieved. Accountability thus becomes a matter of assessing how successfully the teacher has deployed the relevant pedagogy, based on the testing of pupil attainment and teacher performance. This implies a strongly managerialist approach to school leadership which cannot be achieved by collegial shared responsibility since the headteacher has the responsibility to: 'establish clear organizational goals, agree to the means of achieving them, monitor progress and then support the whole process by a suitable system of incentives' (Normore 2004, p. 64).

While schools have been granted increased autonomy over the management of their operational practices to facilitate student performance, so governments have exercised greater control over the curriculum. This trend can be found in most countries where a degree of self-management has been devolved to schools. There is a paradox here, because: 'The decentralization of control over resources can be viewed as consistent with the "market" principles . . . Yet the centralization of control over the curriculum would appear to be . . . more consistent with the principles underlying planned economies' (Bullock and Thomas 1997, p. 211). The link between these two apparently contradictory sets of policies lies in the need to challenge the autonomy of the educational professionals and to link the outputs of schools more closely with the perceived needs of the economy. The centralized elements of educational policy in most countries serve to allow government agencies to hold schools to account for their outputs. Accountability in self-managing schools, therefore, is concerned both with student and teacher performance and with institutional efficiency.

Accountability and resource management

As Karstanje (1999) notes, the effect of both deregulation and decentralization is often to shift the financial responsibility and risk away from governments and in the direction of institutions which, through self-management, become accountable for the deployment of their own resources. In countries such as New Zealand and Australia:

> creating more efficient and cost-effective school administrative struc-
> tures is a . . . central goal for devolution. Typically, this goal is pursued
> through the implementation of an *administrative control* form of site-
> based management which increases school-site managers' accountability

... for the efficient expenditure of resources. (Leithwood 2001, p. 49, original emphasis)

The budgets for self-managing schools are still determined at national level, which may produce a situation in which the resource base is inadequate. In England and Wales for example Local Management of Schools (LMS), which devolved financial responsibility to the institutional level, included an element in the budget for staffing. This element, however, was not determined by the actual costs of staffing in schools but by a formula based on average staff costs for schools of a similar type and size. Consequently, those schools with well-qualified and experienced staff, who had higher salaries, found that their staffing budget was insufficient to meet the actual cost of staffing. The government position was that resource management was the responsibility of the school (Bell 2002). Although the idea that locally managed schools could be run more economically is critical to this approach to accountability, there is no evidence that this is the case (Gaskell 2002).

Fergusson (1994), however, has identified the extent to which the accountability for resource management can result in headteachers becoming embroiled in administration and performance management at the expense of educational matters. Heads no longer have the responsibility for formulating broad educational policy within their schools. Instead, they are accountable for the implementation of externally imposed policies and achieving the outputs determined by those policies. Consequently, unless resources are diverted away from teaching and learning and into administrative structures, there is, on the part of heads and senior staff in schools:

a radically increased emphasis on budgetary considerations ... and less attention to providing leadership about curriculum and instruction ... As an approach to accountability, site-based management is wide spread ... Considerable evidence suggests, however, that by itself it has made a disappointing contribution to the improvement of teaching and learning. (Leithwood *et al.* 2002, pp. 858-9)

Devolving resource management to the institutional level can be seen as shifting the locus of decision making to a more appropriate part of the system, even if accountability is also shifted to that level. Such forms of accountability, however, may be seen as: 'a deliberate process of subterfuge, distortion, concealment and willful neglect as the state seeks to retreat ... from its historical responsibilities for providing quality public education' (Smyth 1993, p. 2). Alternatively, deregulation can be interpreted in a more limited way as a selective withdrawal by the state from areas in which it has had difficulty succeeding, such as providing equality of opportunity through education (Nash 1989). It may also be an example of the way in which the state seeks to cut expenditure on public services during a period of economic stringency induced by global pressures. Whatever the interpretation adopted, school-based management can be seen as a technique for shifting accountability away from government to individual institutions, especially as the failure of individual schools and colleges can be attributed to poor leadership and resource management at local level.

Accountability and dispersed leadership

School-based management accountability also takes yet another form. It requires school leaders either to encourage participation in school leadership and management on the part of teachers, parents and other stakeholders, or to ensure that self-management takes place within a framework of community control. The basic assumption underpinning the community-control model of accountability is that teachers have not been responsive to local preferences. The curriculum of the school ought to reflect the values and preferences of parents and the local community, difficult as this might be to achieve within a centrally controlled national curriculum (Leithwood 2001). Such approaches to accountability might be exemplified by the exercise of parental choice and the operation of market forces discussed earlier in this chapter or, for example, by the role played by the governing bodies of schools in England and boards of trustees in New Zealand. As representatives of their local communities, they are accountable for the management of resources and for pupil performance within their schools (Bell 1999a). As Grace (1997) has pointed out, however, there is ambivalence on the part of many headteachers towards such manifestations of community accountability.

It is also assumed that the role of school leaders within self-managed schools is to empower stakeholders and:

> actively encourage the sharing of power formerly exercised by the principal. School leaders, it is assumed, will act as members of teams rather than sole decision makers ... through participation in decision making teachers and parents will ... be more committed to the results of such decisions. (Leithwood 2001, p. 52)

This dispersal of accountability is essential if school-based management is to work effectively, not least because everyone in the school has a responsibility for its operation. It has been argued that those schools which are most successful in improving school performance have moved from a managerialist approach based on hierarchical organizational operations to: 'a process that nurtures the deep involvement of teachers and parents in the life of the school community' (Silins and Mulford 2002, p. 567).

The development of an accountable relationship between schools and parents represents a complex and sometimes controversial aspect of state intervention in education. In 1994 a survey of teachers and school principals in Hong Kong conducted by the Education Department indicated a positive belief in the desirability of effective home–school co-operation. There was far less agreement about the nature of that partnership or about empowering parents to hold teachers to account. The Hong Kong School Management Initiative, introduced in 1991, encouraged schools to adopt new management practices in order to improve the quality of school education (Cheng 1999). The addition of teacher and parent members to School Management Committees in Hong Kong (Wong 1995) provides a further example of the partnership model of accountability. Ng (1999) noted that the intention of the policy change was for parents to play a much more proactive role in supporting learning and in facilitating the attainment of a much higher level of academic performance by their children. However, only a few schools in Hong Kong permitted parents to become partners in the process of determining school policies (Ng 1999). Nevertheless, the Hong Kong Government remains committed to the promotion and strengthening of this form of accountability through partnership and has produced the School-based Management Consultative Document to pursue this further. Part of the title of the document indicates the strategic direction in which the policy is intended to move: *Transforming Schools into Dynamic and Accountable Professional Learning Communities* (Education Department 2000). This links initiatives to involve parents and teachers jointly in school management closely to the improvement of pupil performance and the development of high-quality school education.

Little wonder then, there is an increased emphasis on leadership training, the creation of national standards for school leaders and even pre-appointment certification such as the National Professional Qualification for Headship in England and Wales. A common theme in such training is that leadership and accountability should be dispersed throughout the organization. This, of course, means that if accountability as well as leadership is distributed throughout an organization, then performance management within the organization becomes a key element in the accountability process. This approach to accountability, as Leithwood *et al.* (2002) indicate, makes unique demands on educational leaders who have to shoulder the burden of responsibility for increased autonomy and accountability: 'It is clear that special kinds of leaders and leadership ... are required for school self-management. For example, there is no place for an autocratic leader who is unwilling to empower others' (Caldwell and Spinks 1992, p. 47).

Headteachers and principals are now expected to base their influence on professional expertise and moral imperatives rather than line authority and they must learn to lead by empowering rather than controlling others (Normore 2004). The contradictions are obvious here. The administrative demands of school-based management take senior staff away from the arena of professional practice while the requirements of performance management are predicated on authority and hierarchy.

Accountability and performance management

In parallel with this emphasis on managing the performance of teachers is the requirement to set standards of performance both for individuals and schools. These often take the form of targets. One of the main management functions of senior staff becomes the monitoring of performance towards achieving both individual and school targets. *The Teaching Standards Framework* (DfES 2001b) states that subject leaders must provide management to secure high-quality teaching, effective use of resources and improved standards of pupil learning: a clear indication that middle managers are now responsible and accountable for performance management. This has implications for workloads, professional relationships and for the training of middle managers. Although in Britain promotion to senior management positions in now subject to more specific criteria and certification, the current level of provision for middle managers is regarded as wholly inadequate (Busher and Harris 2000). In some places, Connecticut and Queensland for example, this extension of the responsibilities of middle managers into the realm of performance management has been accompanied by a more rigorous control over criteria for entry into teaching, and the extension of provision for teacher professional development (Leithwood *et al.* 2002).

In Germany a similar extension of performance management can be found in some universities. Here attempts are being made to strengthen central control within institutions by introducing accountability through contracts (Kreysing 2002). In one university this is based on a process of contract management. Objectives are negotiated between the central board and the faculties as operative units. The heads of faculty, or of the units within the faculty, are responsible for achieving these objectives both within a specified budget and over a pre-determined time period, after which progress is reviewed. This is having a significant impact on the lines of accountability within the university. In the further education sector in Britain, Gleeson and Shain (2003) note that performance management has substantially redrawn the lines of responsibility and accountability which have led to greatly increased regulation of professional workers and intensification of workloads.

The framework for such performance management in schools in Britain is enshrined in legislation that requires headteachers to ensure that all teachers are appraised on a regular basis (DfEE 2000a). The appraisal, now termed performance review, must take place annually and must result in the setting of at least three targets, one of which must relate to pupil performance. Typically the other targets are linked to professional development and management responsibilities. In Britain at least, the performance targets are part of a wider agenda of target setting, culminating in the school's development or improvement plan that sets targets for pupil performance based on nationally determined priorities and standards. Although lay governors are responsible for ensuring that these targets are achieved, the headteachers and subject leaders are directly accountable for the performance of teachers and pupils. With the introduction of the new Ofsted inspection framework in September 2005, every school has to maintain a self-evaluation form that records the judgements made about current performance and priorities for improvement (Bubb *et al.* 2006).

Appraisal in UK schools is now much more closely linked to performance and rewards. Information from the appraisal performance review statement can be used to inform decisions about staff pay and promotion, to the extent that up to the normal pay threshold teachers can expect an annual increment if they are performing satisfactorily. Double increments for excellent performance would need to be justified by review outcomes. Evidence from the performance review is used to inform applications by teachers for elevation to the upper pay spine, while performance reviews form part of the evidence which schools can use to inform decisions about applications for threshold and advanced skills teacher positions, promotion to the leadership group and for the award of performance pay points to eligible teachers. For the first time middle managers in schools and team leaders are involved in the process as appraisers, thus reinforcing the hierarchical management emphasis of the process (DfES 2001c).

Similar performance management measures can be found elsewhere. Tomlinson (2000) identifies a number of performance management mechanisms in the USA, many of which link pay to the appraisal of performance, although these tend to be whole school rather than individually based rewards packages. In Hong Kong schools, there is what Wong (1995, p. 521) describes as 'a bureaucratic system of staff appraisal based on a managerial model'. Here the principal is accountable for the work of the school and has authority to discharge that accountability. In New Zealand, a rigorous performance management system based on teacher appraisal has been in place since 1997. This is predicated on the view, expressed by the New Zealand School Trustees Association (NZSTA), that:

> Performance appraisal ... is a tool by which the board can measure whether the objectives set for the school are being met. Through performance appraisal, the board and the principal can ascertain whether the elements of the job description, the performance object- ives, and the outcomes ... take both the individual and the organization forward. (NZSTA 1999, p. 7)

Concerns have been expressed about the extent to which this process has been used to implement accountability mechanisms: 'What has happened in New Zealand is that the accountability edge and thus the organizational demands of performance appraisal have insidiously been increased' (Middlewood and Cardno 2001, p. 12).

Thus, as Ball (1994) argues, the doctrine of site-based management can be seen as one in which surveillance of school work and holding staff to account is conducted by heads and other senior staff as part of a process of carrying out the intentions of central government. Self-managing schools, like all other modern organizations, can be seen to be concerned with regulation and surveillance, either explicitly or implicitly. As Crozier (1998) notes, the relationship between parents and schools is part of the process of account- ability but also constitutes:

> a device for surveillance. However, this surveillance is not one-way: as well as the accountability of teachers through surveillance, school relationships have been underpinned ... by some form of surveillance and social control of pupils ... and parents. (Crozier 1998, p. 126)

If, as Beare argues, 'Assessing performance is normal practice these days ... for accountability purposes, for efficiency, and for explaining and keeping track of how resources are used' (Beare 2001, p. 170), the implications of the impact of such performance-management mechanisms on the leadership role of the headteacher are extremely significant. In essence, headteachers, especially those in self-managed schools, are in danger of ceasing to be senior peers located within professional groups and are becoming distinctive actors in a managerialist system, in which the pursuit of increasingly centrally determined objectives and methods is their main responsibility. They must account for the deployment of those methods and the achievement of those objectives and, at the same time, ensure the compliance of their teaching staff (Fergusson 1994).

Conclusion

The imperative for a skilled workforce and a competitive economy that has emerged from the socio-political environment over the last two decades has provided the context for the development of rigorous accountability mechanisms within education systems across the world. This movement has been reinforced by the need in many countries for financial stringency in the public sector. These two sets of factors have combined to provide a strategic direction that can lead to the integration of accountability into the organizational principles and establish a range of operational mechanisms for holding self-managed institutions to account. As Bottery (2000) indicates, however, national culture, history and the locus of power all combine to shape the detailed text of national policies in response to global pressures. Green (1999) also notes that while there is clear evidence of the impact of common global forces on education systems in Asia, Australasia, Europe and North America and convergence around broad policy themes such as decentralization and accountability, 'This does not appear to have led to any marked convergence in structures and processes' (Green 1999, p. 6).

Nevertheless, there is a discernable shift towards establishing and maintaining accountability instruments in many countries. Consequently, those within education in many states operate with multiple levels and senses of accountability which often co-exist in a confusing manner (Ferlie *et al.* 1996). Market accountability based on pupil performance and parental choice has been reinforced by the ability of parents to make choices and to determine where their children shall be educated. Schools have to be responsive to client needs if they are to thrive in this new market-led climate. In other words, schools will only provide the outcomes and services, and meet the standards required of them, when they are directly accountable both to their client parents through choice mechanisms and to the state through specified performance targets.

School-based management has in many countries changed the context of accountability within education systems. Some argue that one of the consequences of the emergence of these forms of accountability is that professional accountability, where it existed, has reduced in importance because of government imperatives for higher standards and parental demands for greater responsiveness (O'Neill 1997). Professional norms often have to be subjugated to these public and market pressures, not least through processes of performance management although, as Middlewood (2002) argues, this has also produced an increased emphasis on and extended opportunities for continued professional development. Such opportunities, however, are often closely linked to the achievement of overall national priorities (Bolam 2002). Perhaps the issue here, however, goes beyond the specific nature of teaching as a profession and the nature of professional values and services. Given that the main features of professionalism are not immutable, it is evident that the nature of teacher professionalism has been transformed in parallel with the growing emphasis within the activities of the state on economic performance and the contribution made to the establishing of a national competitive edge by education.

There is also evidence of control over both processes and outcomes in schools and colleges. Much depends on where the balance lies between achieving outcomes through specific processes and the wider continued professional development of teachers and lecturers. How far, for example, does appraisal focus on targets and outcomes and how much attention is given to professional development? If the emphasis is at the outcomes end of the continuum, then accountability and performance management are providing the organizational principles for control through accountability. This is less likely to be the case if the operational practices focus on professional development. Much of the evidence in this chapter suggests that the greater concern is with targets and outcomes. Consequently, questions are raised about the nature of teacher autonomy, responsibility and accountability (Hoyle and John 1995). It would be a mistake not to heed the conclusion of a paper based on the work of the Centre for Educational Research and Innovation: 'The more complex a professional activity becomes, the more policy interventions have to take into account the views of practitioners and leave space for local adaptations ... practical problems cannot be solved for the institutions by central regulations' (OECD 1996, p. 11).

A further consequence of such accountability rooted in the legitimation of economics and the marketplace, has been the diminution of the weight attached to concerns for equality of opportunity, equity and social justice. The operation of market forces through competition and the exercising of parental choice may lead to some schools being oversubscribed and others having rapidly declining enrolments, resulting in a climate that is not conducive to setting and achieving reasonable educational standards for those students that remain. The use of raw measures of pupil achievement as the sole or even the major criterion for making judgments about the efficacy of the performance of schools may also result in discrimination against certain groups of pupils, those with special needs or whose first language is not the language of instruction in the school, for example. The exercise of parental choice may exacerbate these inequities. As Goldring (1997) notes in the cases of both Israel and the USA, one effect of parental choice mechanisms is that students from more affluent families are more likely to leave their neighbourhood schools in favour of magnet schools that cater for students with special skills. There is evidence from both Australia and France that professional families are far more active in exercising choice than are those of manual workers (Hirsch 1997). In Britain, Gewirtz (2002) has pointed out that one of the most significant weaknesses of accountability based on market forces, choice and performance management is that such mechanisms merely tend to produce a redistribution of students among schools and colleges without addressing the root causes of educational under-attainment and issues of equality of opportunity and social justice.

Which Grain will Grow and Which will Not: the Management of Staff – some Issues of Efficiency and Cost-effectiveness

Introduction

The management of schools and colleges is a complex process. At its most strategic it involves formulating a vision for the school or college based on strongly held, shared values and beliefs about the aims and purposes of education. These values and beliefs inform the processes for translating the vision into action through a long-term plan. The strategic level of school management tends to be the preserve of the headteacher, perhaps supported by senior staff and the chair of the governing body. This strategic level, however, is only one level at which management takes place. At the organizational level the strategic view is converted into medium-term objectives supported by the allocation of appropriate resources and the delegation of responsibility for decision making, implementation, review and evaluation. Heads of faculties and departments, subject leaders and year heads play a major role here. In turn, the implementation of medium-term plans requires that they be further sub-divided into the totality of the delegated tasks that have to be carried out at the operational level by teachers in classrooms. At the operational level, therefore, resources are utilized, tasks completed, activities co-ordinated and monitored and outcomes evaluated. The three levels of management must work in harmony towards a common purpose if schools and colleges are to be managed efficiently and effectively and if resources, including staff, are to be deployed in the most appropriate ways. The successful management of staff, therefore, is a vital part of the overall management of the institution.

As a result of a greater degree of autonomy being devolved to schools, the responsibility for managing staff has increasingly fallen to the senior management of schools in conjunction with the school governors, with whom the legal responsibility rests. This is particularly evident as education policy in England and Wales has moved through the Market Phase to the Target Phase and has placed an increasing emphasis on some form of school-based autonomous management. This trend is also evident, however, in many other countries. As Whitty and his colleagues note:

> The past decade has seen an increasing number of attempts in various parts of the world to restructure ... state schooling. Central to these

initiatives are moves to dismantle centralised educational bureaucracies and to create in their place devolved systems ... entailing significant degrees of autonomy and a variety of forms of school based administration. (Whitty *et al.* 1998, p. 3)

This introduction of school-based management has involved, in particular, the decentralization of the budget such that more and more of the financial resources are deployed at school or college level. This shift of the locus of financial control has increasingly placed the responsibility for the management of staff on senior managers in schools. This trend was indicated in 1985 in the UK when a major government report on improving schools concluded that to improve standards, action was necessary in four areas, one of which was staff management:

1. to secure greater clarity about the objectives and content of the curriculum:
2. to reform the examinations system and improve assessment;
3. to improve the professional effectiveness of teachers and the management of the teaching force;
4. to reform school government and harness more fully the contribution which can be made ... by parents, employers and others outside the education service. (DES 1985b, p. 8)

It was further argued that improved teacher effectiveness and better management of staff in schools could only be achieved if information was available about the skills and competences of the individual teacher and if headteachers kept constantly under review the further development and deployment of their staff (Joseph 1985). A scheme for the appraisal of teachers was introduced which included classroom observation and much greater priority was given to developing the management skills of headteachers and their senior colleagues. At the same time, as Bolam (1997) has pointed out, there was a growing emphasis on achieving effective school management. Management training courses funded by local education authorities and the DES gave priority to the management of staff. Management training became a national priority within the education service and a nationally funded development centre for school-management training and a task force on school management were established. Compulsory teacher appraisal, which included classroom observation, a national mentoring scheme for headteachers and a support scheme for newly appointed heads were introduced. More recently the National Professional Qualification for Headship has been introduced for those who aspire to headship and a training programme for experienced heads is about to be launched. All of these initiatives are designed to improve the management of staff in schools.

There is no doubt that the staff in any school or college are its most expensive resource, because, as Hall (1997) has noted, between 75 per cent and 85 per cent of the budget of any educational institution is spent on staffing costs. Hall (1997) suggests that to the extent that the staff of the school are an expensive resource, strategies should be in place to manage that resource at six key stages: recruitment and selection, induction, deployment, development, promotion and exit. These strategies should be informed by a clearly articulated statement at the strategic level about the priorities of the school, a set of policies at the organizational level about the key aspects of resource management and a set of operational tasks to implement those policies. Recruitment to a vacancy opens up a range of choices, the least effective of which may be to succumb to the temptation to replace like with like. Consideration has to be given to the overall priorities of the school, future developments and the extent to which existing work can be reorganized. In many schools budgetary constraints often mean that a senior member of staff may need to be replaced by a less experienced and less expensive person. Frequently, the choice may be whether or not to appoint a teacher at all. A significant proportion of primary school heads now prefer to allocate funding to appointing classroom assistants rather than increasing the number of teachers on their staff (TES 1999; Edwards 1999). Many schools now participate in various forms of teacher training. School-based initial teacher training, licensed teachers and graduate teacher schemes all help to provide opportunities to recruit new teachers who meet the requirements of children in particular schools. Nevertheless, the decision to recruit a new member of staff must be preceded by a careful analysis of present and future staffing needs.

If recruitment is about attracting appropriate applicants, selection is the process of appointing the most suitable person for the job. Since staff are the most valuable and expensive resource in a school, care must be taken over selection. It must be based on a job description that identifies the key tasks for the post, a person specification that states the knowledge, skills, competences and values that are required and a clear description of the way in which selection will be carried out. This approach will go a long way towards preventing the appointment of unsuitable staff by limiting the scope for inappropriate subjective judgements. It will facilitate the appointment of staff who meet the needs of the children in the school, have the appropriate experience and expertise to carry out the duties of the post to which they have been appointed and who understand what is expected of them.

Once in post, staff should be provided with support throughout their induction phase. Arrangements are now in place to provide induction for newly qualified teachers:

> every teacher should have structured support during the first year of full-time teaching. This should build upon their initial training ... and continue to develop their skills in areas identified during initial training. Mentor support will be provided. Schools will be expected to provide a planned induction programme for each newly qualified teacher. (DfEE 2000b pp. 47-8)

Similar help should be given to all staff who are new to the school in order to ensure that they are deployed effectively and can function efficiently. Teachers should not be expected to take on responsibilities for which they have not been prepared and that are not within their sphere of competence. Nor should their work be subject to arbitrary change. Effective deployment matches the competences and experience of staff with the demands being placed upon them.

More flexible staff deployment can be achieved through various forms of in-service training. All staff in schools should, therefore, benefit from a well-structured professional development programme. Appraisal can contribute to the identification of individuals' training needs but the wider requirements of the school, as expressed through its development plan and other policy documents, must also be given priority. Striking the right balance between the needs of individual members of staff and those of the school community as a whole is difficult to achieve, but efficient and effective staff management requires that it must be attempted in as open a way as possible. Similarly, internal promotion opportunities and the nature of support offered to those seeking advancement elsewhere should meet clear criteria. The procedures for obtaining confidential advice in advance of applying for either internal or external posts and feedback after the process should be available. Often such feedback is as important for successful candidates as it is for those who are still seeking promotion. Where a member of staff obtains a post elsewhere it is good practice to conduct an exit interview. This can begin the recruitment process and inform senior managers of many pertinent issues in their schools (Bell and Rhodes 1996).

Staff management in UK schools now has an added dimension, that of performance management (DfEE 1998e). Appraisal was relaunched and became even more rigorous. It is linked to progression through the pay scale for some teachers as well as performance-related pay. The performance of all teachers is assessed against agreed performance objectives and will be subject to ongoing monitoring. Heads and senior staff will be subject to a similar performance-management regime:

> Appraisals of teachers [are] conducted ... on an annual cycle ... The process will lead to a statement assessing each teacher's performance against the previous year's objectives ... The statement will also outline objectives for the coming year. The head will then make a recommendation to the governing body about that teacher's pay, based on the outcomes of appraisal ... Heads will be appraised by the governing body against agreed objectives. Independent advisors will assist ... In considering the level of pay award, the governing body will take into account the head's performance as reflected in the appraisal report. (DfEE 1998e, p. 3)

This rigorous process may or may not lead to the more efficient and effective management of teachers. It is clear, however, that managing staff is, in UK schools and colleges at least, becoming increasing complex and demanding. These complexities require that all of the relevant procedures are known and understood by the staff involved. Hall (1997) concludes, therefore, that it is important for effective staff management that all schools have policies for each area of the staff-management process and that these policies: 'liberate rather than constrain staff performance. In this way, managing staff in autonomous schools successfully balances management accountability and management for freedom' (Hall 1997, p. 160). This has to be achieved, however, within a limited budget, which requires that resources are managed both effectively and efficiently. In short, in all matters of resource management, including the management of staff, schools must be cost-effective.

The cost-effective school

Resource management in any school can best be considered as a system within which resources are transformed into educational outcomes through a number of stages (Simkins 1997). Financial resources are the basis of the budget but, in order to achieve any form of outcomes, money must be converted into other forms of resources that, in turn, are deployed to enable the strategic, organizational and operational priorities of the school to be achieved. Cuthbert (1985) notes that effectiveness is concerned with the extent or quality of educational achievement, whereas efficiency is concerned with the cost of that achievement. An effective school, therefore, is one which deploys its resources, including its staff, in such a way as to match its results with its stated objectives. An effective school may not be either efficient or economic, since these two concepts imply notions of cost. An efficient school is one which achieves its outcomes within its cost limits: 'The efficient school makes good use of all its available resources to achieve the best possible educational outcomes for its children – and in so doing provides excellent value for money' (Ofsted 1995a, p. 121). An economic school is similar to this, but is one which is able to purchase a given standard of goods or services at the lowest cost. Schools in Britain are not particularly good at establishing procedures to ensure that they are efficient or economic: 'Few primary schools had, for example, procedures to monitor the effectiveness of their deployment of support staff; and while awareness about cost-effectiveness is increasing in secondary schools, few schools evaluate the costs of their procedures and plans' (Ofsted 1995b, p. 24).

The task of establishing how far any school is efficient, effective, economic or even cost-effective is made especially difficult because many of the concepts involved in such an analysis are used imprecisely. As Levačić and Glover (1994) point out, the term efficiency tends to be used when processes are being considered while effectiveness is used to refer to achieving outcomes. Frequently, however, the terms are used either in parallel or interchangeably. The criteria for making judgements about value for money, that is detailed information on costs and outcomes, appears to lack precision even if it is available. This is especially true in the management of staff.

The Education Reform Act (DES 1988a) contained major policy initiatives which were intended to make schools cost-effective. There were five key elements to this policy strand that were largely income rather than expenditure driven. These were:

1. The delegation to schools of control over budgets such that, within cash limits, decisions can be taken at school level about numbers and type of staff and other resourcing matters. Thus, schools can make expenditure decisions based on local priorities. This gives senior staff in schools the flexibility to make decisions about the number and type of staff that might be employed in the school.

2. The introduction of a formula to establish how schools are to be funded and to determine what level of funding schools will receive. This is a pupil-driven system through which funding is determined by numbers of pupils on roll and where funding follows pupils. Thus, a popular school that recruits well will receive an increased budget. As a result, more staff may be employed.

3. The delegation to school governors of powers over most staffing matters. The responsibility for identifying the appropriate staffing complement for the school and for certain decisions about the pay of heads and deputies, as well as the appointment of staff, are vested in the governors.

4. The provision of performance information to enable parents to make informed choices about schools. This will, in future, include information about the performance of individual teachers.

5. Admission arrangements that permit relatively easy transfer of pupils between schools.

Here, then, the emphasis is on ways in which the total school budget might be restructured by either gaining or losing pupils, how school policies which determine performance might be influenced to ensure that pupil numbers in any particular school might be increased rather than allowed to decrease and how the overall budget might best be deployed through expenditure on staff and other resources to achieve the school's objectives. As Ofsted inspection reports show, however, there is a wide variety of school-based responses to these aspects of policy (Ofsted 1995b) so what might a cost-effective school look like and how might staff be managed within it?

As Thomas and Martin (1996) suggest, these are questions more easily asked than answered. They note, in seeking to answer these questions, that cost-effectiveness is concerned with the relationship between the learning of children and the human and physical resources which contribute to this learning. It is a way of analysing the relationship between the deployment of resources and educational outcomes. As Mortimore *et al.* (1994) argue, cost-effectiveness is a wider and more challenging concept than effectiveness. They suggest that:

> effective schools are those in which pupils of all abilities achieve to their full potential. Whether that performance is achieved using more rather than fewer resources is not, strictly, part of the assessment of effectiveness. On the other hand, the amount of resources is an essential component of cost-effectiveness. Thus, if two schools that are comparable in other respects are equally effective in terms of performance, the one that uses the smaller amount of resources is the more cost-effective. (Mortimore *et al.* 2004, pp. 21–2)

Thus, cost-effectiveness encompasses efficiency but goes beyond it. To enable their school to be cost-effective, senior staff require information about the entire cost of running their school and they also need to use that information to make decisions about, for example, appropriate staffing levels, types of staff and the deployment of staff. Thomas and Martin (1996) suggest a number of features that are likely to be shared by all cost-effective schools. Such schools will base their work on a periodic *radical audit* focusing on the use of staffing and on the identification of professional development needs related to the school's priorities. Decision making will be informed by detailed information on costs, including staff costs so that alternatives can be assessed in the light of current expenditure. Team meetings, appraisal and surveys will be used to collect information on the quality of teaching and learning from teachers, parents and pupils. Much of this information will be generated independently of the head and senior staff and will lead to the delegation of decision making about priorities to staff with relevant expertise. A dialogue of accountability will be created which will ensure that decisions about resource deployment are made in the light of an overall strategic plan for the school.

These features, in themselves, cannot ensure that staff are managed in a cost-effective way. They provide a framework within which schools can begin to make appropriate staff-management decisions. In their study of 18 schools Thomas and Martin (1996) explored how each school sought to manage its staff in a cost-effective way. Many of the schools achieved this by employing teachers with specific expertise, such as special needs teachers to help colleagues meet the requirements of children with learning difficulties, or an outreach teacher to develop stronger links between the school and its community. Other schools recruited teachers with specific expertise to manage projects for a limited period of time or on contracts which would enable them to cover for absence rather than employing supply staff, thus giving some continuity and flexibility to staff management. One school tackled its falling pupil numbers and, therefore, its declining resource base by deploying a deputy head to develop community-based programmes to increase the school's intake and change its nature.

Often schools took the opportunity to change teaching roles or to appoint teachers with new or different areas of expertise. In some cases these approaches to cost-effective staffing resulted in a change in the management of the school, sometimes at the strategic decision-making level where the input from a key member of staff whose expertise was not in education brought a different perspective to the work of the school. This resulted, in one school, in the collection and presentation of data in a different way to facilitate better decision making. In another, it produced a total restructuring of the school's management systems through the introduction of financial and staff-development databases that provided a wide range of information to inform decision making. In other cases the changes were at the organizational level and even informed the operational activities. Heads of department received better and more understandable budget information about, for example, the cost of staffing field trips. This enabled informed decisions to be made about whether or not to undertake such trips and how best to plan those that were to continue. At the operational level, teachers were able to take informed decisions about their choice of teaching styles and the cost of teaching in particular ways.

Although each school had different needs and adopted different solutions, they had in common the use of some form of audit to provide information on costing and to ensure that staffing matched needs on a fitness-for-purpose basis. In many cases this took the form of changing or enhancing the role of teachers, but in others there was an increased emphasis on the employment of staff with other forms of expertise to support the work of teachers. Several schools used the flexibility that they now had to transfer of some administrative functions from senior teaching staff to bursars, librarians, technicians, site managers and administrative officers or to employ an increased number of clerical and/or technical staff to ease the burden on teaching staff. Mortimore *et al.* (1994) call this group of people who work in schools associate staff.

Managing associate staff

The research by Mortimore *et al.* (1994) shows that many schools have chosen to manage their staffing resource in ways that bring in to the school non-educational expertise as part of the process of being more cost-effective. The largest part of any school's budget is spent on its teaching staff, so how might cost-effectiveness be achieved by providing support in classrooms? There is very little systematic evidence about the deployment of associate staff in schools, especially those that work in classrooms, or about the contribution that they might make to the effective and efficient management of schools. It has been clear since 1967, however, that there is considerable variation in both the provision and the impact on teaching and learning of such staff (Central Advisory Council for Education 1967). The Bullock Report (1975) argued that both teachers and pupils, especially those in disadvantaged areas: 'should have the assistance of trained persons, the nature of whose participation she [the headteacher] will herself decide according to the demands of the situation' (Bullock 1975, para 5.32). In the 1980s concerns over persistent under-achievement by certain groups, the increase in number and range of pupils for whom English was not the first language, changes in the curriculum and its assessment all served to focus attention on the provision of support for teachers. Hargreaves (ILEA 1984) and Thomas (ILEA 1985) both noted the growing importance of associate staff. By the end of the decade it could be argued that:

> it is a prime management function to choose non-teaching staff ... with as much care as teachers ... Thereafter it is desirable ... to ensure that non-teaching staff are fully recognized for their work and included in as many of the appropriate functions as possible. (Reid *et al.* 1988, p. 3)

In the years following the Education Reform Act (DES 1988a) the numbers of associate staff in schools increased significantly. Tight financial controls on educational spending, increased class sizes, curriculum and assessment demands and the growing number of children who are either statemented or regarded as having special needs have combined to lead headteachers and school governors to increase the number of support staff employed in schools:

> According to the most recent official statistics ... between 1991 and 1996 the number of educational support staff in primary schools more than doubled whilst in the same period the number of teachers rose by only 3.2%. This means that, on average, there is now one full time

equivalent non-teaching assistant to every eight teachers. (Moyles and Suschitzky, 1997a, p. 21)

It should also be remembered that financial delegation has created a situation in which heads and school governors now have the power to use their resources to make the decision to employ more support staff without obtaining LEA approval. By 2003 it was evident that primary schools:

> Make excellent use of teaching assistants and other support staff ... seven out of ten headteachers said that they had more than one member of support staff for each teacher in the school; and that the number of hours worked by support staff in the classroom had increased over the last three years. (DfES 2003, p. 65)

So what do these support staff do and what contribution do they make to the effective and efficient management of the school? Razzell, in his commentary on the Plowden Report, described the duties of classroom assistants as follows:

> They issue the milk to the classes, supervize the library, catalogue, classify and cover books with polythene jackets and keep the shelves in good order ... In other schools aides supply the classes with consumable stock, keep the pencils sharpened, the cupboards and stockrooms tidy, repair damaged equipment, undertake duplicating, act as escorts to children, set out audio visual equipment, sort out lost property and not infrequently make tea for staff at lunch time. (Razzell 1968, p. 5)

Kennedy and Duthie (1975) found that many teachers believed that support staff could relieve them of routine non-teaching tasks and so increase the teacher's contact with the children. They note that classroom auxiliaries were used to provide in-class supervision, cleaning and tidying and general school duties such as mounting work and moving furniture. Little appeared to have changed from those activities observed by Razzell although Marland (1978), quoted in Mortimore *et al.* (1994), was already describing classroom assistants as a valuable and cost-effective component of the teaching team. Brennan (1982) commented that non-teaching staff were frequently employed to provide support for children with sensory handicaps and that the helper was the child's eyes, ears and mobility aid. During the 1980s parents were increasingly being used to provide support in classrooms and some were employed as bilingual assistants. There is some evidence that both parents and classroom assistants were starting to be used as apprentice teachers without being trained for the task (Goode 1982). Hodgson *et al.* (1984) noted that assistants in special schools were carrying out educational tasks directed by teachers and Hilleard (1988) established, again in special schools, that assistants spent much of their time on instructional tasks designed by teachers and therapists. By 1989 a study on the deployment of classroom assistants concluded that: 'over 90% stated that they frequently supervised and assisted small groups of children engaged in educational activities set by the teacher ... least time was spent on cleaning and administrative tasks' (Clayton 1989,

p. 106). Mortimore *et al.* (1994) demonstrate that by the early 1990s many classroom assistants are involved in work which previously would have been the domain of teachers. They describe how one classroom assistant who had responsibility for supporting practical activities was given the task of making the practical curriculum more accessible to the children; another assisted in language work for Asian children while a significant number were involved in planning and delivering the curriculum. This marks a significant shift in the role of associate staff who work in classrooms.

This change in the role of classroom assistants from domestic helper to assistant teacher in schools has been recognized in a number of ways (Clayton 1993). A training programme, the Specialist Teacher Assistant Scheme, was introduced in 1994. Its aim was to develop courses specifically to prepare adults to give support to teachers in classrooms in teaching the basic skills of reading, writing and mathematics (Ofsted 1996). Unfortunately, no training was provided for teachers on how best to use their classroom assistants. The deployment of teaching assistants and support staff in schools had now become part of government policy:

> Teaching and learning can be strengthened by using the full potential of teaching assistants and school support staff. All staff should be fully integrated into the schools' activities – enhancing their own role and giving teachers support and information … Teaching assistants are playing an increasingly important role in schools on tasks such as literacy support and helping pupils with special educational needs. We want that contribution to be fully acknowledged for the first time. (DfEE 1998a, pp. 55–6)

Here we see a significant move away from restricting the work of classroom assistants to menial non-teaching tasks towards a direct contribution to teaching and learning as part of an overall policy intended to improve standards. In order to contribute to cost-effectiveness in their schools, associate staff must either undertake duties which release teachers to concentrate more on teaching or make a contribution to supporting teachers in educational activities.

Conclusion

It has been argued above that, increasingly, ancillary staff are becoming more involved in the teaching process in many schools in order to contribute to the cost-effectiveness of their institutions. Mortimore *et al.* (1994) remind us, however, that three general principles must be born in mind when seeking to establish cost-effectiveness. These are, first, 'fitness for purpose' – has the school the right balance and mixture of staff to meet the needs of the pupils and to achieve its objectives? A school staffed almost entirely by associate staff may be efficient but it is hardly likely to be effective or cost-effective. The second is the use of staff audit. This is much the same as the Thomas and Martin (1996) concept of radical audit and should be used to establish where, if anywhere, are the gaps between staff responsibilities and existing skills. The third principle involves recognizing the cost of implementing any choices that are made. This not only means knowing the full cost of a particular course of action, but also being aware of the cost of alternatives and of what may not be possible because a particular choice is made. In other words, opportunity costs must be taken into account. Thus if a school chooses to spend, say, £20,000 on employing two classroom assistants, the true cost of this choice will include premises and equipment costs and a cost associated with the time that will need to be given to supervise and, perhaps, train those assistants. This choice also means that a teacher will not be employed. This is part of the opportunity cost. For such choice to be cost-effective, therefore, the total cost of employing the two assistants must be less than that for the lost opportunities or they must contribute more to the school's overall work than any of the alternative staffing possibilities. Mortimore *et al.* (1994) conclude from their study that this focus on costing alternatives, combined with the increased discretion that heads now have over staffing, has enabled heads to manage the staffing of their schools more cost-effectively. Thomas and Martin (1996) go further and suggest that one of the most important consequences of this approach to managing staff in schools is that it has changed the perceptions of heads as to what is possible.

This review of some of the research evidence on staff management in schools suggests that some, probably most, school managers are using their autonomy over staffing to achieve increased economy and efficiency and to move towards being cost-effective at the operation level of school management. What is less clear, however, is how far heads and senior staff in schools are taking strategic decisions which link choices about resourcing to explicit educational outcomes. Reports from school inspectors indicate that: 'There is little evidence yet of LMS having any substantial impact on educational standards' (DfE 1992, p. 11). Levačić (1995) concludes that there is evidence that local financial management has had a positive impact on the efficiency and effectiveness of schools but it proved difficult to detect any learning improvement as a result of staff or resource management. Researchers, therefore, have to fall back on the perceptions of heads and their staff.

Managing staff in a cost-effective way is about more than simply being creative over the nature of appointments or changing the roles within the school. Cost-effectiveness has to focus on improving the teaching and learning within schools. Even in the limited context of the employment of a classroom assistant for science in one primary school, McGarvey *et al.* (1996) were unable to provide specific evidence of the link between the extra pair of hands and improved pupil performance, although one teacher in the study commented that classroom assistants transform your teaching life. It is dangerous to assume that more adults in classrooms necessarily means better learning opportunities for children (Moyles and Suschitzky 1997b). While extra pairs of hands may contribute to the operational activities of the school, the evidence to support a close link between cost-effective staff management and improved learning outcomes is, at best, superficial. Nor is it clear exactly how far the increased use of associate staff has contributed to the strategic and organizational management of schools. Much more evidence is still required to establish how far cost-effective staff management can have an impact on pupil performance.

Part 3: Management and Leadership in Primary Schools

The four chapters in this section are drawn from a series of projects on management and leadership in primary schools that has spanned almost two decades. The research started in 1988 when a group of primary school headteachers on an in-service course were discussing the likely impact on themselves and their schools of the Education Act that was about to be passed (Bell and Rhodes 1996; DES 1988a). They suggested that somebody ought to research the effects that the proposed policy changes would have on them and their schools, and so a research project was born. This section concentrates on tracing the responses of primary school headteachers to national government policy initiatives. Chapter 8 and Chapter 9 are based on data from an ESRC funded project conducted with my then colleagues at the University of Warwick, Professor David Halpin and Dr Sean Neill. The ESRC funding enabled the research on primary headship to continue through the 1990s and to be extended to a larger number of schools, including a sample from the private sector. Chapter 8 compares the ways in which a group of headteachers in state primary schools responded to the attempts to engender competition between schools through the operation of the educational marketplace, with the marketing activities of heads in similar schools in the private sector. The chapter suggests that in many ways the responses of the state school headteachers represented 'service in every point twice done' as most of them failed to understand the true nature of marketing, yet sought to circumvent or even subvert attempts to make neighbouring schools compete for pupil numbers. In Chapter 9 the increasing importance of school governors is explored and, in particular, the nature of the emerging relationships between heads and their governors, as each sought to come to terms with new responsibilities and new boundaries. Different categories of this relationship are evident as heads and governors strive to provide management and leadership for their schools and to 'Leave no rubs nor botches in the work'. Chapter 10 considers what understandings headteachers have of the planning process to which all schools are subject and how they have responded to these processes. The chapter shows how many heads have been quite successful in reshaping the demands placed upon them to meet more effectively the needs of children in their individual schools, in fact, to make the outcome of such planning 'a tale of some significance' rather than one merely of sound and fury. Chapter 11, written as a collaborative work with my former graduate student

Dr Avril Rowley, incorporates some of the ESRC project data and some of the research data for Avril's doctoral thesis in order to examine the impact of changes in educational policy over a period that spanned the declining years of the New Right and the early years of New Labour. It is evident that although headteachers recognized that 'what's done is done', policy changes were having a significant impact both on their professional identities and on their capacity to cope with the demands being placed upon them.

Service in Every Point Twice Done: Primary Schools and the Nature of the Education Marketplace

Introduction

This chapter considers the ways in which headteachers in primary schools in England have responded to an educational policy based on the establishment of an educational marketplace both in the Market Phase of educational policy and in the early stages of the Target Phase. It will look briefly at the nature of that policy and identify the main characteristics of the educational market. It will consider the reported activities of primary school heads in relation to the competitive nature of the educational marketplace and the strategic marketing of their schools within that environment. It will conclude by offering some observations on the interpretation of those activities in the light of what heads say about their own professional values and the educational marketplace, a critique of the concept of the market as a means of allocating resources and the extent to which heads of primary schools operate from a position of organizational ambiguity in respect of the educational market and the ways in which they manage within that context.

As was argued in Chapter 1, management of schools and the market were closely interrelated in Conservative government policy on the reform and restructuring of state schooling. Both the local management of schools (LMS) and grant maintained (GM) schools policies occasioned not only new conceptions of what it meant to manage a school, but also altered relations between schools and local communities. As Ball (1993) observed, the market and management reforms replaced collective, bureaucratic controls, structures and relationships with individualistic and competitive ones. The model for this fundamental change in perspective and practice is derived from the private sector within which fee-charging schools, managed like small businesses, market and sell their services to parents whose educational requirements they must anticipate and whose confidence they must retain in order to survive. Studies of the impact of particular markets on the management practices of schools, and theorizing about the relationship between local market conditions and the education identities promoted by individual schools, have chiefly been directed at the secondary sector. These studies highlight the extent to which, in secondary schools, management styles are being adopted that stress stricter and more bureaucratic divisions of labour between senior managers and teacher subordinates and involve more explicit ways of managing and marketing the reputation of those schools (see Ball 1992 and 1993). The little research currently available on the impact of recent educational reform on the work of primary school heads and primary school management points up similar developments. For example, findings from the PACE project (Pollard *et al.* 1994), in which 48 primary heads were interviewed, suggest that the local management of primary schools is giving rise to a gradual shift away from collective decision making towards a more 'top-down' directive approach entailing a form of contrived collegiality or 'managed participation'. Similar conclusions are reached by Menter *et al.* (1997) in a study of the effects of education marketization on a group of primary schools in one city. The research reported in this chapter challenges such earlier work by concluding that individualism and competitiveness, while latent in the work of some heads, is not sufficiently pronounced as to lead to the establishment of an education marketplace and thus preclude genuine forms of inter-school collaboration.

The data on which this chapter is based is derived from an Economic and Social Science Research Council funded project (R000221271). The main aim of this project was to examine the extent to which management practices, defined as the formulation of policy and day-to-day decision making, varied between primary schools that had different degrees of managerial responsibility devolved to them. Schools (257) from the LEA maintained and grant maintained (GM) sectors were included in the sample. This provided a comparison between two parts of the maintained sector that had been granted different degrees of institutional autonomy by government legislation. Fieldwork was conducted in two phases. In the first phase a lengthy questionnaire was sent to the heads of 289 primary schools. This sample included every all-through primary school which, at the time of starting the research, had been operating as a GM establishment for a minimum of one year (49 in total), and a randomly selected group of all-through self-governing local authority maintained primary schools located in five LEAs in central England (208 in total). The questionnaire elicited data on 137 primary schools, including 29 from the GM sector. This data comprised basic information on the schools, the perceptions of their heads concerning a range of management roles, practices and functions and details of the characteristics of the education market within which each one operated. The questionnaire data was analysed using the social science statistical package SPSS. These tests enabled us to identify features for each group of respondents which were typical of that group. The principle of typicality, tempered by considerations of geographical proximity, determined the choice of heads for the interview phase of the research. 'Typicality' refers to heads whose responses to the questionnaire in terms of how they described their style of management matched other respondents working in the *same* school sector. This produced a sample of heads whose responses approximated to those that were typical of their sector and a smaller group whose responses were atypical.

The second phase of the research followed the analysis of the questionnaire data. Detailed semi-structured (audio-recorded) interviews were conducted with 12 LEA and 6 GM school heads who had returned a completed questionnaire. These interviews explored further the nature and extent of respondents' sense of professional empowerment and efficacy, including management style and level of job satisfaction. The interviews were also used to obtain additional background information about individual schools and, in particular, the character of the education market environment in which they were set.

Characteristics of the educational marketplace.

A plethora of policy documents bombarded schools, colleges and local education authorities in Britain during the 1980s. These culminated in the Education Reform Act (DES 1988a) and the series of circulars and education acts (e.g. DES 1988b, 1991) which followed it. This legislation was largely derived from a socio-political philosophy based on the work of right-wing political economists such as Friedman and Friedman (1980) and Hayek (1973) who believed that market forces were the most appropriate way of allocating resources and structuring choices in all aspects of human endeavour, including social and educational policy. As was argued in Chapter 1, this belief was translated into a set of organizational principles for public-sector institutions which included the liberty of individuals to make choices based on self-interest; the freedom of individuals to exercise such choices without being subject to coercion from others; the freedom to choose being exercised daily through spending choices (Harris 1980; Joseph 1976; Scruton 1984). Competition becomes the motive force for policy implementation and through it improvement in the nature and quality of service will be brought about as the family becomes a unit of economic consumption, its members make choices about products, and public sector institutions behave as firms seeking to maximize both profits and market share.

Since 1988 legislation has been introduced to implement an educational policy based on creating and sustaining an educational marketplace. Much of this legislation focused on making schools accountable, providing parents with information on which to make judgements about the relative performance of schools and ensuring that funding followed pupils so that schools gained financially if they recruited pupils and suffered financial penalties if they lost pupils. Most of the elements of accountability that provided the impetus for the education market remain under New Labour including the publication of results, league tables and increasingly rigorous inspections by Ofsted whose judgements are now even more telling since the Secretary of State's 'Fresh Start' idea was incorporated into Ofsted strategy. As a result, where a school is significantly underachieving it will immediately be closed and a new school opened with a new staff and a new governing body. Thus, some of the key legislative features designed to foster the education marketplace remain intact or have been strengthened. But how far has an educational market been created? What effect has the attempt to create such a marketplace had on the small and medium-sized enterprises of the educational world, the primary schools?

If schools are to operate in the education marketplace, this presupposes that heads and governors accept the philosophical justifications for the creation of that market which emanate from the wider socio-political environment. If they embrace the education market philosophy and operate in accord with its basic tenets, heads will recognize the need for competition as a motive force and accept it as a mechanism for resource allocation and structuring parental choice. This recognition will then be translated into action in several ways. Heads will seek to recruit the maximum possible number of pupils and, by so doing, maximize the income of the school. In order to achieve this, heads and their governing bodies will develop a coherent marketing plan based on an assessment of parental expectations and the need to communicate the benefits to be accrued from sending children to a particular school. In so doing, heads will understand that: 'Marketing ... can just mean selling, promotion and aggressive competition, or it can mean making the market's requirements central to decision making' (Pardey 1994, pp. 203–4).

Most heads in our sample denied the importance of the educational marketplace to decision making in their schools. They did not acknowledge the centrality of competition to their thinking about the relationship between their school and others in the neighbourhood. Heads of LEA schools, in particular, were more likely to espouse values of collaboration and co-operation with local schools than to recognize that they were in direct competition. A few heads, mainly in GM schools, did see themselves as directly in competition with both LEA and independent schools. One head of a Catholic GM school stated: 'Yes I am in competition. My competitors are the local junior schools and then the private schools. There is a big independent Catholic school which is my main competitor.'

Other GM heads recognized the reality of competition but in a less overt way and sought to minimize its extent and importance as a contributing factor to pupil recruitment: 'Yes I think we are in competition but hopefully competition with a small "c". We try to help parents make the right choices for their children and for some it might be this school.' This head reported that his school was not quite full but he was not prepared to encourage parents to send their children to the school if its pedagogy and ethos did not appear to suit the child. Fully fledged competition was not part of his overall strategy for the school. At most it was an operational exigency. The head sought to deny the centrality of competition and acted to optimize rather than maximize the school's income through the pupil-recruitment process.

Heads of LEA maintained primary schools were even less likely to acknowledge the competitive nature of the marketplace. A typical comment when asked if they were in direct competition with other schools was the following from the head of an inner-city primary school: 'I don't see us in competition. Although we take children from outside our area we are not aggressively competing.' To the same question, a head of a primary school in North Oxfordshire responded:

> Not really, it's sort of swings and roundabouts. There are a number of children in this catchment area that I know go to other schools and I have a number from other areas. We are not competing in that way. There is one school that has very low pupil numbers in our partnership. We support that school as much as possible.

When asked if she would act differently if her school was not full, the same head replied: 'I would like to think not but when it comes to the implications of losing staff I think you would be fighting to keep your numbers up.' The heads of primary schools in this area tended to co-operate over organizing events and to collaborate over pupil numbers. Another head whose school was undersubscribed and which has a GM primary school in its catchment area claimed that: 'We work very closely. We have a close cluster around our secondary school and we are not in competition.' Schools with declining numbers might compete more aggressively, although there appears to be a degree of tolerance about numbers of pupils on roll. Heads appear to be unwilling to use competition as the main mechanism through which to manage their external environment.

Surprisingly, however, the provision of nursery places was one area in which there was competition among LEA schools. Heads with nursery schools were perceived by their peers to have a significant advantage over schools which could not recruit children at such an early age. One head noted that:

> The competition in all honesty has been made by the nursery classes. For a long time we had no problem in filling our numbers but a nearby school has now got newer accommodation and a nursery and so has our next nearest.

The concern here is that once parents place their children in a school they are unlikely to exercise choice and move them. Another head highlighted the importance of a nursery when he remarked that: 'Every other school in this area has got a nursery school. What does that mean? It means that over a period of six years £180,000 is being poured into those schools which is not being poured into mine.' This head perhaps identified the main reasons for such concern. The allocation of nursery provision appears to give some schools a competitive advantage over others on the basis of an allocation process from which some heads felt excluded. Such a process, for those excluded from it, reflected the individualistic, even atomistic nature of the marketplace rather than an approach to socially just decision making based on equality of access and opportunity. Understandably, therefore, heads reacted to what they regarded as an unfair allocation of resources.

In general, however, primary school heads tended not to see themselves as being in competition. They are more concerned about falling below a threshold above which they can staff their schools and sustain an internal structure that is compatible with what they want to achieve than they are about maximizing pupil numbers and thus maximizing their income. Although the overall tenor of responses from heads in GM schools did recognize the need to compete for the attention of parents and to attract the optimum number of children, heads in both LEA and GM schools sought to minimize the importance of competition as a strategy. They tended to deny that it formed a significant part of school management at an organizational level, while recognizing, in some instances, that it might become an operational necessity.

Strategic marketing of primary schools

If heads reject competition as a motive force within the marketplace, to what extent do they manage their schools in accordance with a market ideology? Do they take a strategic view of what it means to exist in a market environment, scan their market for information about consumer preferences and translate these into organizational principles which can then be operationalized through marketing processes? How far are marketing and promotion clearly distinguished at both the organizational and operational levels? Sullivan notes that effective marketing of schools must be based on meeting customer needs by offering a high-quality product using market research and analysis (Sullivan 1991). For heads to market their schools, therefore, they need to have a strategy which, it is argued, should include a concern for the 'Seven Ps of Marketing', namely price, product, people, promotion, place, processes and proof (James and Phillips 1995). Our research, like that of James and Phillips (1995), indicates that such an approach to marketing is not evident. None of the heads in our survey had a clearly formulated and written marketing policy or a marketing plan.

Many heads were fairly explicit about the nature of schools nearby and about the main selling points of their own schools. Our findings support the view that heads were clear about the distinctive features of their schools and: 'had a good understanding of what it was they offered ... Although they did not refer to this explicitly as their product ... they described it confidently and unambiguously' (James and Phillips 1995, p. 276). In the light of this it was interesting to note that these strengths were based far more on what the heads had decided that the school could and should offer than on any analysis of parental choice and preference.

The heads differed in the degree to which they said they employed marketing strategies. At least one appeared not to have a strategy at all. The head of this school, in response to a question about how he marketed the school, replied that he did not advertise. He attracted pupils: 'By standing for principles and standards. By satisfied customers and by talking to parents.' A similar reluctance to become involved in marketing was identified among other heads, one of whom was firm in the view that he did not market his school and he did not often seek coverage in the local press. Nevertheless, the school paid considerable attention to the appearance of the building, which had a revamped entrance, a new technology area and a strictly enforced dress code for the children. The school also ensured that the school logo was on every advertisement for staff in the local press. At the very least, this school was implicitly promoting itself through emphasizing the visible or symbolic aspects of the school as a distinctive place. The head believed that word of mouth and family tradition were far more powerful networks for pupil recruitment than the overt use of advertisements and press coverage. If first impressions count for anything, then any head wishing to benefit from a good local reputation must pay attention to the symbolic aspects of the school, the nature of the place. This emphasis on the visible aspects of the school does not only include the appearance of the building. Clubs, societies and extra-curricular activities are a significant part of schools' self presentation: 'This school is popular for its extra-curricular clubs and its emphasis on music and performing arts. We employ peripatetic music teachers. We achieve good standards, certainly in the standardized test results.'

Another GM school head identified other aspects of the school that played a major part in marketing:

What we do is work very hard at the external face that we present so we put an incredible amount of money into the arts. We put, for example, £1,500 into peripatetic musicians to come in and teach in the school. We have two very good choirs and we sing in the community. We enter national chess competitions and we put a lot of energy into PE. We organize local sports which would not operate unless the school ran them, and then we win them.

This head acknowledged that this was his approach to promoting his school. It is an obvious attempt to benefit from a particular reputation within the local community. His counterparts in LEA schools were far less forthright and were less inclined to believe that it was necessary to have any formal strategy for directly publicizing their schools. Many of these heads claimed not to market their schools at all. They did, however, recognize the importance of the local information network: 'I do give a lot of time to parents that are interested in looking round the school. We set out to be attractive to parents. You can't disregard parents any more.'

Some heads noted the importance of the school brochure:

Our school prospectus I know needs to be good. It needs to fulfil the many regulations that the government has imposed on it but it needs to be good in the sense that it provides good information and promotes the school in a positive way. But I don't want to go down the road of being competitive.

Others argued that they make use of the press to celebrate the work of their schools, to give children a sense of pride in their achievements and to locate the school within its local community, rather than to advertise or promote the school. For example, one head commented that he did ensure that his school appeared in the local press but that this was not marketing, it was: 'The celebration of good education and a shared pride in what we are doing. Yes and it's about the self-esteem of the children. Their efforts can be brought to the attention of a wider audience.'

An LEA primary school head denied marketing the school but recognized the importance of some aspects of place such as the importance of easy access: 'We try to be genuinely open door. We use the grapevine rather than the *Birmingham Evening Mail.*' Another head said of his school:

I know it has a good reputation. It takes a long time to build a good reputation and it could be lost overnight. By far the most important marketing force I have got is word of mouth ... But the old-fashioned thing that people judge a school's performance by, it's the ... grades. So we have a ... tangible record of academic success. One of the other very attractive features to parents is extra-curricular activities. We have an inordinate number. This has lead to a significant amount of success in all sorts of fields of endeavour. If we feel that any group or individual in the school has done something worthy of public recognition, we will let the local press know.

In spite of this extremely perceptive analysis of a well-developed set of promotional and public relations activities based mainly upon the visible, the symbolic and upon the extremely effective use of the information network within the local community, this head stated quite categorically: 'I have never advertised the school in any way, shape or form.'

Almost all of the primary school heads in our sample confuse the term marketing with promotional activities, much of which took the form of public relations exercises. They tend to use local press and television rather than either formal advertising or outreach material, except for prospectuses. Several heads indicate that they have recently increased expenditure on school brochures, although an analysis of the brochures from each school in our sample revealed that these are not of a consistently high standard. Heads obviously treat much of what they termed marketing as an add-on activity and not part of the mainstream of their work. They certainly did not take a rigorous look at: 'what the school most wishes to achieve as a result of a public relations programme ... pinpointing the most relevant target audiences ... decide on the best strategy to reach them ... and ... the most important priorities' (Devlin 1989, pp. 94-5). Even though promotional activities and public relations tended to be the main, if not the only, element of marketing these were, to a large extent, a marginal exercise. They were not based on a strategic view either of the school or the marketplace and were not underpinned by clear organizational principles. The heads in our sample, therefore, did not act in an informed and rational manner in respect of the educational marketplace.

Competitiveness and the educational marketplace

How, then, can such behaviour be explained? At least part of the answer to this question can be found in the way in which the educational market is conceptualized. The free market is a hypothetical construct within the discipline of economics. As a construct it exists within the Newtonian paradigm (Zohar 1997), which presents the world generally, and the marketplace in particular, as an ordered, simple entity that conforms to specific rules. This, in turn, means that its activities should be rational, predictable and controllable. In essence, the rules of the marketplace can be summed up in the statement that firms will seek to maximize profits through competition and consumers make choices based on price and quality.

The perfect market, however, does not exist. It does not obey simple rules, cannot easily be controlled or its outcomes predicted. Those operating in the marketplace do not necessarily follow its tenets. Many firms do not seek to maximize their profits. They continue to trade even when it is unprofitable to do so and when liquidizing assets and reinvesting them would be the most effective way of maximizing profit. Many firms strive for profit optimization rather than maximization, survival being a more attractive option than profit maximization. In every market firms set out to control and influence market operations through such tactics as fixing prices, selling below cost, limiting the supply of products or creating monopolies. Even where firms may choose to behave in accordance with the rules of the market, it cannot be assumed that either they or their customers always have the necessary knowledge to make informed decisions.

Similarly, consumers may not necessarily act as the marketplace dictates that they should. Many consumers may make choices for a wide variety of reasons of which price and the nature of the product are but two. Harmony, equity, geographical proximity, personal convictions and even prejudice may also shape consumer decisions. Furthermore, the concept of the free market presents choice only in the context of competition, ignoring the possibility of other decision-making frameworks within which choice might be made, such as co-operation and collaboration. The possibility of co-operative smart partnerships based on trust, reciprocity of interest and mutual support for the benefit of all is discounted (Hampden-Turner 1997). The market characterizes and explains the totality of human behaviour in terms of self-interest, expressed through buying, selling, consuming and producing. This denies the possibility of altruism, selflessness and concern for others outside the immediate family unit. It also fails to acknowledge that individual self-interest in the marketplace does not operate in isolation. Individual decisions may be, and indeed are, isolated but they impact on the decisions of others and may restrict the choices that others are able to make. This is to deny the existence of community or group interest. The poverty of the market ideology stems from its inability to recognize the existence of community in either an organic or personal sense. Clearly, here is an atomistic view of society within which the public institutions which serve its members are fragmented and placed in opposition to each other. The market, even as a hypothetical construct is imperfect. It is not surprising, therefore, that many heads in primary schools do not act as they might were a true educational market to exist.

It is clear, for example, that competitiveness and individualism, while latent in the work of some heads, is not pronounced in the work of most of them. On the contrary, the extent to which most heads have resisted the temptation to enter into direct competition is surprising. They still, in many instances, prefer to co-operate and collaborate in a number of ways. Husband (1996), for example, draws attention to the existence of patterns of collaboration that include purchasing consortia, professional interchange and partnership development, all of which are inimical to the basic operating tenets of an educational market. Thus, there is, as James and Phillips (1995) note, a special quality about educational relationships. Education is about much more than responding to customer needs in a commercial way and this leads to a rejection of the market ideology.

The rejection of the education market

Primary heads have not marketed their schools intensively nor have they adopted an explicit recruitment strategy for their school. Although they claim to base much of what they do in their schools on parental expectations, scanning the education marketplace in relation to parents and identifying their preferences as consumers of education is not a high priority for many heads (Glatter and Woods 1995). They have preferred instead to rely on word of mouth, presentational, symbolic and opportunist means of commending their institution to parent consumers. Heads have demonstrated a reluctance to become active participants in the educational marketplace. They have not been driven by market forces to maximize income by increasing pupil numbers to excessive levels. Instead, heads in this study have tended to optimize rather than maximize pupil numbers in their schools. They may vary in the extent to which they are willing to adopt accommodatory positions in respect of the education marketplace but, on the whole, they appear to show no enthusiasm for it. It can be seen, therefore that most heads have not subscribed to the market ideology.

The extent to which heads reject the concept of the marketplace can be seen in their behaviour. Heads appear to be supported by a strong set of educational values based on mutual trust, the provision of professional support, the welfare of their pupils and shared views of primary education that transcend their immediate concerns and exist beyond the confines of their schools. It is possible that, for many heads, their socialization into the professional culture of teaching and the extension of this into the realms of primary headship is so strong that it remains uppermost as a predeterminant of their world view. The existence of this professional culture, in itself, provides a foundation upon which supportive networks of like-minded colleagues can be established and sustained. This culture focuses on the educational needs of children and on collegial rather than hierarchical styles of management. As Grace reports of the heads in his sample, their professional caution about the philosophy of the marketplace: 'arose in most cases because they believed that market forces and market values in education would be inimical to educational and professional values' (Grace 1995, p. 208). This value position in respect of the educational marketplace adopted by many heads in our sample finds support among both parents and governors, whose participation is essential if market forces are to operate within an educational environment.

In the theoretical construct of the market, parents are required to act as consumers. It is unclear, however, exactly how far parents are prepared to act in this way. They do not appear to be willing or able to treat the education of their children as a commodity. Parents tend to make educational choices on their perceptions of the best interests of their children. These interests are often couched in terms of sustaining existing friendship groups and proximity of school to home rather than on market considerations such as schools' performance in the standard attainment test league tables. Often children themselves play a central role in this process. 'It is commonplace to assume that parents make choices and yet ... children's own choice of school is a major factor in parental considerations' (Smedley 1995, p. 99).

Nor is it certain just how many parents do exercise the right to move their children during a specific stage of education. There is some evidence to suggest that parents do not have and, in many cases do not seek, full access either to information or processes that might enable them to make these choices (Martin 1995). Furthermore, as Bridges has noted, parents may play many roles in relation to the education of their children, of which that of consumer is but one. These might include supporter, partner, co-educator or even puzzled bystander (Bridges 1994).

At the same time, many governing bodies are equally reticent about managing primary schools as they would in a free market, not least because in many cases they have only partly shouldered the burden of the detailed management of schools. In so doing they also appear to be reluctant to accept the ideology of the market. The range of values espoused by school governors frequently does not include an endorsement of the educational marketplace (Deem *et al.* 1995). At the same time, there is little evidence that governors are anxious to encourage those activities that might be appropriate if a fully fledged educational market were to exist. Thus, there are reservations about this ideology in each of the three key groups whose support is necessary if the educational marketplace is to become a reality.

Conclusion: ambiguity and the education marketplace

There is, however, no doubt that the attempt to introduce market forces to the education sector has had a significant effect (Bottery 1992). Taken as part of a package of measures to reshape the education system, it has been instrumental in creating an extremely turbulent environment. The mechanisms for allocating pupils to schools, the levels of resourcing and processes of accountability and quality assurance are now far more problematic than was the case prior to 1988. As a result, the educational world in England (for Scotland, Northern Ireland and, to a lesser extent, Wales, have been spared some of the more excessive turbulence) can be seen for what it has truly become: a complex set of ambiguous relationships which do not conform readily to any set of rules, the outcomes of which appear to be both uncertain and uncontrollable to those in schools.

In spite of the extremely turbulent nature of their educational environment, many of the primary school heads in this sample did report an increased empowerment and ability to control aspects of work in their schools (Bell, Halpin and Neill 1996a). Nevertheless, they recognized the new realities of this environment. Their sense of empowerment related largely to matters internal to their schools. They felt far less confident about managing their external environment. This is evident both in their relatively unconsidered approach to marketing their schools and in their general unwillingness to become involved in strategic approaches to marketing. This position is based on far more than a lack of knowledge or expertise. It is rooted in value systems which reject, or at least fail to legitimate, marketing as an appropriate activity for this group. Once this is recognized, it is possible to understand how heads can repeatedly deny any involvement in activities which might be termed marketing. There is a clear value conflict here, the result of which is that many heads display those characteristics in relation to the educational marketplace which lead to what Cohen and March (1974) have termed organizational ambiguity (see Chapter 3).

Organizational ambiguity is characterized by unclear goals, a poorly understood technology and fluid membership. In this context, heads in our sample were, in many cases, extremely equivocal about their position in respect of the education marketplace. Some sought to ignore its operation by seeking to collaborate with colleagues in other schools. Others denied that they were influenced by market forces at all, even where their actions might lead observers to conclude otherwise. Still others believed that they had been unfairly treated in some aspects of resource allocation, notably the establishment of nursery schools, and felt compelled to respond to this. When asked what their goals were, each group of heads would reply unambiguously, to do the best for their school. The ambiguity lies in the definition of what is best for primary schools.

Considerable ambiguity also surrounds the technology to be deployed. As James and Philips (1995) have shown, heads have not developed or even set out to develop coherent marketing strategies. At the same time, most heads do not believe that becoming a market leader is necessarily a good thing or something that can be sustained to advantage over time. Even if heads understood the relevant technology, therefore, they are doubtful about its effectiveness and its long-term outcomes, believing that too high a price would have to be paid for becoming an accomplished exponent of the technology derived from the educational marketplace.

The price to be paid might be in terms of a loss of support and professional acceptance by headteacher colleagues. This community of heads, like that in North Oxfordshire, is valued beyond the exigencies of the marketplace and the value of any benefits that participating in the marketplace might bestow. Nevertheless, for some heads, the membership of such professional groupings is fluid to the extent that those heads who felt challenged by the nurseries established in nearby schools were prepared to forego the support of colleagues and seek to maximize pupil recruitment. This fluidity of member-ship is also found, but in a different way, in the schools. The amount of time and effort which heads and their staff are prepared to devote to activities relating to the educational market is very limited. For the staff of most schools, operating within the marketplace is not accorded a high priority. Much of what is done in this regard is a by-product of, and incidental to, the core business of the school and is seen as such by most heads, teachers and governors (Bell, Halpin and Neill 1996b). Marketing the school and competing aggressively within a market environment is not part of the ethos of heads in primary schools.

These relatively small institutions have sought to collaborate despite a formidable array of policy instruments that have been deployed to secure the compliance of headteachers and their staff to a contrary policy. As Wallace (1998) notes, the efforts of the New Right to encourage greater parental choice, the collaborative efforts of these schools and their unwillingness to embrace the demands of the educational market is significant. This unwilling-ness mirrors developments in schools and colleges elsewhere in England and Wales, where voluntary local collaboration was fostered to the extent that such actions: 'represented more than mere resistance to central government reform policies. Rather, they constituted a counter-policy' (Wallace 1998, p. 212). Such collaboration was not universal and nor should it be overestimated. Nevertheless it represented a significant, if implicit, critique of the market-based policies of the New Right.

Leave no Rubs nor Botches in the Work: Primary Heads, Governors and Institutional Autonomy

Introduction

By the late 1980s schools were moving or being moved into the Market Phase of educational policy. They were becoming more autonomous, more accountable and more financially independent, yet more likely to be involved in competition for pupils within an educational marketplace (Bell, Halpin and Neill, 1996b). The organizational model on which these changes were based is of the headteacher as chief executive and the governing body as corporate board. The governing body determines policy and directs its implementation, while the head retains control of the day-to-day management of the school. This chapter examines the extent to which this concept of corporate governance has manifested itself in the management of self-governing primary schools. It is written in five parts. 'Researching the autonomous school' examines the research on managing autonomous schools and the role played by governing bodies in this process. 'Working with governors in schools' reviews the changing role of governors in state schools since 1988 and draws on recent research to explore some of the confusions and conflicts to which this has given rise. 'Empirical focus and methods of inquiry' outlines the background to our own research on the working relations of governors and heads in a sample of state and privately maintained self-governing primary schools. 'Heads and governors' reports some of the results of our research. 'Discontinuities between policy and practice' seeks to explain why the governors of state-maintained primary schools are not presently directing policy implementation or holding heads accountable for their performance in the education marketplace.

Researching the autonomous school

Studies in England of the impact of decentralized educational decision making on the role of the head and of the effects of particular market conditions on the management practices of schools have been directed chiefly at the secondary phase, and hardly at all at private schooling, whether primary or secondary. This research has produced two kinds of finding. One body of research documents the benefits of self-management and indicates how it represents a significant improvement in the way schools now manage their affairs. The second paints a less positive picture of the impact of educational self-management and highlights particularly retrogressive management practices in the overall culture of schooling.

The benefits of delegated decision making on the work of heads, irrespective of phase, are emphasized by Levačić (1995). 'Local management has empowered [them], and by and large they like it' (p. 136). Generally, heads consider local management beneficial in terms of increasing their capacity to plan strategically and concentrate resources on direct teaching and learning. The broad picture appears to be that local management entails heads retaining most of the responsibility for both budget management and financial decision making. However, this is not to suggest that classroom teachers are excluded from the decision-making process altogether. They appear to exercise both influence and genuine decision-taking authority when it comes to spending money which has been delegated to them for specific purposes.

As one would expect, given the formal powers and responsibilities they enjoy with regard to the management of school finance, the governing bodies of locally managed schools play a fuller part than classroom teachers in resource management and allocation, although in the majority of schools studied by Levačić this entails little more than 'mainly acting in advisory or supportive roles and ... [being] ... in an unequal partnership with [heads]' (p. 134). However, these fairly strict divisions of labour related to financial management do not appear to have negative consequences for the allocation of resources. On the contrary, Levačić concludes that, 'local management has improved efficiency on the *input* side ... [and] ... is more successful than LEA administrative allocation in concentrating the resources available on direct teaching and learning' (pp. 162–3).

Similar findings are reported by Thomas and Martin (1996) who identify the pivotal role played by heads in whole-school decision making: 'In all schools, except one, the [head] alone is mentioned as the decision-maker in one context or another' (p. 53). Thomas and Martin also offer examples of classroom teachers taking proposals to the head and of the positive role played by senior management teams in reaching key decisions. Even so, the impression given is that of heads electing to play the most prominent role in suggesting new ideas and generating innovation. Self-management facilitates and legitimates this enhancement in their leadership status. This is not to suggest, however, that the schools investigated by Thomas and Martin were autocratically managed. On the contrary, they found considerable evidence that heads took staff participation very seriously and were not slow to make specific arrangements to facilitate greater levels of collegiality. Here again, school governing bodies do not exercise much, if any, influence on the decisions reached. They tend to hear reports of what heads have already decided.

The research by Ball and his colleagues tells a different story. Two themes in particular stand out in this research. The first concerns the existence of an apparently growing gap between heads and teachers, in terms of values and relationships. 'While the work perspective of classroom teachers remains largely untouched by educational self-management, that of heads is increasingly dominated and contained by financial and administrative concerns. Less and less time remains for educational leadership' (Ball 1994, p. 95). Conversely, more time is dedicated to marketing the school and maintaining its local reputation, tasks which the head, almost single-handedly, takes on.

A second theme revealed in this research concerns the changes educational self-management and the marketization of education bring about in the relationship between heads and parents. This amounts to heads embracing the notion of consumerism and seeing parents as customers rather than co-educators. As Ball (1994) observes, heads are 'now more alert to "market signals", that is, to perceptions of and discontents about their school. They are more likely to be responsive when it seems relevant or expedient to do so' (p. 99). Thus heads are compelled in the current climate to alter their roles in the direction of becoming either exclusively entrepreneurial or mostly manage-rialist. Grace (1995) has argued, however, that heads may take up one of three value stances towards the education marketplace in the face of the market ideology: compliance, accommodation or resistance.

This review of research indicates how difficult it is to draw firm conclusions about the initial effects of institutional autonomy. Some findings represent local management as a significant improvement on previous practice, notably in the area of resource allocation; others draw attention to its limitations. These are the manner in which its financial aspects appear to limit the capacity of heads to exercise effective educational leadership and the extent to which it encourages governing bodies to play an intrusive part in the management of schools (Gewirtz *et al.* 1995). Even when there seems to be agreement about a particular finding, there is dispute about its significance. For example, much of the research reviewed above indicates a growing division of labour within self-managing schools between those who mostly teach and those that mostly manage. The consequences of this are viewed differently by different researchers. Ball sees it as a negative development leading to a fundamental cleavage between educational and entrepreneurial values, while Levačić, who agrees that local management contributes to more specialized management roles within schools, is not able to detect as a result any profound shift in values between classroom teachers and heads. Research which has looked *specifically* at working with governors in schools is somewhat less equivocal.

Working with governors in schools

The changes in school governance introduced by the 1988 Education Reform Act and subsequent legislation have created a potential power shift within schools from the professionals to the lay governing body, because of the responsibilities devolved to the latter. As a result of these new powers, governing bodies and heads are faced with entirely new divisions of responsibility, new patterns of accountability and new partnerships. The devolution of financial powers to schools has moved the locus of decision making from LEAs to schools. At the same time, governors now have a clear and distinctive set of responsibilities, which include overseeing the imple-mentation of the National Curriculum, dealing with parental complaints, implementing admissions procedures and appointing and dismissing staff. Until 1988 many of these responsibilities had been regarded as the province of headteachers. It is hardly surprising, therefore, that Grace (1995) reports that many of the heads in his survey responded to these changes in a defensive rather than a celebratory way. This was partly because of the confusion that now exists about what is the responsibility of governing bodies and what is the duty of headteachers and their staff. It is also because many heads sensed that the changes were underpinned by a dominant ideology that is hostile to the interests of public service professionals.

Many heads are trying to solve this problem by making a distinction between, on the one hand, establishing broad policy, monitoring and evaluating its implementation, which they see as the role of governing bodies, and translating this policy into practice through managing the school in such a way as to ensure that policy objectives are achieved, which they regard as their job and that of teachers (Wilkins 1990). This is at odds with some interpretations of recent legislation. Some governors, especially those with industrial, legal, management or financial experience, wish to see schools run as businesses and are concerned with examination results, standards and other measures of outcomes within a framework of tight budgetary control (Deem *et al.* 1992). As Ball (1994) points out, the values of such groups can bring them into conflict with those heads who wish to run their schools based on educational values. This may lead to disputes about both policy and day-to-day management.

Thus, there is a paradox at the heart of the partnerships between governors and the staff of the schools for which they are responsible concerning the extent to which governors are to act as lay trustees and how far they are to become involved in the routine management of the school. The legislation appears to allow them to play either role while expecting them to do both. The legal and formal duties of governors are clearly spelled out, but their managerial responsibilities in relation to the head are far less explicitly formulated (Deem *et al.* 1995). As Deem (1993) argues, governing bodies are not clear about their roles. Their membership is fluid. There is a high turnover of people acting as school governors, and the structures and processes for carrying out the duties are still to be fully established. Given that the head and the teacher representatives on the governing body are likely to be the only people able to devote their full time to its work, their professional authority is extremely influential and may be able to override effective lay participation (Deem *et al.* 1992). These powerful influences are reinforced by professional definitions of 'appropriate' behaviour and perceptions about who should control school management. As Deem *et al.* (1992) point out, governors may not have the working knowledge of the curriculum, the pupils and the staff to discharge their duties in those areas. These perspectives are supported by the data from our research.

Empirical focus and methods of inquiry

Details of the methodology adopted for this study can be found in Chapter 8. The empirical focus of this research project developed from the assumption that the way in which schools were managed in the past is not necessarily a good guide to how they should be managed in the present. Equally, it was not assumed that, prior to the reforms introduced into English schools by the 1988 Education Reform Act, a culture of co-operation prevailed within state schooling to such an extent that neither competition nor individualism informed the way in which particular schools were managed. It was acknowledged that significant continuities and overlaps exist between what is happening now and what went on in the past. Indeed, for what is happening now to have taken root, a certain amount of fertile ground must already have existed. Competition between schools is not a recent phenomenon. It is an extension of a latent trend and, in the wake of falling rolls, one that was becoming increasingly influential. This research was premised, in part, on a desire to find out what is happening in self-managing primary schools in order to provide an analysis with the potential for improving practice and assisting policy development. Thus, our research orientation was to seek ways in which social scientific insights can be applied in the cause of making things better. Among the data collected from the questionnaires and interviews was information, from the heads' perspective, on the managerial relationship between themselves and their governing bodies.

Heads and governors: some working relationships

There are clear sector differences in the working relationships that heads establish with the governing bodies, especially in the extent to which governors are active in school decision making. These differences are particularly marked between schools in the private sector and those in the other two sectors. Heads in the private sector reported that they were relatively autonomous in all matters pertaining to staffing, the curriculum and short- and medium-term financial decisions, while their governing bodies were marginal to decision making on these matters. One private school head, when asked if he was a member of his governing body, said: 'No, I use the business analogy. I am a managing director of a company, directly answerable to the board. I am in attendance at the meetings but I tend to work more directly with the chairman.' The same head, commenting on the involvement of his governors in the school, said: 'The chairman is around and about quite often. The other governors are invited to social functions. We have three formal meetings a year but we have not set up any formal machinery for sub-committees. It is not necessary. I consult informally.' Another head, when asked about the extent of his control over resource management, replied:

> Virtually total. The governors are not involved in managing resources.
> We have meetings three times a year and one delivers a report. We have
> a financial statement and we look at the budget and review fee levels.
> We do not go in for working parties or sub-committees.

Another private school head noted that, although he would not feel any hesitation about consulting governors and reporting regularly to them, he was concerned about their ability to offer educational advice: 'We have to recognize a weakness here. They aren't educators themselves and we recognize that our governing body has a shortage of educational wisdom.' It appears that governors in the private sector are more than willing to take a general overview and allow heads to manage the school, safe in the knowledge, perhaps, that if they fail, they can be removed. As one head put it:

> I know my target numbers and how likely I am to recruit to them. Once I have agreed the fee level with the Governors, and they have always accepted my recommendations on this, I know my income. I can then make whatever staffing decisions I like within that framework.

All the heads of private schools, however, made it clear that when it came to decisions over major items of capital expenditure, especially new buildings, governors were involved and often made the final decision. Furthermore, heads reported that they would feel it necessary to consult governors about expenditure above a clearly defined limit. A typical comment was:

> If I was spending £1,000, I would certainly touch base with them [the governors]. I don't have to do this by the rules of my contract unless it is over £2,000 but I would feel it correct just to let them know.

Similarly, heads in GM and LEA maintained schools had some autonomy over expenditure, although the spending limits were sometimes much lower than those in the private sector. Although one head was able to spend up to £1,000 without consulting his governors, far more typical was the following comment: 'I don't consult if I am spending less than £200 at any one time, so they allow me that privilege.'

The ways in which governing bodies in the LEA and GM sectors operated was significantly different from their counterparts in the private sector. All heads in both sectors reported that their governing bodies had sub-committees which had been established since the advent of LMS or since opting for GM status. These met regularly and looked at significant parts of school management. A head of an LEA school reported that:

> Governors will be involved in some of the new teams we have, policy teams. They get involved and that tends to be with the things that are total governors' responsibilities, so for sex education, behaviour policy, equal opportunities, they would be very much involved. We have sub-committees. Governors are involved and members of staff are involved as well.

A GM school head made a similar point:

> Basically, we have two governing body meetings a term. We have four committees that service the governing body: finance, curriculum/pupils, personnel and premises and the governing body as a whole are split around those committees. Those committees meet on a regular basis and formulate plans and discuss how things are progressing and look

ahead, and they report back to the main governing body meetings with recommendations.

Many heads in both LEA and GM schools suggested that their position in relation to their governing bodies had changed recently. Immediately after the 1988 Education Reform Act the advice given to heads by their professional associations was to attend governors' meetings but not to be a voting member of the governing body. Although the advice remains the same, heads in our sample indicated that they are choosing to become members of their governing bodies. One LEA head, when asked if he was a full member of his governing body, replied:

> I am now. This year is the first year that I have been a full member because I was invited by the chair of governors to become one. Prior to that I felt that there might be a time when I needed to defend my opinion and the opinion of the staff and then I thought it over and thought it doesn't seem to be like that.

In the GM schools, heads tended to have a similar perspective. As one put it:

> I feel that as a GM school the headteacher has got to be a full voting member of the governing body. I see the governing body as much as a team as anything else. We have made decisions and we haven't really had any conflict.

In terms of relationships with governing bodies, therefore, there are clear differences between private school heads and their state school counterparts. In the case of state schools, however, governors of GM schools were perceived to be more proactive than those in the LEA sector. This reported difference might also shed some light on the reasons for the difference between the private and the state sectors. Almost all LEA heads noted that:

> I have day-to-day executive control. I am the manager for my site. My governors expect me to take day-to-day decisions and carry these out with their support. I report to them at every governor's meeting and meet my chair regularly but the day-to-day management of the school is down to me.

Thus, a clearer understanding is developing about where the duties of the head end and the responsibilities of governors begin. Central to this is the relationship between day-to-day management issues and broader areas of policy. The responses from LEA primary school heads indicated that establishing the demarcation lines has been less problematic here than might have been expected. The areas of ambiguity that surround the boundaries between the two sets of responsibilities may be becoming less blurred or, perhaps, less important to both heads and governors. Governors tend to wish to be more involved in some areas of policy, notably finance, premises and staff appointments. Governors tend to be less involved in other areas such as the curriculum. One LEA school head commented:

> They are quite happy to talk about car parking for an hour, but Key Stage 2 SATS results are discussed and dismissed in 90 seconds. On many issues I produce a policy, I advise and they rubber stamp. I don't see anything wrong with that as long as I maintain a balanced view.

Another noted that: 'There was a reluctance on their part to become involved and it's been a step at a time. With the curriculum there has been a reluctance for them to become involved at all.'

In some GM schools, however, this reluctance was less marked. This may be a by-product of opting for GM status, which requires the governors to be active in decision making, and often results in conflict between different groups within the school community. As a result, governors may feel better informed about the day-to-day management of the school, and more justified in taking an interventionist stance. In answer to the question about the degree of control exerted by the governing body, the head of one GM school stated that:

> By and large I have good relationships with my governors, but there have been some fairly heated discussions. It always hinges on where day-to-day management ends and strategic planning begins. All would be well if the government would only identify what they meant by day-to-day management because the parameters can extend into all sorts of other areas in which the governors feel they may or should have an input.

Another GM head was quite clear about the different areas of responsibility:

> It is my function to manage the curriculum and to look after the well-being of the children, their learning and so on. The governors' role is to make policy and to behave as responsible employers of staff and to give support. We are talking about strategy for the governors in terms of policy and strategy in terms of policy and implementation for the management.

It would be unwise to over-emphasize the differences between the governing bodies of LEA and GM primary schools. In both groups of schools the overwhelming impression given by the responses of heads is that their professional judgements and those of their staff tend to prevail in most debates. There is some indication that GM schools may have governing bodies that are potentially more interventionist than those in LEA schools. There is no doubt, however, that governors in both GM and LEA schools are more closely involved than those in the private sector, especially in decision-taking and policy making. There is a much clearer distinction between the responsibility of heads and governors in the private sector than exists in the state sector. This demarcation is based on the distinction between, on the one hand, professional concerns pertaining to the school curriculum and its management and, on the other, financial and administrative matters. In the state sector, especially in GM schools, this boundary is less distinct and more problematic.

Conclusion: discontinuities between policy and practice

The headteacher–governor relationship is changing, especially in state schools. These changes are located within a policy framework that has been established through a raft by government legislation since 1988. Their impact, however, is not uniform between sectors. Private sector schools experience more autonomy than their counterparts in the other two sectors on all matters relating to curriculum and resource management. This might be termed *extended* autonomy. LEA primary school heads, while being more autonomous than many of their GM colleagues, have less autonomy, especially on staffing and resourcing matters, than private sector heads. This can best be understood as *bounded* autonomy. Heads in GM schools are more likely than those in the other two sectors to experience interventions by governors and, therefore, may be said to experience *restricted* autonomy. For the LEA and GM sectors at least, these relationships are located within the same policy framework. Thus, the findings of our research clearly reveal some disjunction between policy and practice, to the extent that state school governing bodies, in general, have not developed an interventionist stance towards the management of primary schools. How can this be explained?

We want tentatively to suggest an analytical framework to help further our understanding of this complex issue. The framework has four levels: the *socio-political environment* from which policy is derived and within which its overarching guiding principles are formulated; the *organizational principles* which emanate from the socio-political environment and which broadly define policy and establish its success criteria as they apply to spheres of activity such as education; *operational principles* which indicate the parameters within which policy is to be implemented in those spheres of activity; and *management strategies*, based on the operational principles, which are the detailed organizational arrangements that are necessary to implement the policy at the institutional level. Thus, in terms of translating policy into practice, the four levels are in a hierarchical relationship, the first two being concerned with policy formulation and the second two with policy implementation.

It is the socio-political environment that provides the impetus for policy making and from which, in most instances, the legitimation for that policy stems. The language in which these legitimations are couched reflects the dominant ideologies within the socio-political environment. In the last two decades of the twentieth century in Britain the discourse within the socio-political environment has been dominated by the struggle between individualism and collectivism as preordinate determinants of social organization. The outcome of this discourse, as far as education is concerned, is exemplified in the Education White Paper *Choice and Diversity* (DfE 1992), which emphasizes competition and the marketization of education. The educational policies which we have been considering here, and the language in which that policy is expressed, are a product of that discourse.

The organizational principles that define the shape of policy are derived from the same discourse. For example, if an educational market is to operate, then it must, to some extent, be deregulated to enable competition to flourish. This deregulation has, in part, taken the form of reducing the power of LEAs and seeking to minimize the influence of teachers by devolving powers to lay governors. Deregulation has also fostered a diversity of schools from which choice can be made. Without choice, the only competition that can exist is that over scarce resources such as places in schools. Similarly, there have been a number of changes in the extent to which decision making is centralized or decentralized. Resources are allocated centrally to be managed at the institutional level within a centralized National Curriculum. Quality assessment takes place locally at the institutional level but within national frameworks.

Operational principles define, for example, the limits of autonomy, the patterns of accountability and the procedures for assessment and quality control. Management strategies are the activities which contribute to the formulation of internal policy, the day-to-day organization of schools, the specifics of decision making and the nature and extent of delegation of responsibilities. Thus, within schools the key factors in determining the nature of the management strategies and the structuring of responsibilities are the governor/headteacher relationships, the extent to which the day-to-day management of the school is devolved to the head, and the arrangements for making policy in the school. Once these are established, the internal management and decision-making structures, the roles of individual teachers and governors and mechanisms for reporting to and involving parents will follow.

It follows, therefore, that there must be a congruence at all four levels if policy is to be implemented successfully. Within education, the main mechanisms for achieving such congruence have been based on a combination of reward, threat and opportunity. The rewards will accrue to those schools that grow and acquire more resources. The threats are of school closure for some but rigorous inspection for all. The opportunities are for parents to act as consumers and for governors to manage schools. None of these things has quite happened. Heads have demonstrated a reluctance to become active participants in the educational marketplace. They may vary in the extent to which they are willing to adopt accommodatory positions in respect of the interventionist strategies of governors but, on the whole, they appear to show no enthusiasm for it. They have not accepted the prevailing language of legitimation, perhaps because their socialization into the professional culture of teaching is so strong and that culture in itself provides a supportive network of like-minded colleagues. Nor have heads been replaced by school managers or had an extra tier of management imposed above them as appears to have happened to medical staff in the National Health Service. Similarly, most governing bodies have only partly shouldered the burden of the detailed management of schools. It may be that they are also reluctant to accept these legitimations.

To a large extent, however, governing bodies readily acknowledge the distinction between school-based policy formulation, where they may have an input, and the detail of school management, where they may not. At the same time, despite the involvement of individuals drawn from commerce, there is little evidence that governors are anxious to encourage those activities that might be appropriate if a fully fledged educational market were to exist. Many of those responsible for the implementation of government policy do not find it easy to accept in full either its socio-political legitimation, its organizing principles or many of its operational principles. As a result, heads have found that they now have more control over many aspects of school management because of the decline in influence of the LEAs.

It is in this discontinuity between legitimations emanating from the socio-political environment, the organizational and operational principles and the management strategies that we will find explanations about why some aspects of policy have been successfully implemented and some have not. There are significant discontinuities between the four levels and especially, in this case, between the levels concerned with policy formulation and policy implementation. To a lesser extent, similar discontinuities exist between operational principles and management strategies. Such discontinuities go some way towards explaining why the educational marketplace has not fully evolved and why governing bodies are not holding heads to account and directing policy implementation. To sum up, then, it might be claimed that what our research shows is that policy implementers, in this case headteachers, are able to say to policy formulators, the politicians, 'My karma has just run over your dogma!'

A Tale of Some Significance: Primary Headship and Strategic Planning in England

Introduction

The data reported in this chapter has been collected as part of a series of studies on the perspectives of primary headteachers on a range of issues that impact on their work and their perceptions of their roles (Bell 1989b; Bell and Rhodes 1996; Bell, Halpin and Neill 1996a; Bird and Bell 1999; Bell and Rowley 2002; Chan 2002). The research reported here is based on a series of interviews with six primary school headteachers. The interviews took place in the autumn term of 2003 and the spring term of 2004, by which time the Target Phase of educational policy was well established. These interviews focused on what the heads understood by strategic planning, how they implemented such planning processes in their schools and the factors that influenced those processes. The headteachers who are quoted in this study are all experienced; three of the six have had at least two headships and two have had at least three schools prior to their present one. The six schools are not intended to be a random sample of all primary schools. It is an opportunity sample based on schools that have taken part in previous studies. However, while each school is in some way distinctive, the six schools taken together share many characteristics that are typical of most primary schools. School 1 is a relatively new middle school in Milton Keynes with a mixed catchment area. It is soon to become a primary school. School 2 is a junior school in a small town near Northampton and has just emerged from special measures. School 3 is a junior school in another town in Northamptonshire. It has also emerged from special measures. The head at this school was appointed from within the school and this is his only headship. School 4 is a community primary school in a large town hit by the closure of its major industry. School 5 is also a community primary school, in a newly created village on the edge of Solihull. School 6 is a private primary school in a county town in the East Midlands.

Strategy, planning and schools

It has been argued that in English schools strategic planning is the key management process that draws together, and is shaped by, institutional values and goals and which provides a framework for improving the deployment of resources and the quality of provision (Preedy *et al.* 1997).

This may be the case, but it tends to ignore the debate about the nature and efficacy of strategic planning itself. The key issue addressed in this chapter is how primary heads perceive and implement this process. At its simplest, strategic planning may be understood as an approach to establishing the long-term future of an organization and then moving that organization in an appropriate direction to achieve the future state to which its members, or at least its key members, aspire. Quinn (1980) emphasizes the interconnectedness between strategy, planning and the future development of the organization. He defines strategic planning as the integration of an organization's major goals, policies and actions into a cohesive whole. Thus, strategic planning is:

a list of actions so ordered as to attain over a particular time period, certain desired objectives derived from a careful analysis of the internal and external factors likely to affect the organization, which will move the organization from where it is now to where it wants to be. (Puffitt *et al*. 1992, p. 5)

It can be seen, therefore, that strategic planning has become closely associated in management terms with the rational expectations of those who wish to direct and shape an organization towards specific ends. Strategy and planning became synonymous and their essential purposes are to assess the environment in which the organizations operate, forecast the future for the organization and then to deploy resources in order to meet the predicted situation (Whipp 1998). Strategic planning, thus conceptualized, is a top-down process that develops from analysis through the identification of objectives or targets and actions to achieve them. Thus, the deployment of strategic planning as a management technique is predicated on being able to predict the environment and the ability to exercise sufficient control over the organization and its environment to ensure that planned outcomes can be achieved by the deployment and redeployment of available resources. It remains to be seen just how far this pertains to the planning processes adopted by the heads in this study.

Headteachers are central to this process of strategic planning. They are to lead and manage their school's improvement by using pupil data to set targets, especially in literacy and numeracy, for even better performance. As this target driven approach to educational planning has been pursued, a significant change has occurred in the nature of development planning itself. It is no longer sufficient for staff in schools to set their own targets and to be accountable for achieving them. School targets must now be derived from national achievement targets for similar schools (DfEE 1998a, DfEE 1998b). Each individual headteacher must establish such targets in conjunction with the pastoral LEA inspector for the school and incorporate them into the School Improvement Plan. Such plans will be framed by leadership behaviour and values, organizational structure and external forces (Irby *et al.* 2002) and will be based on evidence from the following five areas: 'The external environment (both now and future predictions); the internal strengths of the organization; the prevailing organization culture; the expectations of stakeholders and likely future resources' (Fidler 2002, p. 616). Fidler also notes that these plans may focus on different planning horizons or timescales, including: the very long

term (what will life be like in the future); long-term desirable developments (ten years); medium-term (five year) plans and short-term (three year) institutional development plans. He further suggests that strategic planning:

> is an important aspect of leadership in all organizations. In the past, such considerations were expected to be dealt with by higher levels in education systems but with increasing self-management at institutional level combined with increasing expectations by local communities of their schools, there is now a much wider group of leaders who need to understand the concept and the accompanying process. (Fidler 2002, p. 613)

The model of strategic planning implied above – a linear rational process based on analysis leading to successfully implemented action plans – is not the only approach to planning that may be adopted. Van der Heijden and Eden (1998), in summarizing a body of literature on the subject, claim that there are at least three different main models of strategic planning:

- The Linear Rationalist approach which separates thinking from action and proceeds by analysing the evidence, choosing the best course of action and implementing it (Johnson and Scholes 1989), which approximates to school development and school-improvement planning as it is required of English primary schools.
- The Processual approach accepts that devising an optimum course of action is difficult but should be attempted in a flexible manner in order to adapt to changing circumstances (Senge 1990). This is similar to strategic intent advocated by Davies and Ellison (1999).
- The Evolutionary or Incremental (Quinn 1980) approach which is based on the view that the number of variables make it too complex to identify and implement a specific set of actions: rather, small changes should be made and evaluated in schools over a period of time. It has been argued that the nature of the process, the locus of decision making and the procedures for determining and revising plans over the short term are more important than the formulation of long-term strategic plans and is more appropriate to schools, especially relatively small primary schools. (Bell 2002)

Wallace and McMahon (1994) identify six different approaches to planning in schools. Of these, long-range planning (over five years or more) and strategic planning (three to five years) are subsumed here under the linear rational model. Evolutionary, incremental and flexible planning fit broadly into the evolutionary incremental model and the garbage can model has no direct parallel so it is included in Table 10.1 below as a separate model. This chapter will seek to establish how far strategic planning as deployed in the primary schools in this study approximate to one or more of these models. It can be seen, therefore, that there are a number of dimensions to strategic planning along which the process might be differentiated (see Table 10.1).

Table 10.1 Models of planning

Model of planning	Planning horizon	Main locus of data analysis	Expressing of outcomes	Management technique
Linear rational	Very long or long term	External and internal environments	Single set of consistent aims	Top down and tightly controlled
Processual	Long term	External environment	Broad long-term goals	Participation within a top-down framework
Evolutionary incremental	Short term – one year maximum	Internal environment at whole school or sub-unit level	Targets	Participative-collaborative
Garbage can	Immediate or short term	Internal environment at sub-unit level	Inconsistent and competing objectives	Collaboration within groups but conflict between them

Table 10.1 suggests that there are a number of different approaches that may be adopted to the process of planning. The approach adopted might be an essentially rational one, an incremental one based on short-term adjustments or something in-between the two. Table 10.1 further suggests that, depending on the approach that is adopted, the planning horizon may vary from a very long-term perspective of a possible future state to a short-term view of where the organization might be in a year. Planning might be informed by the analysis of different types of data derived from sources, such as the values that underpin the organizations, the expectations of its key stakeholders or an analysis of the internal and external environments. The view of the future state could be expressed as aims, goals or targets. The management and leadership actions to achieve that future state may also take a variety of forms from a top-down imposition of an action plan to a fully participative approach in which all members of the organization play a full part. It is argued that school improvement planning approximates most closely to the linear rational model because it:

> follows a logical sequence: review takes into account the external and internal environments and the stated aims of the school; priorities, targets and success criteria are set within these aims; action plans make targets operational; and subsequent reviews lead to annual up-dating and rolling forward plans ... for the next few years. (Wallace and McMahon 1994, p. 25)

If the dimensions of strategic planning in Table 10.1 are applied to an analysis of the data collected from the primary headteachers in this study, then a number of key questions emerge that help to shape an understanding of what headteachers in primary schools mean by strategic planning and how far they are able to formulate and implement such plans. These questions are:

- What do heads understand by strategic planning?
- The extent to which values and vision shape the planning process?
- Over what time period do heads believe it is feasible to plan?
- How far do audits of the internal strengths and weaknesses of the school play a part in formulating strategic plans?
- How far do factors in the external environment play a part in formulating strategic plans?
- What role do governors play in formulating strategic plans?
- What is the relationship between strategic planning and the organizational structure and culture of the schools in this study?
- What barriers to strategic planning do heads identify?

How, then, do the primary school headteachers in this study approach the process of strategic planning?

Strategic planning in primary schools

Perceptions of Strategic Planning

The heads in this study certainly took cognisance of many of the factors identified above, especially those listed by Fidler (2002). They did not necessarily subscribe to the linear rational models of strategic planning identified in Table 10.1 as will be seen. Some heads have graphic metaphors for identifying the complexities of the strategic planning processes and coping with those complexities. The head of school 1 saw it as a continuous juggling act while in school 6 it was presented as:

> being on a dance floor. You know you have been involved with various partners but the perception from the balcony might be entirely different so you know that the key factor is being in both places at the same time or moving between the two ... It is incredibly complex. (H6)

In school 3, the head compared his planning process to steering his boat down a river: 'It's the river and rocks and banks and stuff. The skill is actually in knowing what's coming and navigating a course' (H3). In school 4, the head also saw planning in nautical terms:

> We are on deck but from time to time the leader has to climb the rigging and just keep a view on what's happening whether it's outside the school, nationally, whether it's about politics ... then you are back down in the engine room because this sailing boat has got an engine and it's just helping to keep the wheels oiled. (H4)

This is similar to what Mintzberg (1995) calls 'seeing through', looking ahead, behind, above and below, beside and beyond. Whatever the metaphor that heads used to try to understand strategic planning in their schools there is no doubt that for all of them, the process was informed by a commitment to a strongly held set of values and beliefs about their own role and about the nature of their educational enterprise (Bell 2004b).

Values and strategic planning

Heads paid significant attention to the place of values in shaping both their approach to strategic planning and the content of the plans themselves (Chan 2002). In some schools the espoused values emerged as a consequence of debates and discussion:

> How did we arrive at those values? After discussion and debate about what the school should be about, what is important and it was a whole-school approach, all staff were party to that ... We send questionnaires to parents. Our parent governors talked to people ... We asked the children. (H3)

The values that informed the planning in school 5 were also the product of consultation and debate, but this time the whole staff, all children, all parents and governors and representatives of the local community were involved. As a result the head could say: 'We knew where we were when we set up the school ... We had a vision and an idea of what parents wanted from us ... We had our key values' (H5). The core values in other schools were arrived at in somewhat different ways: 'I know what I want from my school and what is best for children ... Children should achieve as much as possible ... The school should be enjoyed' (H1).

Another head was aware that she had a vision based on core values but it was essentially her vision rather than a shared one:

> I have a very strong vision for my school and maybe it's not communicated to all staff as well as it should be. My deputy knows what it is. My senior management, particularly one senior manager who has worked with me in two schools, know exactly what I am after. I have been developing my vision and making the vision not mine but everybody's vision for the school ... The vision is now going out to children. We have asked the parents their views on it. (H2)

The position in which this head found herself is typical of that experienced by many heads who have to seek to reconcile their own strongly held professional values with the need to enable a variety of stakeholders to help to shape the values of a school and the vision that is derived from those values. This gives rise to the other major dilemma that faces many primary school heads: 'We are all different, you cannot offer all things to all people ... so everything we do is in terms of valuing people' (H4).

The planning horizon

It was clear that for most of these heads, strategic planning in primary schools was significantly different from most of the approaches identified in the literature reviewed above. In particular, few of the heads planned over what Fidler (2002) described as the long or medium term. The exception to this was the head of school 6, the private school. In one sense he was in a fortunate position, in that he did not have to implement the national curriculum. However, his situation was more complex in that he had to ensure that the business side of the school ran at a profit. His approach to strategic planning was based on taking a long-term view to inform the medium- and short-term planning:

> We work very much on the idea of long, medium and short term ... based on looking at what education is going to be like in five years' time, what is going to work, bounce things off the wall. We go through this process every year. That sets out our intent for the year, then we build our operational targets. (H6)

This is hardly long-term in the sense that it is normally used in the literature and it is certainly not what Davies and Ellison (1999) term 'futures thinking'. Nevertheless, it is based on a real attempt to give systematic consideration to the future. The head of school 1 noted that, at least for the time being, it was possible for her to consider some form of planning over a three-year period because:

> The school has been given a budget for its first three years based on having 250 children even though it only has 200 at the moment ... I still think planning should focus on what is going to happen in the next academic year. (H1)

The certainty of resources that this provides contrasts to the relative uncertainty experienced by most heads, whose plans tended to be for a period of one or two years: short-term institutional plans in Fidler's terms. This was often a consequence of coming to terms with the reality of strategic planning in primary schools. As the headteacher of school 3 put it:

> We started off very grandly, thinking about getting to grips with what the school development plan needed to be. We tended to make it too detailed. We tried to do a five-year plan but couldn't get to five years. It just became impossible. We are trying for a two-year one now. (H3)

The same head reiterated his point about five-year plans being too difficult at a later stage in the interview and added that the plans in his school: 'Tend to be three years maximum but really they are only two years and these are always led by curriculum issues' (H3). In school 2: 'We have three sets of planning. We have long, medium and short. The long-term plan is the curriculum map which is an overview of all the year's work and it's a really good one' (H2). The curriculum map referred to here is intended to eliminate the overlap between curriculum content that previously occurred as children moved through the school and to provide a basis for children's continuity and progression through the national curriculum. It provided a basis for planning work on a termly and weekly basis. The head of school 4, on the other hand, was concerned about: 'Actually not getting stuck into a piece of paper which tells you what you are going to be doing in your school development plan in June 2005' (H4). In school 5, which at the time of interview was in its second year, the head also planned over the short term: 'The very first plan was about nurturing. What did we want to grow? How we went about it? Who did we want to involve? The second year plan was layered on the first' (H5). In some ways this is a special case because the school is new, but the time period described is similar to that in other schools.

Internal audits and strategic planning

Almost all of the heads in this study relied heavily on forms of internal audit to help to identify and justify planning priorities and to facilitate the implementation of those plans. In school 2 the planning process was informed by a review of teaching methods and materials:

> We reviewed what we were doing, looked at good practice, all the things you would do to make decisions ... We knew we had to adapt because our standards were low ... Very shortly teachers were saying we can't operate like that. We started very quickly to adapt the materials we had and add the dimensions that we needed to it. (H3)

The internal audit of performance in school 6 took an entirely different form. Initially it was led by feedback from the staff to the newly appointed head. This produced a number of changes to the school organization that were not popular with parents, the most obvious of which was the abolition of streaming: 'We went down that route because the feedback from the staff was that the existing system was flawed ... children ended up being streamed in French because of their maths results and things like that' (H6). As a result of this, an evidence-based approach to school-improvement planning was adopted. This was led by an 'On Track' group, established to review sets of issues or single issues based on evidence and to make recommendations for change to be incorporated into the school's plans. As the head of this school reported in a recent article, this group:

> has been the constant 'fertiliser' of development ... It has ensured that as a whole school:
> - We have examined and adapted our own school culture
> - We have produced an extremely streamlined strategic ... school plan
> - We are listening in great detail to, and acting upon, the pupil voice. (Upton 2003, p. 8)

Although this head was the only one to present his planning process as being evidence-based, two other heads commented on the benefit they had gained from a university MBA in Education programme (H1, H2) and another (H5) made use of current research and the ideas developed as part of her MA.

In school 1, where the mission statement is 'Aiming high and achieving together', the head audited the performance of children through a regular review process of results and discussions with staff. She also monitored the performance of staff through performance review meetings:

> The role here is to ensure that teachers are implementing the school improvement plan and moving the children in the direction in which they need to go. Pupil behaviour, IT and creativity are priorities for this year. These were identified by our review process. (H1)

Following the Ofsted inspection in school 2, the head recognized that action had to be taken so she implemented a process of:

> Looking at the children. Looking at where they come from and where they are meant to be going. We found they were standing still . . . but it's not like that any more . . . The idea is that all children who are potential level 5s get there and that our border-level 4s become level 4s. Those who are not level 4 get a good grounding to continue their education . . . This helps with our planning. (H2)

External audits and strategic planning

As was seen above, each school should have a set of specific targets derived from national priorities and benchmarks and agreed with the LEA. When asked how far externally set targets influenced the school's planning process, the head of school 2 remarked that the targets set in conjunction with the LEA inspector were very realistic and largely matched the results of the school's own analysis. Not all heads took such a sanguine view of external targets. The head of school 4 dismissed them as having no value, especially for a school in which a significant proportion of the children have profound learning difficulties. He recognized that there was a danger that such targets:

> Can become rigid and . . . seen as an opportunity to narrow that range of attainment that these youngsters are performing at in a uniform system of target setting. Here we will do whatever we will do . . . in terms of valuing everybody. (H4)

The reaction of heads to another possibly significant set of external influences on their school's strategic planning, namely government policy documents, was equally mixed. In school 1 the head used *Excellence and Enjoyment* (DfES 2003) to shape what happens in the school but: 'I take from these documents what suits us here. I will not be coerced into doing things I don't want to do' (H1). This view was echoed by the head of school 4 who said: 'I know the current framework for Ofsted inspection . . . I don't bury my head in the sand but I focus on what I have got here . . . I want people to be reflecting on that all the time' (H4). On a more positive note, the head of school 2 reported that, with reference to *Excellence and Enjoyment* (DfES 2003):

> I sent away for enough copies for all my staff and governors ... My literacy co-ordinator went on a course last week. She was the only one [on the course] to have been given it to read and discuss ... I am afraid I don't agree with everything in it and nor does my deputy because it's only if you can get the money that all those things in that book work. (H2)

Government publications were far more influential in helping to shape the planning in school 5, perhaps because the school was newly opened and the head had been appointed eight months before the school took its first intake of pupils:

> When we were formulating our development the key documents such as *Excellence and Enjoyment* were, for the first time, giving a kind of overview of how children should be dealt with, what their learning should look like. *Excellence and Enjoyment* gave a feel of what education should look like ... It gives you a rationale in which to fit your own development. It gives you something of a challenge so that if what we are doing is different you can ask why it is different. If our aspirations are the same it gives you an external framework in which to put your thinking. I don't think I have ever lived through an educational age before ... where most people are saying similar things. (H5)

Where they were influential, these government documents were, apart from parents, the most influential form of external influence on the planning process. As shown above, parents were consulted in a number of instances about the school values, mission and plans (e.g. schools 2, 4 and 5). The head of school 4 devoted considerable time and effort to communication with parents:

> Parental letters home become very important and I drive my colleagues potty by ... editing them much more. I spend a lot of time on letters to parents, more than other correspondence that I do, editing and re-editing to make sure it is going to be clear and get the point across ... these people have the confidence to know they can criticize. (H4)

In school 2 the parents were consulted about the content of the strategic plan while in school 5 the parents were involved in drawing up the plan from its inception. Largely, however, consultation with parents tends to be asking for comment on decisions already made. Few heads made any systematic attempt to identify parental opinion more widely or in a rigorous way. One head reported that she closely monitored parental satisfaction: 'All teachers are required to tell me of any concerns or any changes including new babies. I monitor complaints and issues parents bring to me' (H1).

Earlier studies of the extent to which headteachers monitored the parental aspect of their school's external environment found similar differences between schools, with a general tendency in even the most outward-looking schools to not to establish rigorous and systematic procedures (Bell 1999b; James and Phillips 1995). Thus, scanning the external environment is not a significant part of the strategic planning process for most heads.

The role of governors in strategic planning

All heads reported that their governors were supportive partners in the strategic planning process, although the nature of the support that the governors provided varied significantly, from governing bodies that are relatively passive supporters who delegate most things to the head, to those who are actively involved in strategic planning in the school and central to the process. In school 4 the head commented that: 'It's a governing body that seems to feel ... comfortable to delegate to the school whatever they are responsible for' (H4). A similar relationship between the head and governors appears to exist in school 3: 'We have our long-term aim ... We wanted to achieve what the governors had set down. I say the governors, but basically it's me with the governors' approval because that's how it works really' (H3).

In school 1 the head uses the governors as a sounding board and: 'bounces ideas off the chair of governors and discusses ideas with the governors' (H1). In school 2 the governors are more active and closely involved in the life of the school. They accepted some responsibility for the poor Ofsted report and contributed to the work required to enable the school to move out of special measures:

> Well, the governors are brilliant ... all the governors had gone through the previous inspection and stuck with the school because they came out badly, the chair ... worked really hard with the school ... they were regularly in the school working not just as governors but alongside staff. They were helping out, attending meetings. (H2)

It was in school 5, however, where governors appeared to make the most significant contribution to strategic planning. The head explained that this was because the governing body:

> understood the word 'strategic' for a start ... For them strategic means an emphasis on an active role and, in my experience there have been a lot of governing bodies where the role has been passive. They take their monitoring of my objectives absolutely seriously ... The terms of reference of their particular committees are truly enacted. They have all formulated various strategic plans for the development of their committees ... They could happily talk to how that relates to the school's strategic plan ... The chairs of the committees meet with the chair of governors twice a term so there is a definite direction between them all which I find quite unique. (H5)

In this school the governors were more than an adjunct to the planning process, they were central to it. In spite of the differences in the nature of the relationships between heads and governors, in each of the schools the heads regarded their governing bodies as a valuable source of support for what they were trying to achieve in their schools and a useful element in the strategic planning process. Governors were seen as having an important part to play in the planning process. Their contribution was valued by the headteachers both for its specific content and for the overall support that it provided both to the management of the school and to the development of its culture.

School structure and culture

Although the values on which strategic planning was based in each of these schools may not always have been articulated clearly and shared widely, there is no doubt that all the heads in this study wanted to involve their entire staff in the planning process and to empower them to deliver the agreed outcomes, both through using the expertise of the staff and facilitating their further professional development. This intent finds expression in the way in which all of the heads talked about the culture of the school which they differentiated in quite specific ways from the school's management structure. This was particularly true in the schools emerging from special measures:

> I am not a teaching head ... mainly because I had so many issues throughout the school ... I have a deputy and he has two days' management time ... We have a senior management team and that is made up from year leaders and ... my SENCO. (H2)

This head then commented that her deputy had worked with all subject leaders: 'Empowering them to understand their areas and to take responsibility ... teachers are now working together and not working in an isolated way ... a lot of discussion, a lot of time empowering' (H2). She noted, with reference to the formulating of plans for the school, that: 'Everybody has a hand in it. Everybody knows what is required ... I suppose it is a plan owned by all' (H2). Obviously, this shift from isolation and an inability to take responsibility to collaboration and empowerment was an important cultural change both for this head and for the school and those who worked in it. The head of school 2 also noted the importance of school culture: 'It's about providing a safe environment ... I see myself providing support for the people that I employ to do a job ... It's about creating the right atmosphere' (H2).

This emphasis on atmosphere and the role of the head in creating an appropriate atmosphere in which strategic planning could be attempted in a collaborative way was an important theme for all the heads in this study. They were at pains to differentiate between management structures and the cultural aspects of their school's organization. Typical of their comments was that made by the head of school 4:

> Management to me is about having systems in place ... You can have the greatest systems in the world, a beautifully managed school where

nothing happens ... What I try to do in school is to create an atmosphere and ethos where people are valued, where there are high expectations. (H4)

One head noted the difficulties encountered in trying to create a collaborative culture in a new school where staff have been recruited from a range of different contexts:

They are used to being in a school where somebody else has done the policy and you ... follow it, or if they had to write a policy, they have gone away and done it on their own. This idea that we have to share our ideas and share our thinking and make a commitment ... has been quite challenging for people. (H5)

Nevertheless, this head had a clear view of the culture that she wanted to establish in the school. She wanted it to be based on learning communities:

Learning communities in the classroom, learning communities among teachers, learning communities in the broadest sense ... based on reflectiveness, resourcefulness, repositioning, accepting challenge, looking at opportunities, problem solving, creativity. Exactly what I want for the children. (H5)

An even more radical approach to school culture and its relationship to strategic planning can be found in school 6, where the head described his school as: 'A set of loosely coupled systems ... I have to define it like that because I am not keen on structures unless they can be broken down' (H6). His starting point for developing a new culture in his school was to minimize the role played by the formal management structure in the school:

The management team probably ends up meeting once a year if it is lucky because I prefer to work with the whole staff ... there is not much of a hierarchical structure here ... If you are used to a management structure, being in meetings where you leave your rank at the door is quite hard for people ... it is the interaction that is important, not the structure. (H6)

The existing culture of the school also came under scrutiny: 'We went on to look at the school's existing culture and tried actively to define that ... and use it as a base for further development' (H6). The culture of the school now revolved around two significant features. The first was the way in which the staff of the school wanted to see their school culture:

The existing culture of the school was very much ... you work here and work every hour ... That is how it seemed to work ... Staff now go home at a decent hour ... We ended up coming up with the idea that [the school] is a moderate hot-house environment ... The staff coined the term moderate hot house ... The idea was to free up the staff so that they could work on fundamentals. (H6)

The fundamentals for this school were all related to evidence-based planning and their 'On Track' planning group. This group was collaborative, non-judgemental and based on valuing ideas from every source irrespective of the status of the people involved (Upton 2003). It enabled strategic planning to focus on:

What has gone before and work out where we have been successful ... working out how you sustain change, then working out what changes you should be sustaining anyway whilst still allowing people to develop and ensure that you keep a sense of direction. (H6)

This head, like all the others, however, recognized both the complexities of strategic planning and the difficulties involved:

We have to get used to the idea of not being able to have a set strategy, of it not being a linear process in effect and being able to try to work out when and how you jump even before the ideas are past their sell-by date. (H6)

The barriers to strategic planning in primary schools

The difficulties encountered by most of the heads clustered into three main areas, namely: resources, staffing and their inability to predict the future. Several heads commented on the impact that budget uncertainties had on their capacity to plan over a period longer than a year (H1, H2 and H4 for example). Typical of their comments was this: 'If I had a budget over a longer period we could plan more strategically. Not knowing what resources you have got makes planning difficult' (H1). It is not just the knowledge about future funding that is of concern. The level of funding is also a problem: 'Primary education is not funded as well as secondary ... if I had secondary funding I could create a different school' (H4).

Some heads try to overcome their budgetary problems by bidding for external funding but this brings its own difficulties. The uncertainty of the process makes strategic planning difficult (H3) and an unsuccessful bid can mean: 'We were going to do things all in one go; instead we are going to have to do it in little bits ... The timescale has changed' (H2).

If anything, staffing issues cause even more difficulties for heads than budgets. One head described his staffing issues over a year as: 'a roller-coaster ride ... I cannot get Year 6 teachers ... I am also short of a literacy co-ordinator' (H3). The same head noted that sometimes staff changes can be positive but they often create difficulties for strategic planning. This view was echoed the views of the head of school 4 who remarked that he had lost 13 staff over the past few years, most of whom had left to have babies:

We have to be continually moving on and evolving and dealing with staffing difficulties ... Who is going to know what circumstances arise

... what you do will depend on who is going to come in and this affects your major decisions. (H4)

In school 1 the head had similar views: 'You cannot plan any further then a year ahead because of the constraints of staffing and changes in LEA policy' (H1). School 1 also experienced other unanticipated events: 'The school was flooded last summer. This meant that several strategic planning matters had to be put on hold while the school was dried out' (H1). The difficulties of predicting an uncertain future play a major part in shaping the approaches of these heads to strategic planning: 'Because circumstances change in schools ... you can have a view about what might be happening next June but the nonsense is in expecting it to happen' (H4). Some heads perceived their schools to be subject to significant and uncontrollable external forces: 'Even now we cannot predict what external forces are going to be pulling you in this way or that. We can't say we are definitely going there or doing that. This does not help us to be strategic' (H3). This leads many heads to adopt a flexible, perhaps incremental approach to the planning processes in their schools:

In terms of how you can predict the future and the areas that are going to be of interest, I don't think you can ... As a result the greatest strength we have developed is the flexibility to deal with different situations. (H6)

The world of the primary school is complex and, in many ways, uncertain. Such relatively small organizations do not have the capacity to respond easily to changing circumstances. Small wonder, therefore, that one head described his attempts at strategic planning as: 'Being on the edge of chaos' (H6).

Conclusion

It can be seen, then, that the heads in this study do use planning as a management technique in their schools. Most of the dimensions of strategic planning contained in Table 10.1 were recognized and understood by these primary school headteachers. They deployed a range of complex metaphors in order to understand the nature of planning and to cope with the demands that it places upon them and their staff. These heads only planned strategically, however, insofar as they sought to establish coherent and agreed plans for their schools. They wanted to ensure that: 'Everybody is singing from the same hymn-sheet' (H2).

As Lumby (2002) argues, strategic planning is, at least in part, a bureaucratic process, especially when it is required by national policy as it is in England. Headteachers must be able to: 'Develop and implement a cyclical process of goal setting, need identification, priority setting, policy making, planning, budgeting, implementing and evaluating' (Caldwell 1992, p. 16). Nevertheless, as one of the heads in this study notes, primary schools are not bureaucracies, they tend to be are loosely coupled systems although not in the fragmented and disjointed way implied by the garbage-can model (H6). The degree of autonomy enjoyed by the staff of these primary schools, the complexity of both the teaching and learning technology and the relative unpredictability of the external environment: 'renders problematic any simple translation of intention or instruction into planned outcomes ... It is particularly hard to relate specific management activity to improvements in teaching and learning' (Lumby 2002, p. 95). Perhaps for this reason, in formulating and implementing their strategic plans, heads tend to minimize, but not ignore, the importance of the structure of their schools, and place greater emphasis on their collegial and collaborative cultures.

Culture in this context tends to be used, not in the limited sense of: 'The way we do things around here' (Deal and Kennedy 1983, p. 14); the use made of the term by the heads in this study defines culture in a much more fundamental way, seeing it as the deeper level of shared basic assumptions and beliefs (Schein 1985). This reflects the view of culture advanced by Hopkins *et al.* (1994) that includes the dominant values espoused by the school and the philosophy that shapes its approach to teaching, learning and professional relationships. As Hargreaves (1995) notes, cultures have a reality-defining function that enables staff in schools to make sense of their actions and their situation, including the strategic planning processes. As Schein (1985) notes, the integration of the three elements, artefacts, values, and assumptions, can significantly influence how schools build their own culture. In this study heads and their staff deliberately reshaped the culture by integrating these three elements in order to facilitate strategic planning based on a recognition of the importance of developing a collaborative culture where people are valued for what they can contribute and in which ideas can be shared, innovations tried out and where blame is not apportioned: 'It is about creating conditions in which there is openness, where you can agree to disagree' (H4). Although most governing bodies are part of this collaborative culture their role in most schools is relatively marginal since they tend to delegate most of the overall planning responsibility to the headteachers. To some extent this is a result of the very nature of governing bodies themselves in that they are part-time and non-expert groups seeking to deal with complex long- and short-term issues. It may also be a product of the planning process in their schools.

The planning in these primary schools is, at best, incremental and tends to consist of rather small and marginal changes made and evaluated over a very limited planning horizon. The plans themselves are based on a series of internal audits that focus on pupil and teacher performance and which may include some information gleaned from parents. There is no evidence of the careful analysis of external factors that Puffitt *et al.* (1992) argue should form the basis of such strategic plans. The wider policy context of education and beyond is of marginal influence. Heads tend to adopt a reactive and responsive stance rather than a proactive, anticipatory one to matters that emanate from both the national and local environment Even some elements of the internal environment, budgets and staffing for example, are treated in this way over relatively short periods of time. The expectations of stakeholders, particularly governors, are taken into account and espoused values play an important function in determining the content and nature of the plans produced in these primary schools, which do contain specific school development and improvement objectives, relating to agreed targets and focusing on children's learning.

To the extent that it is based on an attempt to identify priorities that will be achieved over time, and that resources are mobilized to achieve those priorities, the planning process in these primary schools can be considered to be strategic. So short is the timespan and so marginal many of the changes that are achieved, however, that the model of planning adopted approximates more closely to an evolutionary or marginal incremental process than to the development and implementation of the type of linear-rational strategic plan that appears to be envisaged in the expectations of the DfES. It is not beyond the realms of possibility that headteachers, governors and teachers could develop a form of planning based on a longer-term time horizon. The evidence here, however, is that they do not do so either out of choice or because the perceived barriers to such planning are too great to be surmounted or to be worth attempting to overcome. Instead, school structures and, more particularly their cultures, are reshaped to facilitate this form of evolutionary incremental planning. What emerged here is a flexible and collaborative planning process more suited to the primary school context than is strategic planning, predicated as it is on the capacity of the school to achieve organizational goals through a rational process that begins with analysis and proceeds in a linear way to implementation. This implies that planning and implementation are orderly and sequential and that schools can be shaped and controlled in order to avoid the unintended consequences of change while realizing strategic objectives. Primary schools cannot do this.

If, as Fidler (2002) suggests, strategic planning is a long-term process that might involve planning horizons of three or five years, or even longer, then the plans that are formulated by the heads in these primary schools are not strategic. The timescale over which heads in this study planned is very short term and even here their approach tended to be based on a degree of flexibility. It approximates more closely to the evolutionary incremental approach (Quinn 1980) than it does to any of the more structured and longer-term models of strategic planning. The inability of heads in these schools to control or even predict their available resources with any degree of certainty of a period of more than a year, however, almost inevitably created a situation in which their planning was short term and highly flexible. To that extent, planning in these primary schools was not strategic, but incremental (see Table 10.2).

It is also far more collaborative than many of the more linear or rationalistic approaches to strategic planning (Bell 2002). In implementing the plans the heads and their staff do seek to reconcile the need to achieve agreed objectives with available resources, but the planning procedure seems to be less of a process of matching resource capabilities to priorities than a matter of shaping priorities to identify what can be achieved within available or uncertain resource parameters. The focus is on coping with short-term or immediate problems but, nevertheless, the process is informed by strongly held values: 'You don't do it because somebody else has told you to or has said that it is a good idea. You have to do it because you believe in a school ... It is all about honesty and integrity' (H5). These tend to provide both a foundation on which planning can be based and a rationale for decisions that are made and priorities that are identified. To some extent, the picture of planning that emerges here conforms to the processual model of planning and Boisot's (1995) concept of

Table 10.2 Dimensions of planning in six English primary schools

Model of planning	Planning horizon	Main locus of data analysis	Expressing of outcomes	Manage-ment technique
Evolution-ary incremen-tal	Short term: one year maximum	Internal envir-onment at whole school or sub-unit level based on values, taking stakeholders' expectations into account	Targets identified with LEA but redefined in the light of school con-text and changing resources	Participative-collaborative with an emphasis on whole staff involvement to minimize garbage-can conflict and uncertainty.

'strategic intention', since it is based on values and vision supported by evidence from institutional evaluation that enables informed and collective decisions to be made and collaboratively implemented. The process described here, however, is one of:

> Coping with turbulence through a direct, intuitive understanding of what is happening in an effort to guide the work of the school. A turbulent environment cannot be tamed by rational analysis alone ... Yet it does not follow that the school's response must be left to a random distribution of lone individuals acting opportunistically ... Strategic intention relies on ... vision ... to give it unity and coherence.
> (adapted from Boisot 1995, p. 36, quoted in Caldwell and Spinks 1998)

However, much of what the headteachers in this study did was concerned with the internal school environment. They demonstrated a relatively low understanding of wider external issues and almost no capacity to control or influence that environment. At best, therefore, planning in these schools consisted of: 'Incremental adjustments to environmental states that cannot be discerned or anticipated through a prior analysis of data' (Boisot 1995, p. 34). The complexity of the issues facing these schools was reflected in the nature of the barriers to strategic planning identified by the headteachers. These barriers appeared to be a product of the size of the schools, the nature of their resourcing and the perceptions of the external environment held by the headteachers. The environment is seen as unpredictable and uncertain in a number of ways, not least of which are the changes in educational policy that seem to occur with singular regularity. These schools are resourced over a very limited time period, typically one year only. Their budgets are small and most schools do not have the resource flexibility to build a contingency fund sufficient to be confident of funding plans in a second year. Consequently, heads are reluctant to commit their schools to strategic plans that span a longer period. This is partly because staffing losses or changes in such relatively small organizations can have significant impact on the school's capacity to develop in specific areas. Therefore, on the evidence of the data collected from these schools it is apparent that primary headteachers and their staff are not attempting to espouse a model of planning that even approximates to long-term strategic planning. Instead, they are redefining the nature of planning to meet the needs of their own circumstances.

What's Done is Done: the Impact of Educational Policy on Headship in Primary Schools in England 1994–2001

Introduction: the policy context

This chapter compares the impact of educational policy on the role of the primary head in the years following the implementation of the main recommendations of the Education Reform Act (DES 1988a), the Market Phase of educational policy, with those reported by headteachers following the introduction of New Labour educational policy in the 1999–2001 period, the Target Phase. The data on which this paper is based was produced by two research projects, one of which, in 1995, looked at the perceptions of primary heads about their roles and management styles, and the other, still in its early stages, which has a similar focus. The head's role is analysed in terms of the balance of activities between the Chief Executive and Leading Professional aspects of that role. This typology of headship, based on the work of Hughes (1976), is used to provide an analytical framework because it still offers a valid and relevant conceptualization of the role of the head, in spite of being one of the earliest to be deployed by any researcher in educational management.

The main thrust of the Education Reform Act (DES 1988a) and the circulars and regulations which followed it (e.g. DES 1988b, 1991) was to create patterns of accountability and autonomy based on a centrally controlled national curriculum that gave children an entitlement to specific curriculum content and enabled direct comparisons to be made between all schools through national assessment (Bell 1992). Organization and management, rather than being vested in LEAs, was devolved to the schools. Here the responsibility for ensuring that the National Curriculum was taught and tested and for the deployment of resources rested not with teachers but with governing bodies on which parents and representatives of the local community are in a majority. The legitimation of these policies was eventually articulated in the White Paper, *Choice and Diversity* (DfE 1992) which identified five great themes: quality, diversity, choice, autonomy and accountability, that provided the context for Conservative educational policy.

The role of the headteacher

Heads have always been required to carry out two different and sometimes conflicting sets of leadership functions in British schools: professional, and chief executive or managerial. Hughes (1985), basing his work on an analysis of the roles of secondary headteachers, drew attention to the importance of understanding this distinction. He noted that the Leading Professional role has both internal and external dimensions. The internal dimensions include the professional guidance of staff, teaching and counselling pupils and parents. The external dimensions are acting as a spokesperson for the school and involvement in external professional activities. The Leading Professional is likely to be involved in:

> Any attempt to identify aims and objectives ... the broad formulation of means by which the resulting decisions are to be implemented ... The measures adopted to judge the extent to which the agreed objectives are being achieved. It will be noted that though the above are unmistakably elements of the management process, the crucial decisions, which have to be taken at each stage, are essentially professional. (Hughes 1985, p. 17)

In a re-evaluation of the Hughes model, Doughty (1998) argued that the Leading Professional role must be reconsidered in the light of developments since 1988. She suggested that the internal dimension of the role now relates specifically to teaching, learning and pupil achievement while the external aspect focuses on professional activities outside school linked to national standards, training and development and establishing links with the school's wider community.

The Chief Executive role also has internal and external dimensions. Hughes suggests that the internal dimension consists of all the allocative and co-ordinating functions within the school, while the external dimension involves relationships with the governing body and the LEA as employing authority. The Chief Executive will be responsible for: 'the division and allocation of work (including the clarification of staff responsibilities and delegation of responsibility); ... the co-ordination and control of organizational activity (including staff supervision ... deadlines and ... efficient procedures)' (Hughes 1998, pp. 175–6). Doughty's (1998) reformulation of this role is based on the view that the Chief Executive's overall responsibility is for the maintenance and defence of the school. The internal dimension of the role is concerned with the allocation, control and co-ordination of the overall functioning of the school while the external focus is on the head's relationship with institutional authority. The role of the governing body, however, is now more ambiguous than when Hughes originally postulated his model. This ambiguity stems from the extent to which the governing body is internal or external to the school. Doughty (1998) argues that the governors are external to the school because the head is accountable to them and they are responsible to parents for the performance of the school.

Other reformulations of these two aspects of the head's role give different emphases. For example, Law and Glover (2000) argue that, although there are complexities and difficulties inherent in combining both Leading Professional and Chief Executive roles, the two roles should be seen as an integrative whole. They suggest that the essential feature of the Chief Executive role is that it is strategic, while the external focus is on undertaking public relations with stakeholders and articulating the school's mission. The Leading Professional role internally is based on acting as a mentor who develops others and offers professional guidance, providing advice for pupils, parents and staff and demonstrating personal competence and teaching skills. The external aspect is two fold: firstly as an ambassador, an organizational envoy within a wide range of professional activities, and secondly as an advocate who is the institutional spokesperson on educational and professional matters.

Hughes suggested that all headteachers carry out professional leadership and executive functions but:

> The professional-as-administrator does not act in some matters as a leading professional and in others as a chief executive. Professional knowledge, skills and attitudes are likely to have a profound effect on the whole range of tasks undertaken by the headteacher. (Hughes 1985, p. 279)

Thus, Hughes claimed, there is a substantial interpenetrating of the two roles such that the Chief Executive function informs that of the Leading Professional and vice versa. He took issue with Morgan *et al.* (1983) who did not recognize the integrative significance of the professional-as-administrator concept since their work emphasized the dichotomous nature of the two aspects of the head's role. The sharp differentiation between the professional and executive proposed by Morgan *et al.* (1983) has been taken a step further by Handy (1984) who argued that schools should have both professional leaders and administrators on the grounds that: 'To combine the two roles in one person is an invitation to stress' (Handy 1984, p. 23). Hughes (1985), Handy (1984) and Morgan *et al.* (1983) all recognized that the two roles are interdependent, although not necessarily integrated, since both sets of functions are necessary for the effective organization and management of schools.

Ribbins (1993), however, argued that the roles are independent not interdependent. He noted that:

> In such a model towards one polar end are located a set of administrative tasks ... and at the other polar end a set of curriculum duties ... This approach assumes that as heads emphasize one aspect of their role they must do so at the expense of the other. Such an approach is unduly restrictive. An alternative approach might be to see the two dimensions as largely independent of each other, rather than antithetical aspects of the orientations which heads bring to their work. (Ribbins 1993, pp. 34-5)

Heads, therefore, can meet the requirements of the two roles at the same time and can, if necessary, treat them independently. Ribbins (1993) also suggested that it is now usual to assume that the role of the head has always had these two basic dimensions, but that the traditional view of headship tended to emphasize the professional while recent developments emphasize the managerial. He contests the view that educational reforms since 1988 have forced heads into giving a much greater priority to administration. He argues that a growing number of heads have come to terms with the administrative demands of the role and are now increasingly active as curriculum leaders (Ribbins 1993). Nevertheless, the National Curriculum and Ofsted inspections imposed significant constraints on heads and their staff while self-management allowed governing bodies to delegate to heads the responsibility for the control and management of resources (Bell, Halpin and Neill 1996a). Great emphasis was placed on the centrality of the head in managing the school, almost to the exclusion of all other significant factors. Headteachers carried almost alone the responsibility for school failure. The then Chief Inspector of Schools emphasized this position. He stated categorically that:

> It is the leadership provided by the headteacher which is the critical factor in raising standards of pupil achievement . . . headteachers must have a clear vision of the curriculum . . . the strength of personality and interpersonal tact needed to engage with teachers in raising standards; [and] the administrative drive to plan programmes of improvement and see that they were carried through. (Woodhead 1996, pp. 10-11)

Thus, headteachers would receive much of the credit for success and have to take responsibility for failure: 'When a school is put into special measures, one of the factors leading to this decision is often poor leadership' (Ofsted 1998a, p. 4). Furthermore, the role of headteachers was to become even more demanding in the future:

> The vision for learning set out in this White Paper will demand the highest qualities of leadership and management from headteachers. The quality of the heads can often make a difference between the success or failure of schools. Good heads can transform a school; poor heads can block progress and achievement. (DfEE 1997a, p. 46)

Heads, therefore, were being cast in the role of 'hero innovator' by this set of policies. Thus, if schools were to take responsibility for their own performance, the individual who shouldered the burden of that responsibility, both for success and failure, was the headteacher. This was particularly true of heads in primary schools.

Primary headship in 1995: Chief Executive or Leading Professional?

The role of the headteacher in primary schools in the UK has experienced significant changes since 1988. By 1995 heads were responsible for their own finances in conjunction with their governing body, more likely to be in competition for pupils within the education marketplace, and subject to public scrutiny through Ofsted inspection reports and the publication of Standard Assessment Test (SATs) results. Small wonder then that many heads initially seemed to find the increased managerial demands made upon them somewhat daunting, as responsibilities were devolved to schools. Mortimore and Mortimore (1991), when commenting on the reaction of primary heads to the provisions of the Education Reform Act (DES 1988a), argued that the generation of pre- and immediately post-1988 heads felt that their past had left them unprepared for the present challenges of leadership. While they felt more than able to give the professional leadership expected of them, they felt ill-equipped to meet the new managerial challenges.

In 1995 an Economic and Social Research Council (ESRC) funded project (R000221271) was established at Warwick University to analyse the impact of different degrees of self-management on the work of primary school heads. Questionnaire data was elicited from 137 schools and 24 were identified for follow-up interviews with headteachers using 'typicality' as the sample selection criteria. Schools from the local education authority (LEA) maintained, grant maintained (GM) and private sectors were included in the sample. The analysis of the data which this research produced explored the effect of educational policy subsequent to the Education Reform Act (DES 1988a) on the work of heads, on decision making within schools and on the partnership between heads and school governors (Bell, Halpin and Neill 1996a; Bell 1996; Bell 1999a; Bell and Halpin 2000). A second research project followed up the first. Questionnaire data was sought from the 24 primary schools in the original interview sample, including those which had GM status, together with 22 from three LEAs in Merseyside. From these, 12 schools were selected using a refined concept of 'typicality' for further investigation during the summer and autumn terms 2001.

The findings from the first project show that educational policies prior to 1995 produced an inherent tension between the need for a strong professional role for heads and the constraints placed upon them by equating the relationship between the head and the governing body with that between a chief executive and a board of directors. It might be expected, therefore, that if the two roles identified by Hughes (1976) are integrated or interdependent then the legislation introduced in the late 1980s and early 1990s would have had an impact on the extent to which primary heads acted as Chief Executive or as Leading Professional. If, on the other hand, the roles are independent then, while heads may report an increase in activity related to one or other role, this would not be at the expense of the other set of functions. The heads in the 1995 sample recognized the interdependence of the two roles when they noted that there was a convincing argument in favour of retaining general oversight of the curriculum and facilitating collegial curriculum decision making while tending to treat resource management somewhat differently. They argued, however, that they could not be expected to possess the subject knowledge needed to oversee every aspect of the National Curriculum, nor be expected to be familiar with the detail of all relevant subject developments. They saw their main priorities as resource management and deployment while recognizing the importance of facilitating curriculum development.

While it was left to the heads in our sample to define in their own words how they provided professional leadership and what such leadership meant to them, it is interesting to note that clear differences were identified in the reported leadership styles of heads in the two different sectors. GM school heads considered that they 'lead from the front'. By contrast, LEA heads were more inclined to think of themselves as 'collegial' and 'consultative' leaders. GM school heads were less willing to delegate decision making compared with heads in the LEA maintained sector. There were, of course, exceptions, but the trend was clear. Nevertheless, both LEA and GM school heads tended to espouse management styles that stressed consultation, collective decision making and delegated responsibility. The same heads reported, however, that teachers were more involved in decisions concerning the curriculum than they were in those relating to staff development, financial and other resource management matters. Typically one head, in the course of describing how financial decisions were made in his school, stated that: 'I check with the chairman of the finance committee and, if necessary, the chairman of governors, but I identify the need and we spend the money.' His approach to curriculum decisions, however, placed considerable emphasis on a team approach and the involvement of class teachers: 'Decisions ... start at teacher level and work up through ... year meetings. Heads of Key Stages 1 and 2, who are very much aware, then feed back to myself with the deputy and administrator so we can take team decisions.' Several heads acknowledged that they lacked expertise to provide professional leadership on the content of some aspects of the National Curriculum. One noted that: 'I have not got a detailed day-to-day knowledge of the working of the whole National Curriculum. I have to accept that limitation and work within it, using the strength of a strong team within the school.' Another went even further, arguing that:

> Planning has become so crucial and has become formalized now. We have short-term planning documents and planning groups, but we also plan long term. The school has a curriculum planning group for this. I don't sit on that. It is a conscious decision. I trust them to do an absolutely first-rate job.

Thus, there is a significant level of teacher involvement in key decisions pertaining to the curriculum. However, the two heads quoted above had a somewhat different approach to resource management from that adopted for curriculum decision making. Here staff were far less involved. In the first school, the head took strategic resource decisions after consulting the finance group of the governing body. For teaching staff, therefore, these decisions: 'Are by and large "decide and tell" in the sense that they are done by me [the head], in conjunction with representatives of the governing body who take decisions that the head is comfortable with.' In the second school, where the head was involved in a pre-LMS pilot project on local financial management, he believed that:

> Heads have never had so much power as they have now ... The criteria that I use at the beginning of the budgetary planning cycle and how I apply them is almost entirely up to me. I am guided by the school development plan that has been formally agreed by the staff and governors.

Many heads in the 1995 sample reported that they felt in overall control of the major decisions that affect the school and believed they were able to manage resources in order to achieve their strategic objectives.

This is not to say, however, that as primary schools became more autonomous, there was a shift away from collective leadership towards a more 'top down' or directive leadership style in these schools. On the contrary, some policy initiatives, especially those relating to the curriculum, either reinforced processes of collective decision making or made them a necessary part of primary school leadership where they did not exist. This was less true of resource management, but even here there was some evidence of increasing consultation. The tensions between collegial and bureaucratic management styles appeared not to emerge either in the management of the curriculum or in resource management. Heads reported that they made every effort to inform and, at times, consult staff on the latter issues while devolving significant decisions to them in the former case.

It is also clear that the heads themselves, and to some extent their staff and governors, made a distinction between those decisions which fell into the realm of professional activity and those regarded as part of their Chief Executive function. Matters pertaining to teaching, learning and the curriculum fell into the former category, while resource management and staffing, sites and buildings came into the latter. Heads tended either to involve staff in curriculum matters or delegate these to colleagues. Thus, in the professional domain heads, on the whole, adopted a collegiate approach to leadership and decision making. In the area of resource management, where heads and their governors were responsible for the totality of the budget, this was less true, although staff were often consulted as part of decision making, and certainly were kept informed about that process. Executive functions, therefore, rested with the head but they devolved much of their professional powers. For some heads the Chief Executive role had an important influence on their overall leadership of the school. These heads felt constrained by their situations and found delegation difficult. The overall view, however, appeared to be that while the demarcation was not always distinct, leadership styles associated with the professional function tended to be more collegial and based on delegation than those associated with the executive function. Thus, it can be seen that the two dimensions of leadership that Hughes (1985) identified are helpful in understanding the impact of autonomy on the reported leadership styles of heads of schools in this sample.

It should be noted, however, that while Hughes (1985) argued that heads would operate as if the two roles were integrated or interdependent, the headteachers in these research samples made a clear distinction between the professional and the executive roles. They tended to operate in each domain as if each were independent of the other, moving between domains on the basis of their perception of the importance of the issues under consideration. Furthermore, the stances adopted by heads in respect of the two aspects of their roles appeared to be related to their overall perceptions of the demands of the policy framework within which they were operating and the level of priority that they accorded to those demands. Although they tended to concentrate attention on the Chief Executive aspects this was not because they necessarily accepted the policy thrust that identified these functions as having overwhelming importance. They did not accepted the prevailing language of legitimation, perhaps because their socialization into the professional culture of teaching was so strong and this, in itself, provided a supportive network of like-minded colleagues. While they gave greater emphasis to it, heads did not fully espouse the Chief Executive at the expense of the Leading Professional role. Governing bodies have not shouldered the burden of the detailed management of schools (Bell and Halpin 2000). As a result, heads have found that they had more control over many aspects of school management because of the decline in influence of the LEAs. Thus, there was, in Conservative education policy, a discontinuity between legitimations emanating from the socio-political environment, the organizational and operational principles, and the management strategies required to implement policy (Bell 1996).

Primary headship in 2001: Chief Executive and Leading Professional

The legitimation of New Labour's educational policy is, in part, couched in terms similar to that of their Conservative predecessors, although there is a significant difference is emphasis and some notable additions. Ball (1999) has suggested that the rhetoric remains the same since it is couched in terms of choice and competition, autonomy and performativity and centralization and prescription. The New Labour approach to all policy making, including that for education, is, however, based on at least one set of assumptions that are not derived from the New Right, that government should 'remake society to fit an *a priori* grand design' (Marquand 1998). New policies and new approaches have been introduced in pursuit of that grand design, many of them driven by performance targets established by the government but to be achieved by those in schools and colleges. This is to be a crusade to overcome social disadvantage and improve economic performance, as the Secretary of State for Education points out in his introduction to the White Paper *Excellence in Schools* (DfEE 1997a).

> To overcome economic and social disadvantage and to make opportunity a reality ... To compete in the global economy ... We must overcome the spiral of disadvantage ... I ask you to join us in making the crusade for higher standards a reality in every classroom and every household in the country. (DfEE 1997a, pp. 3–4)

It is a crusade to deliver excellence: 'There is nothing more important to the Government than raising the standards children achieve in schools. The White Paper *Excellence in Schools* committed us to exacting targets ... Our vision is of excellence for all' (DfEE 1998a, p. 4). Excellence in this context is not an end in itself: 'It is a key element of achieving the Government's goals of a more productive economy, a more cohesive society, a more successful democracy and more fulfilled individuals' (Barber 1999, p. 17). Education, therefore, is to provide the impetus for economic growth. It will enable individuals to gain access to qualifications that will make them employable, productive citizens and will thus restore the social cohesion that was lost during the New Right's flirtation with pure individualism.

If changes in the policy context impinge on educational practice, then it ought now to be possible to begin to establish what, if any, changes there have been in the perceived role of primary heads as a result of the educational policies of New Labour. The phenomenon of the dual role of headship was now to be investigated further within this changing policy context. This research concentrated particularly on exploring the impact of New Labour's education policies on the role of the head as Chief Executive and Leading Professional. It was clear from the questionnaire data that by 2001 a somewhat different situation had emerged. Heads in each sector now had a different perspective and the sector differences were much diminished. This may have something to do with the abolition of GM status and its replacement with the Foundation School concept (DfEE 1997a). By 2001 heads were more closely involved in the totality of their work, rather than concentrating on their executive functions. They were also beginning to feel a growing conflict between the two aspects of their roles and were expressing concerns about their capacity to cope with the increased demands of each function. On the one hand, they felt that their Leading Professional role has had to increase within their schools to ensure that the government policy changes are implemented effectively and to the required standard. On the other hand, this increased professional activity has had to take place against the background of the demands of new government initiatives, which have also increased the demands of the Chief Executive function within their role as headteachers.

Over half the heads in the sample felt that the increase in responsibility in both aspects of their role was leading to an inability to carry out their jobs efficiently. As one head stated: 'Although I support change, the rate of change has become faster since the Labour Party came to power. I feel very overworked like many of my colleagues.' Another head reiterated this viewpoint:

> I am very involved in my post but have to say that as a teaching head, the amount of administration has increased my working hours to 70 hours per week on some occasions. (Never less than 50 hours per week).

Heads generally thought that the added responsibility of ensuring that their schools were implementing new government initiatives such as the Literacy and Numeracy Strategies at the required pace meant that some elements of their roles in school would have to suffer. As one head stated: 'I anticipate constant change. I feel I can't keep up. My job is to facilitate my staff and at present I'm not doing a good one.' Another head felt there was: 'Less time to teach. Demands of office paperwork have brought about changes – e.g. some tasks which I would have ... liked to control ... be involved in ... are now delegated.'

This view of the change to heads' roles in their schools was a theme repeated by most heads in the sample. They felt that the Leading Professional element of their job had become more pronounced as a result of recent policy initiatives over which their staff looked to them for guidance and direction.

Many heads expressed the view that, since the advent of New Labour in 1997, they had been required to become experts in all areas of the curriculum, especially literacy, numeracy and information and communication technology, in order to support their staff and to facilitate and monitor change. One head expressed this in the following way: 'Monitoring the delivery of the curriculum has become much more important in the last two years. I am very involved in this process.' Another head felt that he had to ensure that he has an up-to-date working knowledge of educational initiatives to be able to lead his staff by example, to evaluate their progress against set targets and to monitor progress. He noted that: 'I have had to work hard at promoting literacy and numeracy initiatives. Some of the training pack materials were not really suitable.'

Thus, the duties of the head as Leading Professional were taking on a greater significance for many in this sample. This change was not without its costs. In many cases, heads stated that the increase to their role as the leading professionals in their schools had carried with it the added pressure of dealing with the decline in levels of staff morale in their schools. 'Salaries had risen but staff needed frequent praise to sustain morale. Their poor public image, announcements of yet more changes and critical reports often distressed staff.' Monitoring staff performance and evaluating curriculum change could not be achieved in a vacuum. Heads had to ensure that they continued to show consideration for the concerns of their staff and respect their professionalism while maintaining a certain level of pressure to ensure that policy which impacted directly on work in the classroom was being implemented.

The increase in the responsibilities of headteachers and their accountability for ensuring that their staff implement new government strategies led many heads to believe that there had been a change in their overall style of management. The conflict between their Chief Executive and Leading Professional roles was nowhere more evident than in their responses to any changes in their management styles. Many felt that the pressure of the Chief Executive element of their job had increased with the excessive amounts of documentation that had accompanied government reforms. To cope with this they had to delegate some tasks to their senior management teams. They resigned themselves to the fact that the Chief Executive element of their role was so demanding that, to ensure they could carry out the leading professional element of their role effectively, they had to expect their staff to take more responsibility. One head reported that: 'I have had to learn to delegate more to survive. There are some things that are impossible to delegate.'

Although there appears to have been increased delegation of tasks in schools, many heads felt that their management style had become more autocratic and involved far less consultation since 1997. This, heads felt, was a result of the rapid introduction of significant initiatives, especially related to pupil achievement, and to anticipated demands of performance management processes. For example, one head reported she tried not to compromise in her approach to decision making but that, more often than not, she was forced to take the responsibility herself:

> I still try to involve the staff as much as possible in decision making but there seem to have been so many changes that sometimes in order to get

things done quickly I have to make decisions myself and then sell it to the staff.

Another head was concerned that: 'I am unable to follow my preferred consultative style because many initiatives have to be carried through irrespective of my own or the staff's views.'

A number of other heads held the view that it was becoming far more difficult to balance the demands of the two aspects of their role as Chief Executive and Leading Professional in their schools. They were finding it impossible to juggle both aspects of their job and the management of their schools was suffering. They felt that recent changes in education policy were causing them and their staff unnecessary stress and excessive workloads. As the following two heads stated: 'I sometimes feel the job is managing me, never feel I have got everything running smoothly, forced into crisis management from time to time. "If it ain't broken don't mend it" springs to mind,' and '[The] pressure and pace of government initiatives as a manager having to make change sustainable is a nightmare. Pressure on all staff is far too great.' Heads' accountability for the implementation of government initiated strategies caused pressure to increase on teaching staff who often found it difficult carry out their jobs effectively due to increased stress levels. This affected the day-to-day running of the school adversely. One head summed up the position thus: 'I feel very pressured to sell changes to staff which are being thrust upon us. Stress policy has emerged – more absence through exhaustion which leads to more pressure on everyone. More crisis management!'

In the context of increased pressure and new demands the heads in the 2001 sample appeared to be largely dismissive of training opportunities. Only four had taken the National Professional Qualification for Headteachers (NPQH) and one had done the LPSH and found it very useful. The general view of NPQH was expressed by one head who said: 'It is unstructured. They appear to be making it up as they go along.' Another commented that: 'The focus is OK but the pace is too great.' A third noted that it was far too secondary-focused and unsuitable for primary school heads because it placed too much emphasis on the centrality of the head and failed to recognize the collegial nature of such schools: 'The providers refuse to accept the "we" in small schools.' Nor was NPQH regarded as particularly suitable for deputies. One of the 11 heads in the sample whose deputy had embarked upon NPQH remarked that the course placed far too many demands by being based on tasks, which had to be completed in school: 'It is very difficult in a primary for a deputy head to do NPQH.' Twenty of the heads in the sample had availed themselves of the Headlamp opportunity although, as one head put it, it was silly not to do so since the money was there. This was thought to be more useful to the newly appointed head than NPQH but it was generally regarded as being too little and too late.

The heads the 1995 sample did not have access to most of the current training opportunities but their attitude towards what was available, mainly short courses on specific topics or targeted at new or experienced heads, was far more positive. Perhaps this is linked to the different perspectives on job satisfaction that were identified. In contrast to the situation in 1995, heads in the 2001 sample declared a marked decrease in their levels of job satisfaction.

The conflict between their roles as the Chief Executive and Leading Professional in their schools has caused many heads to claim that they are no longer enjoying their jobs as much as they did two years before. One head reported that his job satisfaction had decreased because: 'Government policies are very prescriptive - spontaneity and innovative ideas are squeezed out.' Another head felt that his job satisfaction was not as it should be due to an inability on his part to deal with the issues that he thought were a priority in his school. Like many of his colleagues in the sample, he argued that government-prescribed changes have caused an inflexible approach to tackling issues that he believed were more important to his school than implementing the Literacy and Numeracy Strategies - strategies that have dominated primary school management since their introduction. 'It is still immensely frustrating not to be able to tackle those initiatives and issues which you know would benefit the children. Lack of funding keeps PTR [pupil–teacher ratio] up to about 1:27, thus absolutely no flexibility.'

The decrease in reported levels of job satisfaction was not universal. A small proportion of heads stated that their levels of job satisfaction had remained constant since 1995 and had even improved. These heads had been in post for less than five years and were still enjoying the challenge of new headship. These heads had little experience of balancing Chief Executive and Leading Professional functions prior to the implementation of New Labour's education policies, and seem to have adapted to the challenges more readily than their more experienced colleagues. As one newly appointed head put it:

> I have a very high level of job satisfaction, I enjoy the challenge, I enjoy the potential for 'making a difference'. I have a strong committed staff but I wish there was a real celebration of the work schools do against the odds.

It is interesting to note, however, that another head stated that:

> [My] job satisfaction [has] improved because of promotion - however, the more I am settling into the job the harder I am finding it. [The] pressure [is] very great, quite stressful, [I] never seem to have the time to get everything done.

Conclusion: the way forward

The overall picture emerging from the analysis of the initial questionnaires from the headteachers sampled in 2001 is one of conflict between the Chief Executive and Leading Professional aspects of heads' roles. There has been an increase in the duties encompassed by each aspect, but heads do not have the time to carry out both and to give them equal emphasis in their approach to school management. As a result, they appear to be delegating some of the Chief Executive elements of their role to their senior management teams to ensure that they maintain their position as the Leading Professional within their schools. This is becoming more important with the implementation of government education policies, which need strong leadership and expertise to enable teaching staff to meet set targets. This recent emphasis on implementing policies that impact directly on schools and on work in classrooms caused a number of heads to agree that overload of information and statutory requirements could lead to inefficiency. Resources were not being well managed and it was difficult to deal with all those requirements and cope with target setting under such conditions. It is clear, therefore, that many heads in the second sample feel increased demands on themselves both as Chief Executives and Leading Professionals in their schools. Policies outlined in the Green Paper (DfEE 1998a) are already requiring heads increasingly to recognize the importance of acting in both capacities, rather than allowing them scope to adopt one role or the other, as heads in the 1995 sample had been able to do. In the Chief Executive role the emphasis is now on performance management, arrangements for accountability and the monitoring of pupil achievement. The Leading Professional emphasis is on establishing a vision for the school, achieving national standards and implementing the next phase of the National Curriculum. Heads now reported a distinct increase in their leading professional responsibilities and acknowledge that this phenomenon has been accompanied by an increase in the importance that they attach to the professional functions. Heads also noted a growth in their work as Chief Executive. Those heads who were in post prior to 1988 suggested that the current developments in both their Leading Professional and Chief Executive roles were generating demands that were greater than those that developed in the wake of the legislation in the last decade of Conservative government. Heads were responding to these demands by treating the two aspects of their roles as independent. In so doing they were seeking to develop coping strategies that were based on shifting the burden of responsibility for one aspect of their role to other colleagues, although which functions were delegated appeared to vary between schools.

Already it is clear, therefore, that although there are similarities in the impact of educational policy on the role of primary headteachers in 1995 and in 2001 there has now been a significant change in that policy. It was now far less concerned with efficiency, with markets and competition, but, as Bottery (1999) noted, it now emphasized civic responsibilities, duties and contributions to the greater well-being of society rather than the individualism and self-interest of the New Right. It focused on targets, standards of performance, citizenship and economic and school effectiveness. Patterns of accountability were now more centralized, with LEAs playing a significant role in helping to raise standards. Policy was increasingly concerned with operational and managerial detail, even to the extent of prescribing curriculum content, pedagogy and processes of performance appraisal. Professional leadership focused on the delivery of a prescribed curriculum. Management activity increasingly became concerned with monitoring a range of different performance indicators both within and between schools. It also included responding to the data provided in order continually to improve pupil attainment, thus enabling policy objectives to be attained. As a result, primary heads increasingly found themselves struggling to establish a balance between the increasing demands of the two independent aspects of their role as they tried to be both Leading Professional and Chief Executive.

Headteachers have viewed these two dimensions as increasingly in conflict, with the former suffering as a result of the exponential increase in the management elements of the primary headteacher's role, including strategic planning, budgeting, resource allocation, working with governors and performance management. (Webb 2005, pp. 69–70)

Heads were struggling to balance their roles as Leading Professionals, particularly working to improve and sustain pupil attainment, with that of Chief Executive, especially responding to the pace of externally driven change and the increasingly complex performance-management agenda.

End Piece: Bring Me No More Reports

Chapter 12 brings us full circle to a critical reconsideration of some elements of education policy, particularly those that continue to form a significant part of the New Labour education policy agenda in the Target Phase. The main focus is on strategic planning as it is applied to schools, on the assumptions that underpin such planning, especially on the conceptualizations of leadership and management, and on the importance attached to school effectiveness. The chapter seeks to establish how far current policy will produce schools which benefit from sound leadership and management or whether that policy agenda is 'full of sound and fury, signifying nothing'. The conclusion to this chapter, and to the book, suggests an alternative approach to planning in schools, based on a reconceptualization of management and leadership that moves away from the hierarchical, performance-driven managerial processes that masquerade as leadership towards a more dispersed, collaborative and less adversarial set of processes.

Strategic Planning in Education: Full of Sound and Fury, Signifying Nothing?

Introduction

This book has been concerned with the strategic, organizational and operational aspects of school management and leadership within the changing educational policy context over time. It concentrates on research carried out largely in schools in England. Chapter 1 argues that education policy has moved through a series of phases which have culminated in the Target Phase. In this phase current education policy, as far as it relates to school management, has come to encapsulate a range of activities associated with planning that now demand that staff in schools at the level of departments, faculties, curriculum areas and even individuals derive their own plans from the overall strategic plan for their school (e.g. DfES 2001a). Such planning has become the required way for schools to prepare for their future. The key issue therefore, is how far does this form of planning enable schools to be well-managed or is such strategic planning simply: 'a tale told by an idiot, full of sound and fury, signifying nothing' (*Macbeth* Act V, Scene v). In seeking to answer this question the chapter will consider the forms in which strategic planning has been adopted in schools in England and examine the conceptual assumptions and the fallacies that underpin the main form of planning currently required of schools. The chapter will then establish whether or not such planning can work in schools and conclude by suggesting an alternative approach to planning that is unlike strategic planning in that it is not based on conflict, competition and hierarchical management.

Strategy and strategic planning

What bloody man is this?
  (*Macbeth* Act I, Scene ii)

In part, the answer to the question about the value of strategic planning can be found embedded in the very concept of strategy itself. As Whipp (1998) points out, the term 'strategy' has military origins and is derived from the Greek word for generalship. Its meaning evolved to encompass a coherent set of actions, the plan, usually concealed from the enemy, intended to achieve a specific military objective. The strategy was to be implemented by using a series of tactics, immediate measures conducted in the presence of the opposition.

Strategy and the development of strategic planning now constitute an important weapon in the armoury of the modern manager. Strategy and planning have became inextricably linked.

At its simplest, strategic planning may be understood as an approach to establishing the long-term future of an organization and then moving that organization in an appropriate direction to achieve the future state to which its members, or at least its key members, aspire. As Schendel and Hofer note, strategic planning is concerned with: 'the entrepreneurial work of the organization, with organizational renewal and growth ... with developing and utilizing the strategy ... to guide the organization's operations' (Schendel and Hofer 1979, p. 11). As was suggested in Chapter 10, strategic planning is based on a series of actions based on an analysis of the organization's internal and external environments that are intended to achieve the targets set for that organization (Puffitt *et al.* 1992).

Strategic planning, based on an analysis of available information, is something an organization uses in order to establish its position in the world of competitive rivalry. It is what makes a firm unique, a winner or a survivor, and is intended to give an organization a competitive advantage over its rivals (Thomas 1993). Strategic planning, therefore, can best be understood as matching the activities of an organization to its environment and to its resource capabilities (Johnson and Scholes 1989). It has been argued that, in schools, developing strategy is a key management process, which draws together institutional values and goals and provides a framework for the quality of provision and the deployment of resources (Preedy *et al.* 1997). How far is this the case?

Strategy, planning and schools

Art thou but a false creation ...?
(*Macbeth* Act II, Scene ii)

Planning in schools over the last two decades has been categorized in a number of ways. For example, Wallace (1994) argues that at both regional and national level frameworks for planning have been produced based on cycles of review, planning and implementation. At institutional level, MacGilchrist *el al.* (1995) claimed that four different types of school plans could be identified: the rhetorical which had no credence within the school; the singular produced by the headteacher alone; the co-operative produced by a group of staff and focusing on finance and staff development; the corporate produced by the staff working together and focusing across an agreed range of the school's priorities. Neither of these typologies, however, takes into the account either the real nature of planning in schools or the extent to which such plans are determined by external factors. It can be argued, for example, that planning in English schools has been largely determined by policy and other environmental pressures external to the school and that such planning has taken at least four different forms, each of which may be regarded as strategic although each has a different emphasis.

1   *Planning at LEA level:* Before the Education Reform Act (DES 1988a) planning, insofar as it related to schools, was largely the province of local

education authorities. It consisted of staffing and resource management, allocating pupils to schools, seeking to match available places to projected pupil numbers, building and maintenance and, latterly, in-service provision. Planning at this level had little direct impact on the curriculum or upon the processes of teaching and learning and it carried with it very little accountability. Indeed most schools were seldom troubled by the need to consider events in the long or even the medium term (Bell 1998).

2 *School Development Plans:* With the increased devolution of responsibility for resource management to schools and the attempts to create an educational marketplace based on competition for pupil numbers came the second form of planning: school development planning, the first systematic attempt to establish strategic planning in schools. While no legislation was introduced to require schools to have a development plan, the Education Act 1987 (DES 1987b) did place a responsibility upon headteachers to define the aims and objectives of the school, to monitor and review the achievement of those aims and objectives, and to manage staff development. The Education Reform Act (DES 1988a) gave a further impetus to the deployment of strategic planning for school development. It linked the introduction of local financial management of schools, the delivery of the new National Curriculum and new patterns of accountability to the school development plan which thus became central to each school's resource management process. At the same time, schools had to respond to the publication of league tables of examination and test results and provide an annual report to parents on the progress of the school. School development plans seemed to provide a way of coping both with this accountability and with the resource management aspects of these new demands.

This view was reinforced in 1989 when the Department of Education and Science commissioned a research project to provide guidance for schools on development planning. The two booklets that resulted from this project were distributed to all schools. The emphasis in the first of these booklets was on staff in schools identifying and justifying their own priorities for change and demonstrating that, by marshalling resources appropriately, the changes had been successfully implemented (Hargreaves *et al.* 1989). By the time the second booklet appeared, the focus had changed somewhat. The purpose of school development plans was now to assist schools to introduce changes successfully, so that the quality of teaching and standards of learning were improved (Hargreaves and Hopkins 1991). Plans were to consist of a statement about key areas for development, set in the context of the school's aims and values, its existing achievements and national and LEA policies and initiatives. A year later, school development plans became one of the focal points of the new national inspection framework. Inspectors from Ofsted were required to make a judgement about the management of the schools through the quality of the school development plan, its usefulness as an instrument of change and development, its realism and the achievement of priorities set (Ofsted 1992). Largely as a result of their incorporation into the inspection process, development plans became the vehicle by which schools specified which improvements in teaching and/or learning were to be brought about. Their main function, however, was to provide a mechanism through which both parents and the Ofsted inspectors could hold staff in schools accountable for priority setting and the meeting of those priorities (Bell and Rhodes 1996).

3 *Business Planning:* At the same time, the original link between a development or strategic plan and the competitive nature of the environment remained as funding followed pupil numbers, schools were encouraged to recruit as many pupils as possible and parents were exhorted to exercise choice over the schools to which they sent their children. It was not merely coincidental that the emergence of development planning coincided with the political intention of the New Right to subject schools and colleges to the exigencies of the marketplace (Bell 1998). Schools, some seduced by the charms of grant-maintained status, were encouraged to adopt a more business-focused approach to their activities and to consider how they might market themselves more effectively, recruit pupils more aggressively and generate funding to support both core and extra-curricular activities. Thus, some schools were subjected to the third type of planning, business planning. This was often led, or at least encouraged, by boards of governors whose members were keen to introduce a more business-like approach to school management. It was certainly financially driven and supported by the Ofsted Inspection Framework (Ofsted 1992) that collected evidence on value for money:

> The need for greater financial planning has created what many schools now regard as a Business Plan. The importance of linking developments with financial planning cannot be over-estimated ... A business plan may be regarded as a fully costed development plan ... and ... give a clear outline of developments over a long time scale ... (Blows 1994, pp. 1–4)

The business plan, therefore, was intended to provide a rationale for resources deployed to meet both school development and individual needs.

4 *School Improvement Planning:* This emphasis on strategic planning in schools continued under the New Labour government after May 1997. The interpretation and use made of strategic planning by New Labour, insofar as it impacts on schools, was however different from that of the outgoing Conservative administration, as was shown in Chapter 1. For New Labour, the purpose of school-based strategic planning was to ensure that schools play a major role both in furthering the government's economic agenda to provide a workforce with appropriate skills and its social agenda to produce good citizens (Bell 1998). 'As well as securing our economic future, learning ... helps make ours a civilised society ... and promotes active citizenship. Learning enables people to play a full part in their community. It strengthens the family, the neighbourhood and consequently the nation' (DfEE 1998a, p. 7). Improving pupil and teacher performance was to be central to both these agendas. This was made clear from the outset: 'From September 1998, each school will be required to have challenging targets for improvement. The use in school of reliable and consistent performance analysis enables ... Headteachers to monitor the performance of classroom teachers' (DfEE 1997b, p. 26). Headteachers are central to this process of strategic planning. They are to lead and manage their school's improvement by using pupil data to set targets for even better performance while being subject to inspection and the

publication of inspection reports. This improvement in performance is concentrated on literacy and numeracy and is expressed in terms of national targets. Specific targets that inform the strategic planning in individual schools are set in conjunction with LEAs, but must move towards those set nationally.

As this target-driven approach to educational planning has been pursued by New Labour, a significant change has occurred in the nature of development planning itself. Schools are no longer expected simply to produce general development plans that focus on any aspect of the school's work that might be identified as a priority at that time. It is no longer sufficient for staff in schools to set their own targets and to be accountable for achieving them. School targets must be derived from national ones for similar schools. The plans into which these targets are incorporated must focus on strategies for bringing about curriculum change that will lead to improvements in pupil performance. All schools are now experiencing the fourth and most tightly focused form of strategic planning, school improvement planning, with its emphasis on the curriculum and the improvement of pupil attainment.

Plans to meet specific school improvement targets for pupil performance are now required. Much of the pedagogy that underpins these plans is expected to conform to centrally determined guidelines about teaching, especially in literacy and numeracy. LEAs are required to provide a range of support and guidance to help their schools achieve the improvement targets set (DfEE 1997b). This is underpinned by close management of teacher performance, the introduction of performance-related pay and the introduction of a new pay scale for advanced skills teachers. In addition, teachers now have to have their own targets for development set out in a personal performance plan. This improvement planning is predicated on the belief that the setting of targets provides a powerful way for schools to raise standards (Hopkins and Harris 1998). Strategic planning as encapsulated in the School Improvement Plan has now become the focus of Ofsted inspections, a mechanism for LEA monitoring and the vehicle for school improvement (Handscomb 2001).

Thus, the emphasis in strategic planning has shifted away from resource management, general accountability and enabling schools to take control of their own development. It has moved towards a specific concern with the curriculum and an explicit accountability for both pupil attainment and for the deployment of resources to achieve improvement targets for pupil performance. The purpose of planning in schools has now become that of ensuring that schools implement the initiatives that are devolved to them by central government. The responsibility of headteachers is now firmly focused on the search, through strategic planning, for enhanced school success to improve both institutional and individual test and examination scores, coupled with the management of teacher performance. Success or failure will not be determined by the operation of market forces but by the extent to which schools meet these predetermined performance targets. Strategic planning for improvement in schools, therefore, is perceived as central both to the implementation of the government's educational policy and to the success of its wider economic and social agenda. But is this confidence in the efficacy of this form of strategic planning justified, and who controls the strategic agenda?

School improvement as strategic planning in schools: three fallacies

What is't you do?
A deed without a name.
(*Macbeth* Act IV, Scene i)

The edifice of strategic planning in schools is based on three sets of fallacies that undermine its efficacy as a management technique for use in educational institutions. These take the form of erroneous assumptions about the nature of leadership and management in schools, about planning as a management technique and about definitions of school effectiveness.

1   *The leadership fallacy.* This derives from the conceptualizations of leadership and management upon which strategic planning in schools is predicated. The headteacher is presented as the locus of management expertise and the individual who carries the burden of responsibility for planning. Thus, headteachership is located within a hierarchical view of school management in which the headteacher is the solitary, heroic and accountable leader who personifies and exemplifies the totality of leadership skills and managerial competences (Bolman and Deal, 1991). This is, as Grace argues: 'a hierarchical form of executive leadership driven by the vision of the self-managed market orientated school' (Grace 1995, p. 313). Such has been the emphasis on the centrality of the role of the headteacher they are required to be: 'critical, transformative, visionary, educative, empowering, liberating, personally ethical, organizationally ethical, responsible' (Grace, 1995, pp. 156-7). If this list constitutes a description of the qualities of a headteacher, it also identifies a person who must seriously be considered for canonization as an educational saint (Grace 1995). This is the myth of the 'hero-innovator' reborn. It requires headteachers, perhaps supported by senior staff, to formulate a vision for the school and then translate this into action. Leadership involves the embodiment and articulation of this vision and its communication to others in the form of a strategic plan.

As Southworth (1999) has pointed out, this model of leadership is based on a concern for control, efficiency, performance of staff and measurable pupil outcomes. It is firmly rooted in the view that education is an integral part of social capital: 'Learning is the key to prosperity ... Investment in human capital will be the foundation of success in the knowledge economy' (DfEE 1998a, p. 7). This is a technical-rationalist approach to education that gives no consideration to the benefits of education other than economic utility (Bottery 2000). There is no notion of education as intrinsically good or aesthetically valuable. This rationale does not emphasize, or even include, the ethical dimensions of leadership and management that should inform the totality of school organization. In fact, matters related to the school as a social and moral organization, living with others in a diverse community and wider issues of social justice are largely ignored in the quest for a narrowly defined form of improvement. Thus the social and the moral are subordinate to the economic in the forms of leadership and management upon which strategic planning in our schools is now predicated.

The presentation of such forms of leadership and management as an appropriate way to conduct the planning process does not recognize the part played by individual teachers in implementing strategies for improvement, and fails to acknowledge the very real dilemmas that confront senior staff in schools. Central to these dilemmas is the extent to which successful planning in schools should be a collective rather than an individual responsibility which must take place at all three levels of management within the institution. There is a failure here to recognize that the vision and the mission at the strategic level are derived from overarching values and beliefs held, not only by the headteacher, but by the whole staff. Similarly, the realization of plans based on them requires a commitment from, and the involvement of, staff at the organizational and operational levels. If, at the strategic level of school management, planning involves translating the vision into broad aims and long-term plans, then it is at the organizational level that the strategic view is converted into medium-term objectives supported by the allocation of appropriate resources and the delegation of responsibility for decision making, implementation, review and evaluation. Here rests much of the managerial responsibility for translating strategy into actions that may produce significant school improvement and the collegial responsibility for supporting and developing colleagues to improve their own performance and enhance the learning of their pupils.

In turn, the implementation of these medium-term plans requires them to be further sub-divided into the totality of the delegated tasks that have to be carried out at the operational level. Here, resources are utilized, tasks completed, activities co-ordinated and monitored. It is at this level, in the classroom, where a collegial framework is most necessary and where those tasks that may bring about improvements in pupil achievement must be carried out. Thus, accountability, resource deployment and management and the responsibility for improvement are located here as much as at the previous two levels. The three levels of management, strategic, organizational and operational, must work in harmony towards a common purpose if strategic planning is to be successful. This will only happen if all members of the school community share the vision and if values are largely communal. Each level depends on the other two. To emphasize one and ignore the others is fundamentally to misunderstand the nature of school as organizations. Headteachers cannot manage schools alone nor can they carry the burden of motivating others to achieve objectives and complete tasks without significant support from colleagues. Headteachers and their staff must move towards inclusive forms of management and leadership that are collegial rather than hierarchical, holistic rather than fragmented and instrumental. The fundamental flaw in this conceptualization of strategic planning is that it leads to the over-emphasis on the role of the headteacher and, at the same time, is based on a narrowly conceptualized perception of leadership itself.

2 *The predictive fallacy*. This concerns the conceptualization of strategic planning itself. The essential purpose of strategic planning is to scan the environment in which the school operates, forecast the future for the school and then deploy resources in order to meet the predicted situation (Whipp 1998). Strategic decisions, therefore, evolve from analysis through planning to the achieving of objectives. Thus, strategic planning is predicated on being

able to predict the future of the school's environment. It assumes that realistic organizational objectives can be identified. It requires the ability to plan effectively and to exercise sufficient control or influence over the organization and its environment to ensure that planned outcomes can be achieved by the deployment and redeployment of available resources. Thus, strategic planning in schools, if it is to succeed, must be based on an analysis of both the present situation and possible future states. Such planning presupposes that senior staff in schools have the capacity to control the environment and not be controlled by it. Strategic planning demands that headteachers and teachers be proactive to the extent that they do not take the external environment to be immutable, but seek to influence and shape it by deploying resources to create change.

To achieve this it must be assumed that schools can be managed so as to respond in a rational way to environmental factors and that organizationally acceptable means and desired ends can be rationally linked. This implies that planning and implementation are orderly and sequential and that schools can be shaped and controlled in such a way as to avoid the unintended consequences of change while realizing strategic objectives. Mintzberg (1994) has drawn attention to the mistake of assuming that means and ends can be linked in this way, that significant changes in the environment can be predicted and that organizations can make rational choices about ways in which to respond to their environments. Quinn (1980) and Pettigrew (1973) have exploded the myth that strategic planning evolves in a neat linear progression from analysis to implementation. The rationality of their plans and the inherent power of their positions will be insufficient for senior managers to ensure that those plans can be successfully implemented (Quinn 1993). This is, at least in part, because decisions and choices are often not made by a careful matching of means to ends. As March and Olsen (1979) argue from their analysis of decision making in education, the linking of solutions to problems is frequently the result of oversight, accident, flight or loose association, none of which is either rational or strategic.

Furthermore, to treat organizational activity as a rational response to an analysis of the environment is to assume that there is a range of actions which match environmental circumstances and from which rational choices can be made. The fallacious nature of this position was noted by Puffitt *et al.* (1992) who pointed out that in most circumstances there are only a very limited number of options available to staff in schools, and by March and Olsen (1979) who demonstrated that although organizations do act within environmentally constrained boundaries, a similar environmental situation may produce a different organizational response and the same organizational action may produce different environmental outcomes at different times. Thus the planning model which underpins school development is defective because it is insufficiently responsive both to short and long-term changes in the environment.

3 *The effectiveness fallacy.* The current approach to strategic planning is derived from conceptualizations embedded in its ideological antecedents, namely school effectiveness. As Slee and Weiner point out: 'The effective schooling research, in conjunction with ... the school improvement movement has been adopted by policy-makers pursuant to the resolution of ... the

alleged crises in state education' (Slee and Weiner 1998, pp. 1-2). It is here, then, that the agenda for strategic planning in schools is set and its parameters defined. The problem is that the discourse of effective schooling and school improvement overstates what planning can achieve. This discourse is largely based on an extremely narrow set of criteria against which to identify the effect of schools on pupil performance, and tends to reduce learning to limited, discrete, assessable and comparable segments of academic knowledge; witness the emphasis on literacy, numeracy and little else in the current strategic targets which are set for schools (Slee and Weiner 1998). This is an extremely value-laden approach for, as Beare (2001) argues, once you have educational provision focused on:

> literacy and numeracy testing, competition among schools, rewards for schools with demonstrably good outcomes ... and a kind of excellence based on beating your peers ... there [is] not much enthusiasm for sentiment, human kindness ... respecting the worth of every person. (Beare 2001, p. 5)

Such reductionism makes simplistic assumptions about the nature and purposes of education. The strategic planning based on it suffers from an impoverished, mechanistic and narrow view of what counts as educational achievement, ignores the impact of context and disregards the effects of differential funding, school selection policies and, above all, social and economic disadvantage (Gray and Wilcox 1995).

In taking this stance, the school effectiveness discourse labels entire schools as good or bad after measuring them against conformity to disconnected criteria and brands entire institutions as failing or even pathological (Teddlie and Reynolds 2000) when the anticipated conformity is not observed. This is an inappropriate level of analysis. Identifying schools as good or bad, in effect treating them as units of analysis in themselves, is problematic because the dominant organizational entity within schools is the classroom and the main point of reference is either the age, stage or the subject. This aspect of the school effectiveness discourse fails to recognize that it is not necessarily the difference between schools that affects achievement most significantly but the differences within them (Lingard, Ladwig and Luke 1998). Even inspection reports confirm that in many failing schools, examples of good practice can be found. The sources of differential achievement within schools must be carefully considered (Gamoran and Berends 1987). School planning, if it is to contribute to sound school management, must pay far more attention to intra-school differences and less to inter-school comparisons through league tables and other differential performance indicators.

Perhaps the most significant weakness of all in the school-effectiveness discourse is the fundamental vacuum at its very core. It lacks any clear conceptual rationale that links the characteristics that commonly describe an effective school with a dynamic model of school leadership and management in such a way that it might be possible to explain the relationships between those characteristics and improved pupil performance. As Ouston (1998) has pointed out, the precise nature of the relationship between an effective headteacher, the classroom performance of an individual teacher and the learning of a particular child is largely ignored in the school effectiveness literature. New Labour policy in this regard rests largely on exhortation and a battery of tactics, the precise outcomes of which are, at best, indeterminate. A form of planning must be developed that makes planning possible in a complex and unpredictable environment. Planning for school improvement, therefore, should rest on a much more fundamental understanding of the nature of schools, the main features of appropriate management and leadership in those schools, and of the world in which schools exist than is the case at present.

Planning for the future: can strategic planning work in schools?

> *Stay you imperfect speakers, tell me more. Say from whence you owe this strange intelligence*
>
> (*Macbeth* Act I, Scene iii)

The world view on which much strategic planning is predicated is based on the Newtonian paradigm that presents the environment as a place of order, simplicity and conformity, where everything operates according to specific, knowable and predetermined rules. The world is perceived as an orderly place where the whole is equal to, but no greater than, the sum of its parts. This, in turn, means that all activities are predictable and controllable. The search for truth from such a world view is a search for the rules that order that world. Gaining knowledge is based on the identification of the discrete components that make up the whole. Learning, therefore, is rooted in deductive logic and dissection, so that the parts can be isolated and understood. In a hierarchically controlled organization this is an individualistic process that proceeds in a linear way through analysis and the construction of generalizations based on empirical evidence. The atomism, fragmentation and concern with predictability and control which shape this approach to strategic planning produce an underlying set of cognitive processes that are reductive, reactive and unable to cope with rapid change and uncertainty. This is because the cognitive processes which underpin this form of planning are rigid, inflexible and exclusive. Its outcomes, therefore, are merely the disjointed acquisition of disconnected elements of knowledge and the limited acquisition of context-specific competences.

Thus, strategic planning is reduced to the identification, by a small group of senior managers, of long-term goals and the one way to achieve them. Implementation rests with the majority, who had no part in its formulation. Strategic planning, as it exists in most contemporary organizations including schools, therefore, is based on the monopolization of power by a few and social relationships derived from modes of activity which are rooted in conflict, competition, hierarchy and social control as the prime determinants of social order. In an unpredictable, rapidly changing environment strategic planning of this sort is unhelpful as a way of enabling schools to prepare for the future. Such planning is not conducive to the sound management of groups of well-qualified, motivated professional teachers whose predominant concern is the welfare of the pupils in their care. It inhibits creativity and imaginative thinking. It fails to employ much of the talent in the organization and it cannot readily take account of forces emanating from the external environment in a period of rapid and extensive change (Zohar 1997). Such an approach to change through strategic planning in education is overly prescriptive and is based on the assumption that there is only one way to achieve improvement. It has taken the fun, the excitement and the creativity from what many of us do and has limited the horizons that we can offer to the children in our care by producing a narrow, examination-based curriculum.

In schools, the link between strategic planning and school management is made even more problematic by the operation of the very policy mechanisms that are meant to serve those working within educational institutions. The implementation of educational policies which seek to define the nature, scope and direction of such planning and which, ultimately, determine the strategies available for that implementation, make it difficult, if not impossible, for managers in schools to predict or exercise control over the future. The most important example of this is the breakdown in the government's own strategic planning which has led to a failure in adequate levels of teacher recruitment and supply (TES 2001). If headteachers are to manage schools successfully it must be possible for headteachers to recruit and retain a suitability qualified and motivated staff. If it is impossible for the government and its agencies to implement its own strategic policies, how can those responsible for school management be expected to plan strategically?

Thus the formulation and implementation of school improvement plans is constrained by the very policy context that shapes planning in schools and evaluates the success of that planning. It is based on an inadequate model which is linear and two dimensional (Forshaw 1998). As a result, the planning process focuses on either the immediate or the small scale while concentrating on maintenance functions rather than on considering alternatives and developing independent solutions to difficult, long-term problems. So complex has the world become that it can be argued that those responsible for strategic planning in schools have little chance of knowing sufficient about the environment, even if they wished to do so. Making accurate predictions on which to base planning becomes an almost impossible task. The rate and impact of technological change, the extent of social change, the speed of political change and the global influences on local environments combine to make it impossible for schools to have a complete understanding of their environments. This, in turn, means that the knowledge base on which school improvement planning can be based is totally inadequate (Davies 1998). Strategic planning as a management technique for staff in schools, therefore, is deeply flawed, based on inappropriate assumptions about the nature and purpose of education, and founded on an ill-conceived model of schools as organizations and the management of those schools. It is unlikely, then, to make a useful contribution to the processes of school management. It is indeed, full of sound and fury that has little significance. As Wheatley (1999) has argued:

> For many years ... we have invested in the planning process derived from Newtonian beliefs. How many schools made significant and consistent progress because of elaborate and costly strategic plans? ...

Instead of the ability to analyse and predict, we need to be better, faster learners from what has just happened. Agility and intelligence are required ... (Wheatley 1999, p. 38)

Does this mean that all attempts to develop insights into the future should be abandoned? Clearly not, since schools, like other organizations, cannot be left to drift aimlessly on a turbulent sea of change. How then, might the future be addressed?

Planning in schools: a way forward

I ... wish the estate o' the world were now undone
(Macbeth Act V, Scene v)

As Handy (1995) has argued, we are faced with an unpredictable world in which the only certainty is uncertainty. Such an environment requires an approach to planning which can be based not on a set of immutable, externally imposed targets, but on reaching agreement on a series of short-term objectives derived from negotiated and shared common values (Bell 1999a). It needs to take into account the nature of the questions that may be asked about the future while recognizing that the answers to them may be either unknown or unknowable. It has to be recognized that in coping with the new future, important information may not be available, important alternatives may be ignored and important possible outcomes neglected. The capacity to retain a distinct separation between means and ends and to rely on the linear relationship between them is greatly reduced in this new environment. Thus, plans will not be made and implemented. Rather, they will be made and remade endlessly as the school proceeds through a process of successive approximations to agreed objectives derived from policy, both of which may change before being achieved. Lindblom (1959) termed this approach to policy formulation and planning the 'Science of Muddling Through' while Pinchot (1985) called it 'Intrapreneurship' and Wallace (1994) saw it as 'rationalistic flexibility based on pragmatic contingency'.

This approach to planning is an extremely sophisticated form of responding to unknown and perhaps unknowable organizational futures. It locates the capacity to respond rapidly to changing situations within an agreed view of what might be possible, based on a series of incremental responses to external change. It requires a coherent sense of purpose that does not rest on the fruitless pursuit of vision or targets (Hargreaves 1994). In order for such an approach to planning to succeed, however, there must be an agreement within the school about basic values and broadly acceptable means which are not rooted in the traditional hierarchical management model with its rule-bound inflexibilities and emphasis on the separation of functions. Work relationships must move towards being less hierarchical, more multi-functional and holistic, based on a wider distribution of power within the organization. Whole-school perspectives must be developed. These are too important to be left to a small group of staff, however senior. It will then be seen that there are many ways of getting things done, each of which may be equally legitimate and that co-operation, responsiveness, flexibility and partnership must replace our present inflexible structures. This is a most difficult but a most exciting challenge.

To succeed in the reformulation of planning at school level will require a different mindset, perhaps similar to that based on the distinction between connected and separated modes of knowing developed through an investigation into problem solving by women in management positions in schools (Tarule 1998). Separated knowing is Newtonian. It seeks objectivity, is abstract, adversarial, critical, exclusive and detached from personal relationships. It is inherent in strategic planning. As Wheatley suggests, however: 'There is no objective reality out there waiting to reveal its secrets. There is only what we create through our engagement with others and events' (Wheatley 1999, p. 7). If this is the case, then the world for which we all seek to plan is neither predictable nor controllable. Rather, it is the product of our shared understandings and interactions with our environment. It is from this starting point that planning must evolve. Such planning should be based on connected knowing, a collaborative process of looking for what is right, through sharing rather than competition, and by accepting the validity of a range of different perspectives. Meanings are constructed and developed through reasoning with others and through narratives rather than analysis. These take place within inclusive and communal relationships, the foundation of which is a commonality of experiences, not a defence of differences. Knowledge, therefore, is distributed, shared and circulated throughout the school, not located in the office of the headteacher or a cadre of senior staff. Such connected knowledge and the processes inherent within it provide a foundation on which flexible yet inclusive policy formulation, based on different but shared values and perspectives, can be developed.

The emphasis will be on holistic relationships and policies which focus on integration rather than fragmentation, recognize that the sum is greater than the parts and celebrate the imaginative and the experimental. The mode of discourse will shift from debate to a dialogue which focuses on finding out rather than knowing, on questions not answers, which proceeds through listening not criticizing, sharing rather than winning and losing, and exploring new possibilities not defending established positions. The cognitive processes which support this approach are such that they enable each individual to make a distinctive contribution within a flexible framework rather than expecting a series of limited contributions, the sum of which make up the predetermined whole. Issues will be addressed, reinterpreted, readdressed and redefined in the light of communal understandings and common knowledge.

Planning, therefore, will become a shared, incremental and flexible process that is based on the creation, monitoring and the continual adjustment of plans for the short, medium and longer term (Wallace 1994). Planning may be updated whenever new information comes to light or unpredicted circumstances occur. Such information and circumstances may have different implications for different aspects of the school organization. This may mean that parts of the school may change at different rates from each other, one department developing while another is stable, thus limiting innovation fatigue. Management of the three levels of school organization will also change. At the strategic level there will be much more emphasis on the collaborative revision of the overall plan. At the organizational level there will be far more opportunities for differential implementation of aspects of the plan between parts of the school and a greater concern for collegial support, while at the operational level the plan will be reviewed frequently in the light of continually changing circumstances and resource constraints. Schools may thus become loosely coupled in the sense that freedom and autonomy allows for such different rates of development within the overall framework of the institution (Marion 1999). In many ways, it will require school leaders and managers to experience 'walking between two worlds' (Fitzgerald 2006, p. 210) where the terrain is complicated and contested.

Such an approach to strategic planning is far removed from the bureaucratic, linear, rational, positivist methods rooted in the unequal distribution of power and a belief in the sanctity of order and control, on which the deployment of strategic planning in schools is currently based. It requires a new form of leadership predicated on openness, collaboration and power sharing, where flexibility, creativity, imagination and responsiveness can flourish and genuine accountability for school improvement can exist. If this can be achieved then planning for school improvement may be successfully linked to good management practices, such that educational purposes based on the experiences of the wider membership of the school can shape the school planning processes and not the other way round. Indeed, it may even be possible for staff in schools to eliminate the sound and fury of planning and to replace the nothingness with something much more positive so that we can all say to policy makers, beware for:

Birnham Wood be come to Dunsinane
        (*Macbeth* Act V, Scene vii)

Bibliography

Adamson, S. (1998), *Education Action Zones: How to Apply: Guidance on Completing the Form*. DfEE: London.

Alexander, R., Rose, J. and Woodhead, C. (1992), *Curriculum Organization and Classroom Practice in Primary Schools: a Discussion Paper*. London: Department for Education and Science.

Ball, S. (1992), 'Changing management and the management of change', paper presented at the Annual Meeting of the American Educational Research Association, San Francisco, April.

—— (1993), 'Education policy, power relations and teachers' work', *British Journal of Educational Studies*, 41 (2), 106-21.

—— (1994), *Education Reform: a Critical and Post-structural Approach*. Buckingham: Open University Press.

—— (1999), 'Labour, learning and the economy, a policy sociology perspective', *Cambridge Journal of Education*, 29 (2), 195-206.

Banks, O. (1976), *The Sociology of Education*. London: Batsford.

Barber, M. (1996), *The Learning Game: Arguments for an Education Revolution*. Victor Gollancz: London.

—— (1999), 'Teachers' place in the big picture', *Times Educational Supplement*, 12 February, p. 17.

Baron, G. and Howell, D.A. (1974), *The Government and Management of Schools*. London: Athlone Press.

Baron, G. and Taylor, W. (eds), (1969), *Educational Administration and the Social Sciences*. London: Athlone Press.

Bass B.M. and Alvolio, B.J. (1993), 'Transformational leadership: a response to critics', in M.M. Chemers and R. Ayman (eds), *Leadership Theory and Research: Perspectives and Directions*. San Diego: Academic Press.

Beare, H. (2001), *Creating the Future School: Student Outcomes and the Reform of Education*. London: Routledge Falmer.

Beckhofer, F. (1974), 'Current approaches to empirical research - some central ideas', in J. Rex (ed.), *Approaches to Sociology: an Introduction to Major Trends in British Sociology*. London: Routledge and Kegan Paul.

Bell, D. and Ritchie, R. (1999), *Towards Effective Subject Leadership in the Primary School*. Buckingham: Open University Press.

Bell, L. (1980), 'The school as an organization: a re-appraisal', *British Journal of Sociology of Education* 1 (2), 183-93.

—— (1985), 'An investigation of a new role in schools: the case of the TVEI co-ordinator', in T. Simkins (ed.), *Research in the Management of Secondary Education, Sheffield Polytechnic Papers in Educational Management, (59)*. Sheffield: Sheffield City Polytechnic.

—— (1987), 'The school as an organization: a re-appraisal' in A. Westoby (ed.), *Culture and Power in Educational Organization: a Reader*. Milton Keynes: Open University Press.

—— (1988), 'Technical and vocational educational initiative: criticism, innovation and response', in L. Bondi and M.H. Matthew (eds), *Education and Society: Studies in the Politics, Sociology and Geography of Education*. London: Routledge.

—— (1989a), 'Ambiguity models and secondary schools: a case study', in T. Bush (ed.), *Managing Education: Theory and Practice*. Milton Keynes: Open University Press.

—— (1989b), *Management Skills in Primary Schools*, London: Routledge.

—— (1992), *Managing Teams in Secondary Schools*, London: Routledge.

—— (1994a), 'Research on school amalgamation: some broad perspectives on the Oakfield School Project', in T. Maddocks and J. Woods (eds), *Theory, Research and Action in Educational Administration*. Victoria: ACEA Pathways Series: Australian Council for Educational Administration.

—— (1994b) 'When worlds collide: school culture, imposed change and teacher's work', in F. Crowther, F. Caldwell, J. Chapman, G. Lakomski and D. Ogilvie (eds), *The Workplace in Education: Australian Perspectives. First Yearbook of the Australian Council for Education Administration*. Sydney: Edward Arnold.

—— (1996), 'Educational management, some issues of policy and practice', Inaugural Professorial Lecture, Liverpool: Liverpool John Moores University.

—— (1998), 'The quality of markets is not strain'd. It droppeth as the gentle rain from Heaven upon the place beneath: Primary schools in the education marketplace', paper presented at the American Education Research Association Conference, San Diego, April.

—— (1999a), 'Back to the future, the development of education policy in England', *Journal of Educational Administration*, 37 (3 & 4), 200-28.

—— (1999b), 'Primary schools and the nature of the education marketplace', in T. Bush, L. Bell, R. Bolam, R. Glatter and P. Ribbins (eds), *Educational Management: Redefining Theory, Policy and Practice*. London: Paul Chapman Publishing.

—— (2000), 'The management of staff: some issues of efficiency and cost-effectiveness' in L. Anderson, and M. Coleman (eds), *Managing Finance and Resources in Education*. London: Paul Chapman Publishing.

—— (2001), 'Cross-curriculum co-ordination' in N. Burton and D. Middlewood (eds), *Managing the Curriculum*. London: Paul Chapman Publishing.

—— (2002), 'Strategic planning and school management: full of sound and fury, signifying nothing?' *Journal of Educational Administration*, 40 (5), 407-24.

—— (2004a), 'Throw physic to the dogs. I'll none of it! Human capital and educational policy: an analysis', paper presented at the Athens Institute for Education and Research 6th International Conference on Education, Athens, Greece, May 2004.

—— (2004b), 'Visions of primary headship', *Primary Headship*, June, 8–9.

—— (2006), 'Five models of schools as organizations: summary document', unpublished monograph: University of Leicester, Centre for Educational Leadership and Management.

Bell, L. and Halpin, D. (2000), 'Primary heads, governors and institutional autonomy' in K. Stott and V. Trafford (eds), *Partnerships: Shaping the Future of Education*. London: Middlesex University Press.

Bell, L. and Hodge, S. (1990), *The Final Evaluation Report of the Powys TVEI Pilot Project*. Department of Education, University of Warwick.

Bell, L. and Rhodes, C. (1996), *The Skills of Primary School Management*. London: Routledge.

Bell, L. and Rowley, A. (2002), 'The impact of educational policy on headship in primary schools in England, 1994–2001', *Journal of Educational Administration*, 40 (3), 195–210.

Bell, L. and Stevenson, H. (2006), *Education Policy: Process, Themes and Impact*. London: Routledge.

Bell, L., Bolam, R. and Cubillo, L. (2003), *A Systematic Review of the Impact of School Headteachers and Principals on School Performance. Review Conducted by the School Leadership Review Group (EPPI-Centre Review)*. London: EPPI-Centre, Social Science Research Unit, Institute of Education.

Bell, L., Halpin, D. and Neill, S. (1996a), 'Managing self governing primary schools in the local authority, grant maintained and private sectors', *Educational Management and Administration*, 24 (2), 253–61.

—— (1996b), 'Management and the marketplace: perspectives from primary headteachers', paper presented to the British Educational Management and Administration Society Research Conference, Cambridge, July.

Beynon, J. (1985), 'Institutional change and career histories in a comprehensive school', in S.J. Ball and I.F. Goodson (eds), *Teachers' Lives and Careers*. Lewes: Falmer Press.

Bidewell, E. (1965), 'The school as a formal organization', in J.G. March (ed.), *Handbook of Organizations*. London: Rand-McNally.

Bird, A. and Bell, L. (1999), 'The culture of school management; an infant school experience', in H. Gunter, H. Tomlinson and P. Smith, *Living Headship: Voices, Values and Vision*. London: Paul Chapman Publishing.

Blair, T. (1998), *The Government's Annual Report 1997–98*. London: The Stationery Office.

—— (2002) 'A second term to put secondary schools first', *The Times*, 5 September.

Blows, M. (1994), *Whole School Planning: a Practical Guide to Development and Business Planning for Schools*. Dudley: Local Education Authority Advisory Service.

Bobbit, F. (1913), 'Some general principles of management applied to the problems of city school systems', in *The Supervision of City Schools*. Chicago: University of Chicago.

Boisot, M. (1995), 'Preparing for turbulence: the changing relationship between strategy and management development in the learning organization', in B. Garret (ed.), *Developing Strategic Thought: Rediscovering the Art of Direction-giving*. London: McGraw-Hill.

Bolam, R. (1997), 'Changes in educational management training', paper presented to the First ESRC Seminar: Redefining Educational Management, Leicester, June.

—— (2002), 'Professional development and professionalism', in T. Bush and L. Bell (eds), *The Principles and Practice of Educational Management*. London: Paul Chapman Publishing.

Bolman, L.G. and Deal, T.E. (1991), *Reframing Organizations: Artistry, Choice and Leadership*. San Francisco: Jossey-Bass.

Bottery, M. (1992), *The Ethics of Educational Management: Personal, Social and Political Perspectives on School Organization*. London: Cassell.

—— (1998), ' "Rowing the Boat" and "Riding the Bicycle" – Metaphors for school management and policy on the late 1990s', paper presented to the Third ESRC Seminar: Redefining Education Management, Open University: Milton Keynes.

—— (1999), 'Education under the new modernizers, an agenda for centralization, illiberalism and inequality?', *Cambridge Journal of Education*, 29 (2), 103–20.

—— (2000), *Ethics, Policy and Education*. London: Continuum.

Boyle, E. (1963), *The Newsom Report*. London: HMSO.

Brennan, W.K. (1982), *Special Education in Mainstream Schools*. Stratford-upon-Avon: National Council for Special Education.

Bridges, D. (1994), 'Parents: customers or partners?', in D. Bridges and T.H. McLaughlin (eds), *Education and the Marketplace*. London: Falmer Press.

Bubb, S., Realey, P. and Ahtaridou, E. (2006), 'The self-evaluation form in the changing educational landscape of educational leadership: how are schools completing it and is it helping?' Paper presented to the British Educational Leadership, Management and Administration Society Annual Conference, The Changing Landscape of Educational Leadership and Management, Aston, Birmingham, 6 October.

Bullock Report (1975), *Committee of Inquiry into Reading and the Use of English*. London: HMSO.

Bullock, A. and Thomas, H. (1997), *Schools at the Centre? A Study of Decentralization*. London: Routledge.

Burgess, R. (1986), *Sociology, Education and Schools: an Introduction to the Sociology of Education*. London: Batsford.

Burgess, T. (1992), 'Accountability with confidence', in T. Burgess (ed.), *Accountability in Schools*. Harlow: Longman.

Bush, T. (1989), (ed.), *Managing Education: Theory and Practice*. Milton Keynes: Open University Press.

—— (1995), *Theories of Educational Management*. London: Paul Chapman Publishing.

—— (2002), 'Educational management: theory and practice', in T. Bush and L. Bell (eds), *The Principles and Practice of Educational Management*. London: Paul Chapman Publishing.

Bush, T., Bell, L., Bolam, R., Glatter, R. and Ribbins, P. (1999), (eds), *Educational Management, Redefining Theory, Policy and Practice*. London: Paul Chapman Publishing.

Busher, H. and Harris, A. (1999), 'Leadership of school subject areas: tensions and dimensions of managing the middle', *School Leadership and Management*, 19 (3), 305-17.

—— (2000), *Leading Subject Areas: Improving Schools*. London: Paul Chapman Publishing.

Caldwell, B. (1992), 'The principal as leader of the self-managing school in Australia', *Journal of Educational Administration*, 30 (3), 6-19.

—— (1997), 'The future of public education: a policy for lasting reform', *Educational Management and Administration*, 25 (4), 357-70.

—— (2002), 'Autonomy and self-management: concepts and evidence', in T. Bush and L. Bell (eds), *The Principles and Practice of Educational Management*. London: Paul Chapman Publishing.

Caldwell, B. and Spinks, J. (1988), *The Self-Managing School*. London: Falmer Press.

—— (1992), *Leading the Self-Managing School*. London: Falmer Press.

—— (1998), *Beyond the Self-Managing School*. London: Falmer Press.

Campbell, R. (1985), *Developing the Primary School Curriculum*. London: Holt, Rinehart and Winston.

—— (1989), 'The Education Reform Act 1988: some implications for curriculum decision-making in primary schools', in M. Preedy (ed.), *Approaches to Curriculum Management*. Milton Keynes: Open University Press.

Central Advisory Council for Education (1967), *Children and their Primary Schools (The Plowden Report)*. London: HMSO.

Centre for Policy Studies (1988), 'Advice to the Education Secretary' in J. Haviland, (ed.), *Take Care Mr Baker!* London: Fourth Estate.

Chan, D. (2002), *How Primary School Principals Manage Strategic Planning: a Comparative Study between Hong Kong and England. A Report for the National College of School Leadership*. Leicester: University of Leicester, Centre for Educational Management and Leadership.

Charoenwongsak, K. (1998), 'Higher-value products and better education seen as vital', *Bangkok Post*, 25 November p. 2.

Cheng, Y. (1999), 'Recent educational developments in South East Asia', *School Effectiveness and Improvement*, 10 (1), 3-30.

—— (2000), 'Educational change and development in Hong Kong: effectiveness, quality and relevance', in T. Townsend and Y. Cheng (eds), *Educational Change and Development in the Asia-Pacific Region: Challenges for the Future*. Lisse: Swets and Zeitlinger.

Clayton, T. (1989), 'The role and management of welfare assistants', in T. Bowers (ed.), *Managing Special Needs*. Milton Keynes: Open University.

—— (1993), 'From domestic helper to "assistant teacher" - the changing role of the British classroom assistant', *European Journal of Special Educational Needs*, 8 (1), 11-23.

Cohen, M.D. and March, J.D. (1974), *Leadership and Ambiguity: the American College President*. New York: McGraw-Hill.

Cohen, M.D., March, J.G. and Olsen, J.P. (1972), 'A garbage can model of organizational choice', *Administrative Science Quarterly*, 17, 1-25.

Coleman, M. and Earley, P. (2005), *Leadership and Management in Education: Cultures, Change and Context*. Oxford: Oxford University Press.

Coleman, M., Middlewood, D. and Bush, T. (1995), *Managing the Curriculum in Secondary Schools.* Northampton: Educational Management Development Unit, University of Leicester.

Cox, C.B. and Dyson, A.E. (eds), (1969), *Fight for Education: a Black Paper.* London: Critical Science Quarterly.

Crozier, G. (1998), 'Parents and schools: partnership or surveillance?', *Journal of Educational Policy*, 13 (1), 125-36.

Cuthbert, R. (1985), 'Do we get value for money from value for money studies?' in *Value for Money in Further Education - Combe Lodge Report*, 18 (1), 5-11.

Cyert, R.M. and March, J.G. (1963), *A Behavioural Theory of the Firm.* Englewood Cliffs: Prentice Hall.

Davies, B. (1998), *Leadership in Schools: Inaugural Lecture.* Lincoln: University of Lincolnshire and Humberside.

Davies, B. and Ellison. L. (1999), *Strategic Direction and Development of the School.* London: Routledge.

Davies, B. and Ellison, L. (eds), (1997), *School Leadership for the 21st Century.* London: Routledge.

Davies, L. (1990), *Equity and Efficiency? School Management in an International Context.* Lewes: Falmer Press.

Deal, T. (1988), 'The symbolism of effective schools', in A. Westoby, *Culture and Power in Educational Organizations.* Milton Keynes: Open University Press.

Deal, T. and Kennedy, A. (1983), 'Culture and school performance', *Educational Leadership*, 40 (5), 11-14.

Deem, R. (1993), 'Educational reform and school governing bodies in England 1986-1992; old dogs, new tricks or new dogs, new tricks?' in M. Preedy, (ed.), *Managing the Effective School.* London: Paul Chapman/Open University.

Deem, R., Brehony, K. and Heath, S. (1995), *Active Citizenship and the Governing of Schools.* Buckingham: Open University Press.

Deem, R., Brehony, K. and Hemming, S. (1992), 'Social justice, social divisions and the governing of schools', in D. Gill and B. Mayor (eds), *Racism and Education: Structures and Strategies.* London: Sage.

DES (1977a), *Ten Good Schools.* London: HMSO.

—— (1977b), *Education in Schools: a Consultative Document* (Green Paper). London: HMSO.

—— (1977c), *Educating our Children: Four Subjects for Debate.* London: HMSO.

—— (1979), *A Framework for the School Curriculum.* London: HMSO.

—— (1981), *The Secondary Curriculum 11-16, a Report on Progress.* London: HMSO.

—— (1983), *Teaching Quality.* London: HMSO.

—— (1985a), *Better Schools.* London: HMSO.

—— (1985b), *Quality in Schools: Evaluation and Appraisal.* London: HMSO.

—— (1985c), *Education Observed 3: Good Teachers.* London: HMSO.

—— (1986), *The Education Act.* London: HMSO.

—— (1987a), *The Education (School Teachers' Pay and Conditions) Order.* London: HMSO.

—— (1987b), *The Education Act*. London: HMSO.

—— (1988a), *The Education Reform Act*. London: HMSO.

—— (1988b), *Circular 7/88. The Education Reform Act: Local Management of Schools*. London: HMSO.

—— (1991), *The Education (School Teacher Appraisal) Regulations*. London: HMSO.

Devlin, T. (1989), 'Planning an effective public relations programme', in J. Sayer and V. Williams (eds), *School External Relations*. London: Cassell.

DfE (1992), *Choice and Diversity: a New Framework for Schools*. Cardiff: Welsh Office.

DfEE (1997a), *Excellence in Schools*. London: The Stationery Office.

—— (1997b), *From Targets to Action: Guidance to Support Effective Target-setting in Schools*. London: The Stationery Office.

—— (1997c), *Extending Opportunity: a National Framework for Study Support*. London: The Stationery Office.

—— (1998a), *Teachers: Meeting the Challenge of Change. A Green Paper*. London: The Stationery Office,

—— (1998b), *Excellence for all Children: Green Paper on Special Educational Needs*. London: The Stationery Office.

—— (1998c), *The National Literacy Strategy*. London: The Stationery Office.

—— (1998d), *The Implementation of the National Numeracy Strategy*. London: The Stationery Office.

—— (1998e), *Teachers: Meeting the Challenge of Change: Technical Consultation Document on Pay and Performance Management*. London: The Stationery Office.

—— (2000a), *Performance Management in Schools; Performance Management Framework*. London: The Stationery Office.

—— (2000b), *Performance Management in Schools: Guidance Note*. London: DfEE.

DfES (2001a), *Schools Achieving Success*. London: The Stationery Office.

—— (2001b), *The Teaching Standards Framework*. London: The Stationery Office.

—— (2001c), *Statutory Instrument 2001 No: 2855 Education (School Teacher Appraisal), (England), Regulations 2001*. Online. Available HTTP: www.legislation.hmso.gov.uk/si2001/20012855.htm#5 (accessed 3 August 2004).

—— (2003), *Excellence and Enjoyment: a Strategy for Primary Schools*. London: DfES Publications.

—— (2005), *School Teachers' Pay and Conditions Document*. London: The Stationery Office.

DTI (1994), *Competitiveness Helping Business to Win*. London: HMSO.

Dimmock, C. (1995), 'School leadership. securing quality teaching and learning', in C.W. Evers and J.D. Chapman (eds), *Educational Administration: an Australian perspective*. Sydney: Allen and Unwin.

Doughty, J. (1998), 'The changing role of the secondary school headteacher', unpublished Ph.D. thesis, University of Leicester.

Downes, P. (1988), (ed.), *Local Financial Management in Schools*. Oxford: Blackwell.

Dreeben, R. (1973), 'The school as a workplace', in J. Ozga (ed.), (1990),

Schoolwork: Approaches to the Labour Process of Teaching. Milton Keynes: Open University Press.

Duffy, M. (1988), 'The school curriculum', in D. Firth (ed.), *School Management in Practice*. Harlow: Longman.

Duigan, P. (1987), 'Leaders as cultural builders', *Unicorn*, 13 (4), 208–10.

Education Department (2000), *Transforming Schools into Dynamic and Accountable Professional Learning Communities: School-based Management Consultation Document*. Hong Kong: Advisory Committee on School-based Management.

Edwards, E. (1999), 'A study of the development of the specialist teacher assistant scheme (STA), in England', unpublished draft Ph.D. thesis, Liverpool John Moores University.

Edwards, W. (1991), 'Accountability and autonomy: dual strands for the administrator', in W. Walker, R. Farquhar and M. Hughes (eds), *Advancing Education: School Leadership in Action*. London: Falmer Press.

Egan, K. (1999), 'Education's three old ideas and a better idea', *Journal of Curriculum Studies*, 31 (3), 257–67.

Elmore, R.F. (1996), 'Getting to scale with good educational practice', *Harvard Educational Review*, 66 (1), 1–26.

Etzioni, A. (1964), *Modern Organizations*. Englewood Cliffs: Prentice Hall.

—— (1997), *The New Golden Rule*. London: Profile Books.

Fergusson, R. (1994), 'Managerialism in education', in J. Clarke, A. Cochrane and E. McLaughlin. (eds), *Managing Social Policy*. London: Sage.

—— (2000), 'Modernizing managerialism in education', in J. Clarke, S. Gewirtz and E. McLaughlin (eds), *New Managerialism New Welfare?* London: Sage.

Ferlie, E., Ashburner, L., Fitzgerald, L. and Pettigrew, A. (1996), *The New Public Management in Action*. Oxford: Oxford University Press.

Fidler, B. (2002), 'Strategic leadership and cognition', in K. Leithwood and P. Hallenger (eds), *Second International Handbook of Educational Leadership and Administration*. Norwell, MA: Kluwer Academic Publishers.

Field, K., Holden, P. and Lawlor, H. (2000), *Effective Subject Leadership*. London: Routledge.

Finn, B. (1991), *Young People's Participation in Post-Compulsory Education and Training*. Report of the Australian Education Council Review Committee, Melbourne: Australian Education Council.

Fitzgerald, T. (2006), 'Walking between two worlds: indigenous women and educational leadership' in *Educational Management, Administration and Leadership*, 34 (2), 201–13.

Forshaw, J. (1998), 'Establishing a planning framework for Rhyddings School for the year 2000 and beyond', *School Leadership and Management*, 18 (4), 485–96.

Foskett, N. (1998), 'Linking market to strategy', in D. Middlewood and J. Lumby (eds), *Strategic Management in Schools and Colleges*. London: Paul Chapman Publishing.

—— (2003), 'Market policies, management and leadership in school', in B.

Davies and J. West-Burnham, *Handbook of Educational Leadership and Management*. London: Pearson Longman.

Foucault, M. (1977), *Discipline and Punish: the Birth of the Prison*. Harmondsworth: Penguin.

Friedman, M. and Friedman, R. (1980), *Free to Choose*. New York: Harcourt, Brace and Jovanovich.

Fullan, M. (1993), *Change Forces: Probing the Depths of Educational Reform*, London: Falmer Press.

Fullan, M. and Hargreaves, A. (1992), *What is Worth Fighting for in Your School?* Milton Keynes: Open University Press.

Gamoran, A. and Berends, M. (1987), 'The effects of stratification in secondary schools: synthesis of survey and ethnographic research', *Review of Educational Research*, 57 (4), 415-35.

Gaskell, J. (2002), 'School choice and educational leadership: rethinking the future of public schooling', in K. Leithwood and P. Hallinger (eds), *Second International Handbook of Educational Leadership and Administration*. Norwell, MA: Kluwer Academic Publishers.

Gewirtz, S. (2002), *The Managerial School: Post-welfarism and Social Justice in Education*. London: Routledge.

Gewirtz, S., Ball, S. and Bowe, R. (1995), *Markets, Equity and Choice*. Buckingham: Open University Press.

Glatter, R. (1972), *Management Development for the Education Profession*. London: Harrap.

— (1977), 'Foreword', in B. Baron *The Managerial Approach to Tertiary Education: a Critical Analysis*. Studies in Education 7, London: University of London Institute of Education.

Glatter, R. and Woods, P.A. (1995), 'Parental choice and school decision-making: operating in a market-like environment', in A.K.C. Wong and K.M. Cheng (eds), *Educational Leaders and Change*. Hong Kong: Hong Kong University Press.

Glatter, R., Woods, P. and Bagley, C. (eds), (1997), *Choice and Diversity in Schooling: Perspectives and Prospects*. London: Routledge.

Gleeson, D. (1987), 'General introduction: TVEI and secondary education', in D. Gleeson (ed.) *TVEI and Secondary Education*. Milton Keynes: Open University Press.

Gleeson, D. and Shain, F. (2003), 'Managing ambiguity in further education', in N. Bennett, M. Crawford and M. Cartwright (eds), *Effective Educational Leadership*. London: Paul Chapman Publishing.

Goldring, E. (1997), 'Parental involvement and school choice: Israel and the United States', in R. Glatter, P. Woods and C. Bagley (eds), *Choice and Diversity in Schooling: Perspectives and Prospects*. London: Routledge.

Goode, J. (1982), 'The development of effective home school programmes – a study of parental perspectives in the process of schooling', unpublished M.Phil. thesis, University of Nottingham.

Grace, G. (1995), *School Leadership: Beyond Educational Management: an Essay in Policy Scholarship*. London: Falmer Press.

— (1997), 'Politics, markets, and democratic schools: on the transformation of school leadership', in A.H. Halsey, H. Lauder, P. Brown and A.S. Wells (eds), *Education, Culture, Economy and Society*. London: Oxford University Press.

Graham, D. with Tytler, D. (1993), *A Lesson for Us All: the Making of the National Curriculum*. London: Routledge.

Gray, J. and Wilcox. B. (1995), *Good School, Bad School*. Buckingham: Open University Press.

Green, A. (1999), 'Education and globalization in Europe and East Asia: convergent and divergent trends', *Journal of Educational Policy*, 14 (1), 55–72.

Gronn, P. (1996), 'From transactions to transformations: a new world order in the study of leadership', *Educational Management and Administration*, 24 (1), 7–30.

Hacker, R. and Rowe, M. (1998), 'A longitudinal study of the effects of implementing a National Curriculum Project upon classroom practices', *Journal of Curriculum Studies*, 9 (1), 95–103.

Hall, V. (1997), 'Managing staff', in B. Fidler, S. Russell and T. Simkins (eds), *Choices for Self Managing Schools*, London: Paul Chapman Publishing.

Hallinger, P., Chantarapanya, P., Sriboonma, U. and Kantamara, P. (2000), 'The challenge of educational reform in Thailand: *Jing Jai, Jing Jung and Nae Norn*', in T. Townsend and Y.C. Cheng (eds), *Educational Change and Development in the Asia-Pacific Region: Challenges for the Future*. Lisse: Swets and Zeitlinger.

Hampden-Turner, C. (1997), 'Globalization/global values: two concepts of globalizing value', paper presented at 'New Paradigms in Human Resource Development', 26th International Federation of Training and Development Organizations, Kuala Lumpur, 28–30 October.

Handscomb, G. (2001), 'Flexible Planning', *Managing Schools Today*, June/July, 30–3.

Handy, C. (1984), *Taken for Granted? Understanding Schools as Organizations*. London: Longman.

—— (1995), *The Empty Raincoat: Making Sense of the Future*. London: Arrow Business Books.

Hannay, L. and Ross, J. (1999), 'Deputy heads as middle managers? Questioning the Black Box', *School Leadership and Management*, 19 (3), 345–58.

Hargreaves, A. (1992), 'Cultures in teaching: a focus for change', in A. Hargreaves and M. Fullan (eds), *Understanding Teacher Development*. London: Cassell.

—— (1994), *Changing Teachers, Changing Times*. London: Cassell.

Hargreaves, D. (1967), *Social Relationships in Secondary Schools*. London: Routledge and Kegan Paul.

—— (1995), 'School culture, school effectiveness and school improvement', *School Effectiveness and Improvement*, 6, 23–46.

Hargreaves, D. and Hopkins, D. (1991), *Development Planning, a Practical Guide. Advice to Governors, Principals and Teachers*. London: DES.

Hargreaves, D., Hopkins, D., Leask, M., Connolly, J. and Robinson, P. (1989), *Planning for School Development: Advice to Governors, Headteachers and Teachers*. London: DES.

Harris, R. (1980), *The End of Government . . . ?* London: Institute of Economic Affairs Occasional Paper 58.

Harrison, B. (1998), 'Managing pastoral care in schools: taking responsibility for people', in M. Calvert and J. Henderson (eds), *Managing Pastoral Care*. London: Cassell.

Harwood, D. (1992), 'In at the deep end: a case study of the co-ordinator role in a "low key" innovation', *School Organization*, 12 (1), 17–28.

Hayek, F. (1973), *Law, Legislation and Liberty, vol 1*. London: Routledge and Kegan Paul.

Hilleard, F. (1988), 'The role of the non-teaching assistant in the special school', unpublished M.Ed. thesis, King Alfred's College, Winchester.

Hirsch, D. (1997), 'Policies for school choice: what can Britain learn from abroad?', in R. Glatter, P.A. Woods and C. Bagley (eds), *Choice and Diversity in Schooling: Perspectives and Prospects*. London: Routledge.

Hodgson, A., Clunies-Ross, L. and Hegarty, S. (1984), *Learning Together: Teaching Pupils with Special Needs in the Ordinary School*. Windsor: NFER-Nelson.

Holland, G. (1996), 'Raising achievement', Speech to the North of England Education Conference, Harrogate, January.

Hopkins, D. and Harris, A. (1998), 'Improving city schools, the role of the LEA', *Education Journal*, December: 22–3.

Hopkins, D., Ainscow, M. and West, M. (1994), *School Improvement in an Era of Change*. London: Cassell.

Hoyle, E. (1965), 'Organizational analysis in the field of education', *Educational Research*, 7 (2), 97–114.

—— (1969), 'Organizational analysis and educational administration', in G. Baron and W. Taylor (eds), *Educational Administration and the Social Sciences*. London: Althone Press.

—— (1973), 'Strategies of curriculum change', in R. Watkins (ed.), *In-service Training: Structure and Content*. London: Ward Lock Educational.

Hoyle, E. and John, P. (1995), *Professional Knowledge and Professional Practice*. London: Cassell.

Hughes, M. (1976), 'The professional-as-administrator, the case of the secondary school head', in R.S. Peters, *The Role of the Head*. London: Routledge and Kegan Paul.

—— (1985), 'Leadership in professionally staffed organizations', in M. Hughes, P. Ribbins, and H. Thomas, (eds), *Managing Education; the System and the Institution*. London: Holt, Rinehart and Winston.

—— (1998), 'Research report, the professional-as-administrator' in M. Strain, B. Dennison, J. Ouston and V. Hall (eds), *Policy, Leadership and Professional Knowledge in Education*. London: Paul Chapman Publishing.

Hughes, M. (ed.), (1975), *Administering Education: International Challenge*. London: Athlone Press.

Hummel, R.C. and Nagle, J.M. (1975), 'The character of bureaucracy in urban schools' in R.C. Stob, (ed.), *The Sociology of Education: a Source Book*. Homewood: Dorsey Press.

Humphrey, C. and Thomas, H. (1985), 'Giving schools the money', *Education*, 165 (19), 419–20.

200   *Perspectives on Educational Management and Leadership*

Husband, C. (1996), 'Schools, markets and collaboration: new models for educational policy', in D. Bridges and C. Husband (eds), *Consorting and Collaborating in the Educational Market Place*. London: Falmer Press.

ILEA (1982), *Keeping the School under Review*. London: ILEA.

—— (1984), *Improving Secondary Schools (The Hargreaves Report)*. London: ILEA.

—— (1985), *Improving Primary Schools (The Thomas Report)*. London: ILEA.

Irby, B., Brown, G., Duff, J. and Tautman, D. (2002), 'The synergistic leadership theory' *Journal of Educational Administration*, 40 (5), 425-66.

James, C. and Phillips, P. (1995), 'The practice of educational marketing in schools', in M. Preedy, R. Glatter and R. Levačić (eds), (1997), *Educational Management: Strategy, Quality and Resources*. Buckingham: Open University Press.

Johnson, G. and Scholes, K. (1989), *Exploring Corporate Strategy*. Hemel Hempstead: Prentice Hall.

Joseph, Sir K. (1976), *Stranded on the Middle Ground*. London: Centre for Policy Studies.

—— (1985), Speech to the North of England Education Conference, Chester, 4 January.

Karstanje, P. (1999), 'Decentralisation and deregulation in Europe: towards a conceptual framework', in T. Bush, L. Bell, R. Bolam, R. Glatter and P. Ribbins (eds), *Educational Management: Redefining Theory, Policy and Practice*. London: Paul Chapman Publishing.

Kennedy, K. and Duthie, J. (1975), *Auxiliaries in the Classroom*. Edinburgh: Scottish Education Department, HMSO.

Kogan, M. (1986), *Education Accountability*. London: Hutchinson.

—— (1997), 'Education management in hard times', in J. Mortimore and V. Little (eds), *Living Education: Essays in Honour of John Tomlinson*. London: Paul Chapman Publishing.

Kreysing, M. (2002), 'Autonomy, accountability, and organizational complexity in higher education: the Goettingen model of university reform', *Journal of Educational Administration*, 40 (6), 552-60.

Kroeber, A. and Kluckhohn, C. (1952), 'Culture: a critical review of concepts and definitions', *Papers of the Peabody Museum of American Archaeology and Ethnology*, 47, 3-223.

Lacey, C. (1970), *Hightown Grammar*. Manchester: Manchester University Press.

Law, S. and Glover, D. (2000), *Educational Leadership and Learning: Practice, Policy and Research*. Buckingham: Open University Press.

Lawn, M. (1991), 'Social construction of quality in teaching' in G. Grace and M. Lawn (eds), *Teacher Supply and Teacher Quality: Issues for the 1990s*. Claverdon: Multi-lingual Matters.

Lawton, D. (1980), *The Politics of the School Curriculum*. London: Routledge and Kegan Paul.

—— (1983), *Curriculum Studies and Educational Planning*. London: Hodder and Stoughton.

Lee, J. and Dimmock, C. (1999), 'Curriculum leadership and management in secondary schools: a Hong Kong case study', *School Leadership and Management*, 19 (4), 455-81.

Leithwood, K. (2001), 'Criteria for appraising school leaders in an accountability policy context', in D. Middlewood and C. Cardno (eds), *Managing Teacher Appraisal and Performance*. London: Routledge Falmer.

Leithwood, K., Jantzi, D. and Steinbach, R. (2002), 'Leadership practices for accountable schools', in K. Leithwood and P. Hallinger (eds), *Second International Handbook of Educational Leadership and Administration*. Norwell, MA: Kluwer Academic Publishers.

Levačić, R. (1995), *Local Management of Schools: Analysis and Practice*. Buckingham: Open University Press.

Levačić, R. and Glover, D. (1994), *Ofsted Assessments of Schools' Efficiency*. Milton Keynes: Centre for Educational Policy and Management, Open University.

Lindblom, E. (1959), 'The science of muddling through', in A. Faludi (ed.), (1973), *Reader in Planning Theory*. Oxford: Pergamon Press.

Lingard, B., Ladwig, J. and Luke, A. (1998), 'School effects in postmodern conditions', in R. Slee and G. Weiner with S. Tomlinson (eds), *School Effectiveness for Whom? Challenges to the School Effectiveness and School Improvement Movements*. London: Falmer Press.

Lo, Y. (1999), 'School-based curriculum development: the Hong Kong experience', *Journal of Curriculum Studies*, 10 (3), 419-42.

Lumby, J. (1995), *Managing the Curriculum in Further Education*. Northampton: Education Management Development Unit, University of Leicester.

—— (2001), 'Framing teaching and learning in the twenty-first century', in D. Middlewood and N. Burton (eds), *Managing the Curriculum*. London: Paul Chapman Publishing.

—— (2002), 'Vision and Strategic Planning', in T. Bush and L. Bell (eds), *The Principles and Practice of Educational Management*. London: Paul Chapman Publishing.

MacBeath, J. (2006) 'New relationships for old: inspection and self-evaluation in England and Hong Kong', *International Studies in Educational Administration*, 34 (2), 2-18.

MacGilchrist, B., Mortimore, P., Savage, J. and Beresford, C. (1995), *Planning Matters: Impact of Development Planning in Primary Schools*. London: Paul Chapman Publishing.

Maclure, S. (1997), 'The Tomlinson years', in J. Mortimore and V. Little (eds), *Living Education: Essays in Honour of John Tomlinson*. London: Paul Chapman Publishing.

Maes, F., Vandenberghe, R. and Ghesquiere, P. (1999), 'The imperative of complementarity between the school level and the classroom level in educational innovation', *Journal of Curriculum Studies*, 31 (6), 661-77.

Mahoney, P., Mentor, I. and Hextall, I. (2004) 'The emotional impact of performance-related pay on teachers in England', *British Journal of Educational Research*, 30 (3), 435-56.

Manzer, R. (1970), *Teachers and Politics*. Manchester: Manchester University Press.

March, J. and Olson, J. (1979), *Ambiguity and Choice in Organizations*. Bergen: Universitetsforlaget.

Marion, R. (1999), *The Edge of Organization: Chaos and Complexity Theories of Formal Social Systems*. London: Sage.

Marland, M. (1978), 'The teacher, the ancillary and inner-city education', unpublished paper.

Marquand, D. (1998), 'The Blair paradox', *Prospect*, May, 19–24.

Marsh, C. (1997), *Perspectives: Key Concepts for Understanding the Curriculum*. London: Falmer Press.

Martin, S. (1995), 'Choices of secondary school: the experiences of eight urban families', unpublished Ed.D. thesis, University of Bristol.

Mayer, E. (1992), *Employment-related Key Competencies for Post-compulsory Education and Training*. Canberra: Australian Government Printing Office.

McCulloch, G. (1987), 'History and policy: the politics of TVEI', in D. Gleeson (ed.), *TVEI and Secondary Education: a Critical Appraisal*. Milton Keynes: Open University Press.

McGarvey, B., Marriott, S., Morgan, V. and Abbott. L. (1996), 'A study of auxiliary support in some primary classrooms: extra hands and extra eyes', *Educational Research*, 38 (3), 293–305.

Megahy, T. (1998), 'Managing the curriculum: pastoral care – a vehicle for raising student achievement', in M. Calvert and J. Henderson (eds), *Managing Pastoral Care*. London: Cassell.

Menter, I., Muschamp, Y., Nicholls, P., Ozga, J. with Pollard, A. (1997), *Work and Identity in the Primary School: a Post-Fordian Analysis*. Buckingham: Open University Press.

Merson, M. and Bell L. (1987), *The Evaluation of the Solihull TVEI Project*. Department of Education, University of Warwick.

—— (1988), *The Evaluation of the Walsall TVEI Project*. Department of Education, University of Warwick.

Middlewood, D. (2002), 'Appraisal and Performance Management', in T. Bush and L. Bell (eds), *The Principles and Practice of Educational Management*. London: Paul Chapman Publishing.

Middlewood, D. and Burton, N. (eds), (2001), *Managing the Curriculum*. London: Paul Chapman Publishing.

Middlewood, D. and Cardno, C. (2001), 'The significance of teacher performance and its appraisal', in D. Middlewood and C. Cardno (eds), *Managing Teacher Appraisal and Performance: a Comparative Approach*. London: Routledge Falmer.

Midthassel, U., Bru, E. and Idse, T. (2000), 'The principal's role in promoting school development activity in Norway', *School Leadership and Management*, 20 (2), 247–60.

Midwinter, E. (ed.), (1972), *Projections: an Educational Priority Area at Work*. London: Ward Lock Educational.

Mintzberg, H. (1994), *The Rise and Fall of Strategic Planning*. London: Prentice Hall.

—— (1995), 'Strategic thinking as seeing', in B. Garrett (ed.), *Developing Strategic Thought: Rediscovering the Art of Direction-Giving*. London: McGraw-Hill.

Mok, K. (2003), 'Decentralization and marketization of education in Singapore: a case study of the school excellence model', *Journal of Educational Administration*, 41 (4), 348-86.

Moore, J. (1992), 'The role of the science co-ordinator in primary schools: a survey of headteachers' views', *School Organization*, 12 (1), 7-15.

Morgan, C. (1976), *Management in Education: Dissimilar or Congruent. E321.1.* Milton Keynes: Open University Press.

Morgan, C., Hall, V. and Mackay, H. (1983), *The Selection of Secondary School Headteachers*. Milton Keynes: Open University Press.

Morgan, G. (1989), *Teaching Organization Theory*. Newbury Park CA: Sage.

Mortimore, P. and Mortimore, J. (1991), *The Primary Head. Roles, Responsibilities and Reflection*. London: Paul Chapman Publishing.

Mortimore, P. and Mortimore, J. with Thomas, H. (1994), *Managing Associate Staff: Innovation in Primary and Secondary Schools*. London: Paul Chapman Publishing.

Moyles, J. and Suschitzky, W. (1997a), 'The employment and deployment of classroom support staff: headteachers' perspectives', *Research in Education*, 58, 21-34.

—— (1997b), *Jills of all Trades? Classroom Assistants in KS1 Classes*. London: Association of Teachers and Lecturers.

MSC (1981), *A New Training Initiative*. London: Manpower Services Commission.

—— (1983), *TVEI Review 1983*. London: Manpower Services Commission.

Nash, C. (1995), 'Flexible learning and outcomes', in J. Burke (ed.), *Outcomes, Learning and the Curriculum: Implications for NVQs, GNVQs and Other Qualifications*. London: Falmer Press.

Nash, R. (1989), 'Tomorrow's schools: state power and parent participation', *New Zealand Journal of Educational Studies*, 24 (2), 113-28.

Neville, M. (1995), 'School culture and effectiveness in an Asian pluralistic society', *International Studies in Educational Administration*, 23 (2), 28-37.

Newland, C. (1995), 'Spanish American elementary education 1950-1992: bureaucracy, growth and decentralization', *International Journal of Educational Development*, 15 (2), 103-14.

Ng, S.-W. (1999), 'Home-school relations in Hong Kong: separation or partnership', *School Effectiveness and Improvement*, 9 (4), 551-60.

Nias, J., Southworth, G. and Yeomans, R. (1992), *Staff Relationships in the Primary School: a Study of Organizational Cultures*. London: Cassell.

Normore, A. (2004), 'The edge of chaos: school administrators and accountability', *Journal of Educational Administration*, 42 (1), 55-77.

NZSTA (1999), *Guidelines for Boards of Trustees: the Management of the Principals by the School Board of Trustees*. Wellington: Government Printer.

O'Neill, J. (1997), 'Teach, learn, appraise; the impossible triangle', in J. O'Neill (ed.), *Teacher Appraisal in New Zealand*. Palmerston North: ERDC Press.

OECD (1996), 'An overview of OECD work on teachers, their pay and conditions, teaching quality and the continued professional development of teachers', paper presented to the 45th International Conference on Education, 30 September–5 October, Geneva: UNESCO.

Ofsted (1992), *Framework for the Inspection of Schools*. London: HMSO.

—— (1995a), *The Ofsted Handbook: Guidance on the Inspection of Secondary Schools*. London: HMSO.

—— (1995b), *The Annual Report of Her Majesty's Chief Inspector of Schools*. London: HMSO.

—— (1996), *The Specialist Teacher Assistant Pilot Scheme: Final Evaluation Report on the First Year*. London: HMSO.

—— (1998a), *Making Headway*. London: The Stationery Office.

—— (1998b), *School Evaluation Matters*. London: The Stationery Office.

—— (1999), *The National Literacy Strategy: an Interim Evaluation*. Bedford: Nenworth Print Limited.

Olssen, M., Codd, J. and O'Neill, A. (2004), *Education Policy: Globalization, Citizenship and Democracy*. London: Sage.

Ong, T. and Chia, E. (1994), 'The pastoral care and guidance programme in an independent school in Singapore', in P. Lang, R. Best and A. Lichtenberg (eds), *Caring for Children: International Perspectives on Pastoral Care and PSE*. London: Cassell.

Osborn, M. and Black, E. (1994), *Developing the National Curriculum at Key Stage 2: the Changing Nature of Teachers' Work*. Bristol: NAS/UWT.

Ouston, J. (1998), 'The school effectiveness and school improvement movement: a reflection on its contribution to the development of good schools', paper presented to the Third ESRC Seminar: Redefining Education Management, Open University: Milton Keynes, June.

Owen, G. (1992), 'Whole-school management of information technology', *School Organization*, 12 (1), 29–40.

Packwood, T. (1989), 'Return to the hierarchy', *Educational Management and Administration*, 5 (2), 1–6.

Pardey, D. (1994), 'Marketing for schools', in H. Green (ed.), *The School Management Handbook*. London: Kogan Page.

Parsons, T. (1964), *Structure and Process in Modern Societies*. London: Prentice Hall.

Pettigrew, A. (1973), *The Politics of Organizational Decision Making*. London: Tavistock.

Pinchot, G. (1985), *Intrapreneuring*. New York: Harper and Row.

Pollard, A., Croll, P., Broadfoot, P., Osbourne, M. and Abbott, D. (1994), *Changing English Primary Schools*. London: Cassell.

Preedy, M., Glatter, R. and Levačić, R. (eds), (1997), *Educational Management: Strategy, Quality and Resources*. Buckingham: Open University Press.

Prosser, J. (1992), 'Becoming a school and the development of school culture', paper presented to the British Educational Management and Administration Society Research Conference, April 1992, University of Nottingham.

Puffitt, R., Stoten, B. and Winkley, D. (1992), *Business Planning for Schools*. London: Longman.

Quinn, J. (1980), *Strategies for Change: Logical Incrementalism*. Honewood, IL: Irwin.

—— (1993), 'Managing strategic change', in C. Mabey and B. Mayon-White (eds), *Managing Change*. Buckingham: Open University Press.

Razzell, A. (1968), *Juniors, a Postscript to Plowden*. Buckingham: Penguin Books.

Reid, I. (1978), *Sociological Perspectives on School and Education*. London: Open Books.

Reid, K., Bullock, R. and Howarth, S. (1988), *An Introduction to Primary Organization*. London: Hodder and Stoughton.

Ribbins, P. (1993), 'Telling tales of secondary heads, on educational reform and the National Curriculum', in C. Chitty (ed.), *The National Curriculum, is it Working?* London: Longman.

Ribbins, P. and Marland, M. (1994), *Headship Matters: Conversations with Seven Secondary School Headteachers*. Harlow: Longman.

Richards, C. (1998), 'Curriculum and pedagogy in Key Stage 2: a survey of policy and practice in small rural primary schools', *Curriculum Journal*, 19 (3), 319-32.

Robertson, D. (1995), 'Aspirations, achievement and progression in post-secondary and higher education', in J. Burke (ed.), *Outcomes, Learning and the Curriculum: Implications for NVQs, GNVQs and Other Qualifications*. London: Falmer Press.

Salim, J. and Chua, E. (1994), 'The development of pastoral care and career guidance in Singapore schools', in P. Lang, R. Best and A. Lichtenberg (eds), *Caring for Children: International Perspectives on Pastoral Care and PSE*. London: Cassell.

Schein, E. (1985), *Organizational Culture and Leadership*. San Francisco: Jossey-Bass.

Schendel, D. and Hofer, C. (1979), *Strategic Management: a New View of Business Policy and Planning*. Boston: Little, Brown.

Scott, P. (1989), 'Accountability, responsiveness and responsibility', in R. Glatter (ed.), *Educational Institutions and their Environments: Managing the Boundaries*. Milton Keynes: Open University Press.

Scruton, R. (1984), *The Meaning of Conservatism*. London: Macmillan.

Senge, P. (1990), *The Fifth Discipline: the Art and Practice of the Learning Organization*. New York: Random House.

Shakespeare, W. *Macbeth*, quoted in S.J. Ervine (ed.), (1923), *The Complete Works of William Shakespeare*. London: Literary Press, pp. 1100-27; first published in J. Heminge and H. Condell (eds), (1623), *The Workes of William Shakespeare. His Comedies, Histories and Tragedies*. First Folio Edition.

Shipman, M. (1968), *Sociology of the School*. London: Longmans.

—— (1985), 'Ethnography and educational policy making', in R. Burgess (ed.), *Field Methods in the Study of Education*, Lewes: Falmer Press.

Silins, H. and Mulford, W. (2002), 'Leadership and school results', in K. Leithwood and P. Hallinger (eds), *Second International Handbook of Educational Leadership and Administration*. Norwell, MA: Kluwer Academic Publishers.

Simkins, T. (1997), 'Managing resources', in B. Fidler, S. Russell and T. Simkins (eds), *Choices for Self-Managing Schools*. London: Paul Chapman Publishing.

Slee, R. and Weiner, G. (1998), 'Introduction: school effectiveness for whom?', in R. Slee and G. Weiner with S. Tomlinson (eds), *School Effectiveness for Whom? Challenges to the School Effectiveness and School Improvement Movements*. London: Falmer Press.

Smedley, D. (1995), 'Marketing secondary schools to parents – some lessons from the research on parental choice', *Educational Management and Administration*, 22 (2), 96-103.

Smyth, J. (ed.), (1993), *A Socially Critical View of the Self-Managing School*. London: Falmer Press.

Sockett, H. (1980), 'Accountability: the contemporary issues', in H. Sockett (ed.), *Accountability in the English Educational System*. London: Hodder and Stoughton.

Southworth, G. (1999), 'Primary school leadership in England, policy, practice and theory', *School Leadership and Management*, 19 (1), 49-65.

Southworth, G. and Conner, C. (1999), *Managing Improving Primary Schools: Using Evidence-based Management and Leadership*. London: Falmer Press.

Sugarman, B. (1975), 'The school as a social system', in V. Houghton, R. McHugh and C. Morgan (eds), (1975), *Management in Education*, London: Ward Lock.

Sullivan, M. (1991), *Marketing your School: a Handbook*. London: Longmans.

Swift, D. (1969), *The Sociology of Education*. London: Routledge and Kegan Paul.

Tan, E. (1994), 'Teacher training in pastoral care: the Singapore perspective', in P. Lang, R. Best and A. Lichtenberg (eds), *Caring for Children: International Perspectives on Pastoral Care and PSE*. London: Cassell.

Tarule, J. (1998), 'The characteristics of connected and separate modes of knowing', paper presented to the Joint UCET/AATCDE Seminar, London: Institute of Education, March.

Taylor, E. (1971), *Primitive Culture*. London: John Murray.

Teacher Training Agency (TTA) (1998), *National Standards for School Leaders*. London: TTA.

Teddlie, C. and Reynolds, D. (eds), (2000), *The International Handbook of School Effectiveness Research*. London: Falmer Press.

TES (1999), 'Heads vote for support staff', *Times Educational Supplement*. London: 4 February.

—— (2001), 'Anyone there with a pulse?', *Editorial, Times Educational Supplement*. London: 31 August.

Thomas, H. (1993), 'Perspectives on theory building in strategic management', *Journal of Management Studies*, 30 (1), 3-10.

Thomas, H. and Martin, J. (1996), *Managing Resources for School Improvement: Creating a Cost-effective School*. London: Routledge.

Tomlinson, H. (2000), 'Proposals for performance-related pay for teachers in English schools', *School Leadership and Management*, 20, 281-98.

Tomlinson, J. (1986), *Crossing the Bridge*. Sheffield Papers in Educational Management: Sheffield City Polytechnic.

Torrington, D. and Weightman, J. (1989), *The Reality of School Management*. Oxford: Blackwell.

Turner, C. (1977), 'Organizing educational institutions as anarchies', *Education Administration*, 5, 6-12.

Upton, M. (2003), 'Evidence-based improvement: creating a change culture in your staffroom', *Primary Headship*, March/April: 8-9.

Van der Heijden, A. and Eden, C. (1998), 'The theory and praxis of reflective learning in strategy making', in C. Eden and J.-C. Spender (eds), (1998), *Managerial and Organizational Cognition: Theory, Methods and Research*. London: Sage.

Wallace, M. (1994), 'Towards a contingency approach to development planning in schools', in D. Hargreaves and D. Hopkins (eds), *Development Planning for School Improvement*. London: Cassell.

—— (1998), 'A counter-policy to subvert educational reform? Collaboration among schools and colleges in a competitive climate', *British Educational Research Journal*, 24 (2), 195-215.

Wallace, M. and McMahon, A. (1994), *Planning for Change in Turbulent Times: Case of Multiracial Primary Schools*. London: Continuum.

Waller, W. (1932), *The Sociology of Teaching*. New York: Wiley.

Waters, M. (1996), *Curriculum Co-ordinators in Primary Schools*. London: Collins Educational.

Webb, R. (2005) 'Leading teaching and learning in the primary school: from "educative leadership" to "pedagogical leadership" ', *Educational Management, Administration and Leadership*, 33 (1), 69-92.

Weick, K. (1976), 'Educational organizations as loosely coupled systems', *Administrative Science Quarterly*, 21 (1), 1-19.

Weston J. (2000), 'The National Literacy Strategy and its effect upon literacy teaching and the management structures in the primary and secondary school. A pilot study', unpublished Ed.D. assignment, University of Leicester.

Wheatley, M. (1999), *Leadership and the New Sciences*. San Francisco: Berrett-Koehler.

Whipp, R. (1998), 'Creative deconstruction: strategy and organizations', paper presented to the Second ESRC Seminar: Redefining Educational Management, University of Cardiff, Cardiff.

Whitty, G. (1997), 'Social theory and education policy: the legacy of Karl Mannheim', *British Journal of Sociology of Education*, 18 (2), 149-63.

—— (2005), 'Foreword', in M. Coleman and P. Earley, (eds), *Leadership and Management in Education: Cultures, Change and Context*. Oxford: Oxford University Press.

Whitty, G., Power, S. and Halpin, D. (1998), *Devolution and Choice in Education: the School the State and the Market*. Buckingham: Open University Press.

Wilkins, J. (1990), *Restructuring Education after the Reform Act and the Role of School Governors; a Head Teacher Perspective*. Open University Education Reform Study Group, Occasional Paper No. 1, Milton Keynes.

Wong, E., Sharpe, F. and McCormick, J. (1998), 'Factors affecting the perceived effectiveness of planning in Hong Kong self-managing schools', *Educational Management and Administration*, 26 (1), 67-81.

Wong, K.-C., (1995), 'Education accountability in Hong Kong: lessons from the

School Management Initiative', *International Journal of Educational Research*, 23 (6), 519–29.

Woodhead, C. (1996), *The Annual Report of Her Majesty's Chief Inspector of Schools: Standards and Quality in Education 1994/95*. London: Office for Standards in Education.

—— (1997), *The Annual Report of Her Majesty's Chief Inspector of Schools: Standards and Quality in Education 1995/96*. London: Office for Standards in Education.

Wragg, E. (1997), *The Cubic Curriculum*. London: Routledge.

Zohar, D. (1997), *Rewiring the Corporate Brain: Using the New Science to Rethink how we Structure and Lead Organizations*. San Francisco: Berrett-Koehler Publishers.

Index

A

accountability 16, 22, 25, 30, 54, 61, 90–102, 106, 109, 119, 127, 129, 138, 159, 168, 169, 171, 177, 181
action plans 22, 143
Acts of Parliament
    Education Act 1944 11, 12
    Education Act 1986 18
    Education Reform Act 1988 11, 19, 76, 107, 110, 119, 131, 133, 135, 159, 163, 176, 177
administration 96
agricultural colleges 85
ancillary staff 112
appraisal 102, 109
art 28
Asia 101
assessment 61, 64, 79, 82, 110, 138
Assisted Places Scheme 30
associate staff 110
audits *see also* external audits, internal audits 109
Australasia 101
Australia 78, 79, 94, 95, 102
autonomy 30, 32, 45, 61, 63, 92, 102, 103, 159

B

basic skills 17
beacon schools 30
Better Schools 18
Blair, Tony 24, 27
breakfast clubs 29
budget 110
    constraints 105
    management 130
Bullock Report 110
bureaucracy, Weberian concept of 49
bursars 110
Business Excellence Model 28
business plans 178

C

Callaghan, Jim 16
    Ruskin College speech 16
Canada 82, 89
Carnegie Commission on Higher Education 51
Centre for Educational Research and Innovation 102
Chile 94
China 94
Choice and Diversity: a New Framework for Schools (white paper) 21, 28, 137, 159
church schools 36
City Technology Colleges 30, 75
class sizes 30
classroom assistants 105, 111, 112, 113
classroom observation 104
classroom teachers 130
collectivism 137
commerce 65
communication technology 28
community-based teaching 13
competition 119, 120, 121, 124–5, 133
    public/private sector 115
comprehensive education 21
comprhensive schools 12
compulsory schooling 90
Connecticut 98
Conservative government 19, 171, 178
    policy 117, 159, 166
Conservative New Right 11
consumerism 131
contracts 99
corporal punishment 41
cost-effectiveness 52, 107–10, 112, 113
crisis management 169
curriculum *see also* National

Curriculum 11, 12, 14, 15, 16, 20, 21, 22, 27, 37, 61, 63, 76, 77, 78, 79, 81, 82, 86, 87, 88, 92, 95, 110, 112, 132, 133, 137, 146, 163, 164, 165, 168, 171, 177, 179
content 66, 67, 84, 92-3
development 64, 69, 73, 74, 75, 85
planning 12
primary 11

D
decentralization 23, 93, 95, 104
Department for Education and Skills (DfES) 156
Department for Trade and Industry (DTI) 17, 63
Department of Education and Science (DES) 19, 63, 104, 177
deprivation, definitions 13
deregulation 93, 94, 95, 96
DES *see* Department of Education and Science
development planning 178
DfES *see* Department for Education and Skills
differential funding 183
disruptive pupils 41
diversity 22
division of labour 48, 49
drama 28
DTI *see* Department for Trade and Industry

E
EAZ *see* Education Action Zone
Eccles, David 14
Economic and Social Research Council (ESRC) 115, 163
Economic and Social Science Research Council (ESSRC) 118
economic growth 26
Education Act 1944 11, 12
Education Act 1986 18
Education Act 1987 177
Education Act 1988 115
Education Action Zone (EAZ) 25, 31, 32
education budget 16
Education in Schools: a Consultative Document (Green Paper) 14, 17
education policy 9, 11, 20, 24, 159, 169, 171
Conservative 166
Market Phase 23, 24, 90, 103, 117, 129, 159
Partnership Phase 90

New Labour 166, 167, 170
Resource Constrained Phase 33
Social Democratic Phase 90
Target Phase 90, 103, 117, 140, 159, 175
Education Reform Act 1988 11, 19, 76, 107, 110, 119, 131, 133, 135, 159, 163, 176, 177
education system, structure 16
Educational Development Plan 31
educational goals 52, 56, 59
Educational Priority Areas (EPAs) 13, 14, 31, 32
educational reform 14, 118
educational standards 13
11+ selection procedures 12
EPAs *see* Educational Priority Areas
equal opportunities 13, 15, 16, 102
equity 61, 91, 102
ESRC *see* Economic and Social Research Council
ESSRC *see* Economic and Social Science Research Council
ethnic minorities 36
Europe 101
Excellence and Enjoyment 148-9
Excellence in Schools 25, 26, 166
exclusion 28
Extending Opportunity: a National Framework for Study Support 29, 31
external assessment 12
external audits 148-50

F, G
Foundation Schools 30, 167
France 102
funding 15, 119
external 153
further education 78, 85, 86, 99
colleges 85
GCSE *see* General Certificate of Secondary Education
General Certificate of Secondary Education (GCSE) 42
General Election 1977 24
Germany 99
GM schools *see* grant-maintained schools
GM sector 163
goal orientation 48
governing bodies 132
government policy documents 148
government publications 149
governors 54-5, 103, 108, 110, 111, 115, 119, 126, 127, 129, 131, 133-

7, 138, 143, 145, 149, 150-51, 155, 156, 163, 178
graduate teacher schemes 105
grammar schools 12
grant-maintained (GM) schools 21, 30, 118, 120, 121, 134, 135, 136, 137
headteachers 137, 164
grant-maintained status 178
abolition 167
grants 13

H
Headlamp opportunity 169
heads of department 109
headteachers 18, 21, 23, 26, 33, 36, 49, 61, 69, 70, 87, 89, 96, 97, 99, 100, 103, 104, 106, 110, 113, 115, 119, 120, 122, 127, 128, 130, 131, 132, 133-7, 141, 145, 146, 149, 154, 155, 156, 157, 160-2, 164, 177, 178, 179, 180, 181
GM schools 137, 164
job satisfaction 23
as managers 18
primary schools 115, 117, 124, 125, 137, 140, 141, 143, 157, 162-70, 171
secondary schools 160
hierarchy of authority 49
higher education 85
Hong Kong 87, 93, 97, 100
School-based Management Consultative Document 98
School Management Committees 97
School Management Initiative 97
House of Commons 14
Expenditure Committee 16
human capital 24

I, J
ICT *see* information and communication technology
ideologies, educational 53
ideologies, political 53
ILEA *see* Inner London Education Authority
independent schools 120
individualism 45, 82, 91, 125, 137
industry 65
inequalities 19
information and communication technology (ICT) 79, 168
information technology (IT) 19, 25, 28, 83

Inner London Education Authority (ILEA) 64
in-school training 86
in-service education and training (INSET) 44, 70, 79, 106
inspection 138
reports 183
inspectorates 92
internal audits 147-8, 155
Israel 102
IT *see* information technology
job satisfaction 169-70

K, L
Key Stage 1 164
Key Stage 2 164
Key Stage 3 84
Labour administration 11
Labour government 16
education policy 31
Labour Party 167
language 86
LEA headteachers 164
LEA inspectors 141
LEA maintained schools 134
LEA primary schools, headteachers 137
LEA schools 120, 121, 123, 135, 136
leadership 11
league tables 1, 30, 119, 126, 183
learning difficulties 109, 148
Learning Game, The (book) 27
learning outcomes 113
learning process 53, 79
learning strategies 13
learning styles 67
LEAs *see* Local Education Authorities
legislation 119
librarians 110
licensed teachers 105
lifelong learning 85
literacy 25, 28, 29, 76, 80, 86, 168, 179, 183
Literacy Advisors 81, 84
Literacy Hour 29
Literacy Strategies 167, 170
LMS *see* Local Management of Schools
Local Education Authorities (LEAs) 13, 15, 16, 17, 18, 20, 22, 25, 28, 30, 31, 32, 33, 36, 52, 63, 64, 66, 67, 69, 70, 73, 74, 75, 111, 118, 130, 131, 138, 139, 154, 159, 160, 163, 166, 171, 176-7, 179
local government 51
Local Management of Schools (LMS)

96, 134

M
Major, John 11
management 15
Manpower Services Commission
  (MSC) 15, 17, 63, 64, 65, 75, 69
  TVEI unit 65, 66
market forces 1, 20, 22, 51, 52, 92,
  97, 102, 126, 127
marketing 115, 117, 120, 127
marketization 131
marketplace 117
middle class 14
mixed ability teaching 14, 54, 57
modular courses 85
MSC *see* Manpower Services
  Commission
music 28

N
national assessment 159
National Childcare Strategy 28
National College for School
  Leadership (NCSL) 27
National Curriculum *see also* cur-
  riculum 2, 14, 19, 22, 23, 28, 31,
  75, 79, 80, 81, 83, 84, 94, 97, 131,
  138, 146, 159, 162, 163, 164, 171,
  177
National Curriculum Council 12
National Foundation for Educational
  Research (NFER) 66
national government 51
National Health Service 138
national identity 90
national inspection framework 177
National Literacy Project, Literacy
  Advisors 86
National Literacy Strategy 29, 75, 80–
  81, 84
National Numeracy Strategy 29, 75
National Professional Qualification
  for Headship (NPQH) 27, 98, 104,
  169
National Special Studies 66
National Steering Group 66
national targets 179
NCSL *see* National College for School
  Leadership
neo-conservatism 91
neo-liberalism 91
Netherlands 78
New Labour 24, 26, 27–8, 29, 116,
  119, 168, 179
  education policies 11, 26, 159,
  166, 167, 170, 184

government 2, 178
New Right 23, 24, 26, 92, 116, 128,
  166, 167, 171, 178
  education policy 21
New Zealand 78, 94, 95, 97, 100
  National Curriculum 78
New Zealand School Trustees
  Association (NZSTA) 100
NFER *see* National Foundation for
  Educational Research
non-selective education 40
non-teaching staff *see* associate staff
North America 101
Norway 78, 87
NPQH *see* National Professional
  Qualification for Headship
Nuffield Foundation 9
numeracy 25, 28, 29, 76, 80, 168,
  179, 183
Numeracy Strategy 167, 170
nursery provision 121
nursery schools 121
NZSTA *see* New Zealand School
  Trustees Association

O, P
Oakfields School Project 9
Ofsted 22, 23, 28, 29, 80, 86, 119,
  148, 150, 177–8
  inspection reports 108
  inspections 30, 162, 179
Ofsted Inspection Framework 99,
  178
oil crisis of 1973 15
organizational cultures 34–5, 38, 40,
  41–6
organizational structure 85
outcomes 95, 101, 107, 182
outreach teachers 109
PACE project 118
parental choice 16–17, 120, 128
parents 18, 21, 51, 54–5, 66, 97, 101,
  111, 117, 126, 131, 138, 145, 149,
  155
pedagogy 14, 57, 90, 91, 92, 93, 95
performance appraisal 30
performance management 2, 61, 171,
  172
performance related pay 106, 179
performance review *see* teacher
  appraisal
performance targets 24
performing arts colleges 85
personal performance plans 179
Personal, Social and Health Education
  (PSHE) 79
planning 115, 154, 176

Plowden Report 13, 14, 111
Poland 94
post-compulsory education 84
post-Fordism 32
post-16 provision 83
pre-LMS pilot project 164
primary schools 14, 28, 29, 79, 80,
  81, 82, 107, 110, 115, 118, 119,
  128, 142, 156
  grant maintained 136
  headteachers 105, 115, 117, 124,
    125, 140, 141, 143, 157, 162–70,
    171
  National Literacy Strategy 80–81
  self-governing 129
  self-managing 133
  staffing 153–4
  strategic marketing 121
  strategic planning 144–54
primary sector 85
private sector 117, 133, 134, 136,
  163
  schools 129,137
professional development 102
  programmes 106
Professional Development
  Co-ordinators 79
professionalism 62, 101, 168
PSHE see Personal, Social and Health
  Education
PTR *see* pupil–teacher ratio
public examinations 42
public relations 124, 161
pupil attainment 52, 61, 171
pupil forces 126
pupil numbers 16
pupil performance 53, 183
pupil recruitment 122,128
pupil under-achievement 12
pupil–teacher ratio (PTR) 170

Q, R
quality assurance 127
quality control 138
Queensland 98
racial minorities *see* ethnic minorities
Records of Achievement 79
redundancy 16
research workers 68
resource allocation 22, 30, 31, 120,
  127, 130, 131
resource management 15, 18, 80, 96,
  133, 137, 163, 164, 165, 177, 181
resources 15, 20, 98, 107, 156

S
SATs *see* Standard Assessment Tests

school amalgamations 47
school brochures 124
school budgets, restructuring 108
school development plans 106, 146,
  147, 164, 177
School Evaluation Matters 28
school finance 18, 130
school governors see governors
School Improvement Plans 141, 147,
  148, 179, 185
school inspection 21
school inspectors 113
School Management Initiative (SMI)
  93
school organization 87
school selection policies 183
Schools Council 14
Schools Excellence Model (SEM),
  Singapore 93
schools, admissions policy 22
science 19
science and technology 15
secondary schools 12, 14, 20, 79, 81,
  82, 83, 84, 107, 117
  headteachers, 160
secondary sector 85
selective education 36, 40
selective schools 36
self-assessment 94
self-evaluation 99
self-management 162
self-managing schools 92–4
SEM *see* Schools Excellence Model
SEM schools 94
SENCO *see* Special Needs
  Co-ordinators
Sinagpore 86
  Schools Excellence Model (SEM)
  93
site-based management 18, 19, 20,
  21, 22, 23, 25, 27, 30, 92, 95, 100
site-based managers 29
sixth form colleges 85
skills-based qualifications 85
SMI *see* School Management Initiative
social change 16
social cohesion 90
social inequality 12
social justice 19, 61, 90, 91, 102, 180
social science statistical package
  (SPSS) 118
South America 93
special educational needs (SEN) 67,
  76
special measures 151
special needs 41, 102, 110

Special Needs Co-ordinators
  (SENCO) 79
special needs teachers 109
special schools 111
Specialist Teacher Assistant Scheme
  112
Spiritual, Moral, Social and Cultural
  (SMSC) development 79
SPSS *see* social science statistical
  package
staff audit 112
staff deployment 104, 105-6
staff development 104-5, 109
staff exit 105
staff induction 104, 105
staff morale 168
staff promotion 105, 106
staff recruitment 104, 105
staff selection 104, 105
staff turnover 54, 157
staffing 165, 177
  primary schools 153-4
Standard Assessment Tests (SATs)
  126, 162
standards 29, 57
state schools 137
state sector 136
statemented children 110
strategic planning 2, 140-54, 155,
  157, 175-6, 179, 180-6, 188
  primary schools 144-54
stress levels 169
subject departments 82
subject-specific teaching 82
Summer Numeracy Schools 29
supply staff 109
support staff 107, 112
Supported Self Study 79
surveys 109
Switzerland 78

T
Taiwan 29
target setting 2, 30
targets 27, 28, 95, 98, 141, 178, 179,
  186
Taylor Committee 16

teacher appraisal 18, 21, 29, 92, 99,
  104, 106
teacher autonomy 12, 16, 18
teacher morale 13, 15
teacher recruitment 185
teacher salaries 13
teacher training 105
teachers 132
  conditions of service 81
teaching assistants 111
Teaching Standards Framework 98
teaching styles 67
team meetings 109
Technical and Vocational Educational
  Initiative (TVEI) 17, 61, 63, 65, 67,
  68, 71, 72, 73, 74, 75, 76, 79
  school co-ordinators 68, 70
technicians 110
technology 19, 53, 54, 56, 57
tertiary colleges 85
Thailand 88
Thatcher, Margaret 11, 19
Third Way 24
Threshold Assessment 29
trade unions 66
TRIST *see* TVEI Related In-Service
  Training
truancy 28, 42, 43
TVEI *see* Technical and Vocational
  Educational Initiative
TVEI projects, National Guidelines 69
TVEI Related In-Service Training
  (TRIST) 64

U, V, W, Y
Uganda 94
USA 94, 102
vandalism 42
vocational training 85
vocationalism 15
Warwick University 163
Woodhead, Chris, Chief Inspector of
  Schools 1994-2000 162
work experience 63, 64, 65, 68, 70
working class 14
youth unemployment 15, 16